Critical Studies of the Asia Pacific Series

Series Editor: **Mark Beeson**, Professor of International Politics, Murdoch University, Australia

Critical Studies of the Asia Pacific showcases new research and scholarship on what is arguably the most important region in the world in the twenty-first century. The rise of China and the continuing strategic importance of this dynamic economic area to the United States mean that the Asia Pacific will remain crucially important to policymakers and scholars alike. The unifying theme of the series is a desire to publish the best theoretically-informed, original research on the region. Titles in the series cover the politics, economics, and security of the region, as well as focussing on its institutional processes, individual countries, issues, and leaders.

Titles include:

Jonathan D. London (*editor*)
POLITICS IN CONTEMPORARY VIETNAM
Party, State, and Authority Relations

Arndt Michael
INDIA'S FOREIGN POLICY AND REGIONAL MULTILATERALISM

Joel Rathus
JAPAN, CHINA AND NETWORKED REGIONALISM IN EAST ASIA

Claudia Tazreiter and Siew Yean Tham (*editors*)
GLOBALIZATION AND SOCIAL TRANSFORMATION IN THE ASIA-PACIFIC
The Australian and Malayasian Experience

Sow Keat Tok
MANAGING CHINA'S SOVEREIGNTY IN HONG KONG AND TAIWAN

William Tow and Rikki Kersten (*editors*)
BILATERAL PERSPECTIVES ON REGIONAL SECURITY
Australia, Japan and the Asia-Pacific Region

Barry Wain
MALAYSIAN MAVERICK
Mahathir Mohamad in Turbulent Times

Mikael Weissmann
THE EAST ASIAN PEACE
Conflict Prevention and Informal Peacebuilding

Robert G. Wirsing, Christopher Jasparro and Daniel C. Stoll
INTERNATIONAL CONFLICT OVER WATER RESOURCES IN HIMALAYAN ASIA

Critical Studies of the Asia Pacific Series
Series Standing Order ISBN 978–0–230–22896–2 (Hardback)
978–0–230–22897–9 (Paperback)
(*outside North America only*)

You can receive future titles in this series as they are published by placing a standing order. Please contact your bookseller or, in case of difficulty, write to us at the address below with your name and address, the title of series and one of the ISBNs quoted above.

Customer Services Department, Macmillan Distribution Ltd, Houndmills, Basingstoke, Hampshire RG21 6XS, England

Politics in Contemporary Vietnam

Party, State, and Authority Relations

Edited by

Jonathan D. London
Professor, City University of Hong Kong

First published 2014 by
PALGRAVE MACMILLAN

Palgrave Macmillan in the UK is an imprint of Macmillan Publishers Limited,
registered in England, company number 785998, of Houndmills, Basingstoke,
Hampshire RG21 6XS.

Palgrave Macmillan in the US is a division of St Martin's Press LLC,
175 Fifth Avenue, New York, NY 10010.

Palgrave Macmillan is the global academic imprint of the above companies
and has companies and representatives throughout the world.

Palgrave® and Macmillan® are registered trademarks in the United States,
the United Kingdom, Europe and other countries

ISBN: 978–1–137–34752–7

This book is printed on paper suitable for recycling and made from fully
managed and sustained forest sources. Logging, pulping and manufacturing
processes are expected to conform to the environmental regulations of the
country of origin.

A catalogue record for this book is available from the British Library.

A catalog record for this book is available from the Library of Congress.

Transferred to Digital Printing in 2014

For the Vietnamese People

Contents

List of Illustrations

Figures

Tables

Acknowledgments

The publication of this volume marks the culmination of efforts by its contributing authors, all of whom I wish to thank for their energy and enthusiasm through multiple discussions, revisions, and updates. The idea for this volume was conceived at a workshop entitled "Authoritarianism in East Asia: Vietnam, China, and North Korea", held in Hong Kong in June–July of 2009, in which all but two of the contributors to this volume participated. I wish to thank the City University of Hong Kong and its Centre for Southeast Asian Studies for their generous sponsorship of that workshop. I wish to express particular gratitude to Professor William F. Case, then SEARC Director, for his consistent and good-natured support. Edward Friedman, Mark Selden, and Stephan Haggard provided valuable guidance in the early planning of this manuscript. The volume has also benefited from critical feedback from Series Editor Mark Beeson and anonymous reviewers. In the preparation of this volume I was continually impressed with the editorial and production staff at Palgrave MacMillan. I wish to thank countless friends and colleagues in Vietnam for helping me to understand the country. Finally, I wish to thank Nankyung Choi and our two children, Jesse and Anna, for their support, love, and affection.

Jonathan D. London

Notes on Contributors

Thomas Jandl is Scholar-in-Residence at the School of International Service at American University in Washington, DC, where he teaches courses on the East Asian development model and Vietnam's political economy. His research interests are economic development with focus on economic governance, rent seeking, and decentralization. He now investigates whether economic decentralization can offer the benefits of pluralistic contestation generally associated with democratic institutions as promoted by "Western" democracies. He received his PhD in International Relations from American University. He has published on the political economy of development in Malaysia and Vietnam, including a recent book titled *Vietnam in the Global Economy: The Dynamics of Integration, Decentralization and Contested Politics*.

Jonathan D. London is a political economist and professor at the City University of Hong Kong where he is program leader for the university's Master's program in Development Studies and Core Member of the Southeast Asia Research Center. With interests that span politics, policy analysis, and academics, London has published extensively on social, political, and economic themes pertaining to Vietnam. He holds a PhD in Sociology from the University of Wisconsin-Madison.

Edmund J. Malesky is Associate Professor of Political Economy at Duke University, who specializes on the political economy of Vietnam. He is currently on sabbatical as a visiting associate professor at the National University of Singapore Business School. In 2012, Malesky received a state medal from the Government of Vietnam for his role in promoting economic development as the lead researcher for the US AID's Vietnam Provincial Competitiveness Index. In 2013, he was appointed by President Obama to serve on the board of the Vietnam Education Foundation; a program dedicated to identifying talented Vietnamese for doctoral training in the United States. He is a noted specialist in economic development, authoritarian institutions, and comparative political economy in Southeast Asia. He has published in leading political science and economic journals, including the *American Political Science Review, Journal of Politics, Quarterly Journal of Political Science, British Journal of Politics,* and *Journal of Law, Economics, and Organization*. Malesky has been awarded the Harvard Academy Fellowship, the Gabriel Almond

Award for best dissertation, the International Political Economy Society Best Paper Award, and the Rockefeller Bellagio Residency Fellowship.

Carlyle A. Thayer is Emeritus Professor, University of New South Wales (UNSW) at the Australian Defence Force Academy, Canberra. He was educated at Brown and holds an MA in Southeast Asian Studies from Yale and a PhD in International Relations from the Australian National University. Carlyle served in South Vietnam with the International Voluntary Services (1967–68), conducted field work for his PhD thesis there in 1972, first visited reunified Vietnam in 1981, and has returned annually ever since. He is the author of over 480 publications including: *Southeast Asia: Patterns of Security Cooperation* (2010), *Vietnam People's Army: Development and Modernization* (2009), *The Vietnam People's Army under Doi Moi* (1994), and *War by Other Means: National Liberation and Revolution in Vietnam, 1954–1960* (1989).

Benedict J. Tria Kerkvliet is Emeritus Professor at the Australian National University and is currently doing research on public political criticism in Vietnam. One resulting publication is "Workers' Protests in Contemporary Vietnam (with Some Comparisons to those in the Pre-1975 South)." *Journal of Vietnamese Studies* 5, no. 1 (2010): 162–204. Among his other publications about Vietnam is *The Power of Everyday Politics: How Vietnamese Peasants Transformed National Policy* (2005). He has also published on agrarian politics elsewhere in Southeast Asia, especially the Philippines.

Thaveeporn Vasavakul received a PhD in Government from Cornell University's Department of Government in 1994. She was a postdoctoral research fellow at the Department of Political and Social Change, then the Research School of Pacific and Asian Studies, Australian National University, from 1994 to 1997. From 1994 to 2006, she taught Southeast Asia politics and government, Vietnamese politics, and comparative revolutions in her capacity as a visiting professor at the University of Michigan, the University of California, Los Angeles, the Yale University, the University of California, Berkeley, and the Australian National University. Since the late 1990s she has worked as a governance consultant with expertise in the areas of public administration reform, local governance, and anticorruption policy. Her assignments, also focusing on Vietnam, are in the forms of policy research, result-based program design and evaluation, and capacity-building training. She has written extensively on Vietnam's politics and policies in the era of doi moi. She is currently lead specialist at Governance Support

Facility Initiatives (GoSFI), where she works on projects on Asia, the Pacific, and Africa.

Tuong Vu is Associate Professor of Political Science at the University of Oregon, and has held visiting appointments at the National University of Singapore and Princeton University. A PhD from Berkeley, his book *Paths to Development in Asia: South Korea, Vietnam, China, and Indonesia* (2010) received a 2011 Bernard Schwartz Award Honorable Mention. He is co-editor of *Dynamics of the Cold War in Asia: Ideology, Identity, and Culture* (2009) and *Southeast Asia in Political Science: Theory, Region, and Qualitative Analysis* (2008). He is on the editorial board of *Journal of Vietnamese Studies* and *Philippine Journal of Political Science*. His articles have appeared in many scholarly journals such as *World Politics, Journal of Southeast Asian Studies, Journal of Vietnamese Studies, Studies in Comparative International Development* and *Theory and Society*. Currently he is completing a book about the Vietnamese revolution as a case of radical movements in international politics.

Andrew Wells-Dang is Researcher and Practitioner on civil society and governance. A resident in Vietnam since 1997, he works as Team Leader for the Advocacy Coalition Support Program implemented by Oxfam and funded by the UK Department for International Development (DFID). The views expressed in his chapter in this volume are his own and do not necessarily reflect the views of Oxfam or DFID. Andrew holds a PhD in political science from the University of Birmingham (UK) and an MA in international development from the Johns Hopkins School of Advanced International Studies (Washington, DC), where he is a visiting scholar in Southeast Asian studies. He is the author of *Civil Society Networks in China and Vietnam: Informal Pathbreakers in Health and the Environment* (Palgrave Macmillan, 2012) as well as essays and articles in *Asia Times, Foreign Affairs, Foreign Policy in Focus*, and *Pacific Review*.

1
Politics in Contemporary Vietnam

Jonathan D. London

Vietnam's political development has entered an extraordinary, if indeterminate, phase. Politics in Vietnam, long a predictable affair, are
today characterized by a sense of uncertainty and possibility that has no
precedent in the country's postwar history. Changes are apparent on a
variety of levels. At the pinnacle of state power, competition among elite
members of the Communist Party of Vietnam (CPV) has produced no
clear victor, lending to a sense of acute political gridlock. The degree of
dissensus was laid bare in October of 2012, when the entire Politburo was
subjected to unprecedented criticism by the Party Central Committee. It
was evident again in early 2013, when Vietnam saw a bitter and unchar-
acteristically public proxy struggle for control over the party Politburo.
Nor have evolutionary processes been limited to the sphere of elite politics. Recent changes in Vietnam's political culture are a case in point.
Unfiltered political speech and contentious politics, only recently a rarity
in Vietnam, have swiftly become commonplace. While the art of political
commentary, dormant for decades, has seen a spirited revival. Underlying
all of these political developments is a set of tensions and contradictions
within Vietnam's political economy itself. While the country's economy
retains considerable potential, two decades of rapid economic growth
has given way to a flagging economic performance. Today in Vietnam
there is a sense that economic mismanagement, corruption, skills and
infrastructure bottlenecks, and sheer incompetence are conspiring to
dim the country's prospects. Intensifying social inequalities and ineq-
uities have contributed to political restlessness. Nor, however, should
political discontinuties be exaggerated. In late 2013 Vietnam's National
Assembly edorsed a revised constitution that ignored calls for reform that
have emerged both within and outside the Party. While Vietnamese are
taking a greater interest in politics, organized dissent is severely repressed.

This volume places Vietnam's recent political evolution in perspective through a rigorous analysis of politics in contemporary Vietnam.

Comprising contributions from leading Vietnam scholars, this volume drills deeply into core aspects of Vietnam's politics. Thematic focuses include the development and decay of the Communist Party of Vietnam, the politics of (in)accountability within the state administrative apparatus, the recent evolution of relations between central and local authorities, the functions of representative institutions, the activities of political dissidents, the growth of incipient forms of secondary association and "civil society," and state repression. Unlike much of the scholarship on Vietnam, the contributions in this volume take special care to consider Vietnam in light of broader debates concerning politics in Asia. China is of particular interest, even as much of the literature on China is itself insular and noncomparative. Yet Vietnam is not China and indeed recent experience in Vietnam speaks to broader debates in comparative politics concerning such matters as regime survival and decay, elections and representation, civil society, and dissident politics. Finally, there are differing characterizations and explanations of the state of Vietnamese politics today. Indeed, the chapters in this volume find agreement in some areas and discord in others, facilitating a lively discussion and contributing to a better if imperfect understanding of the dynamics of power relations in one of Asia's most important but least understood countries.

This introductory chapter has three aims. The first is to establish a common foundation by way of a concise and up-to-date overview of Vietnam's political institutions that also introduces contributions to this volume. The second is to highlight a crosscutting theme around which the chapters in this volume coalesce; namely, the nature of authoritarian politics in Vietnam and the significance of the Vietnamese case in relation to broader debates in comparative politics, political sociology, and related fields. The final aim of this introduction is to identify salient tensions and disagreements that emerge across the various contributions to this volume, some of which are raised by the authors themselves. I will return to these tensions in the volume's concluding chapter, in which I take stock of this volume's contributions and consider Vietnam's political outlook and future research on the subject.

Politics in Vietnam

Contemporary Vietnam exhibits a one-party regime in which secondary association is highly circumscribed and dissident behavior is subject to severe punishment. This and other institutional attributes suggest that

Vietnam's political regime remains solidly authoritarian. Yet beyond this simple characterization, Vietnam's politics are not widely understood. Vietnam's politics are complex and they are changing. And yet, too often, prevailing understandings of politics in Vietnam tend to be simplistic or outdated, or both. Another common mistake is to assume that Vietnam's politics may be simply "read-off" from the Chinese case. While the volume of scholarly literature on politics in Vietnam has increased, Vietnam is often overlooked in literature on comparative politics. Next to China, Vietnam seems small and inconsequential. There is a tendency to forget or be ignorant of the fact that Vietnam today is the world's 13th most populous country and that after two decades of sustained economic growth, Vietnam has entered the ranks of the world's lower-middle income countries. Vietnam is significant in its own right and its politics are distinctive from that of China. Indeed, the differences between Vietnam and China are ripe for comparative and theoretically informed analysis.

That politics in Vietnam remains enigmatic also owes to its limited accessibility. In the past and up to the present, the country's leadership has remained suspicious of and resistant to external scrutiny. Still, Vietnam in the last two decades has become much more accessible and there is by now a significant scholarly literature on the country's political economy, though heavily concentrated on analysis of social and economic conditions in the country. Indeed, from a situation of too little data, analyses of social conditions in Vietnam today seem frequently overwhelmed by data. Worse, it is very often the case that studies of social and economic conditions and processes in Vietnam ignore politics altogether, forgetting that all social and economic processes are intrinsically political. A likely reason for this is that a good deal of social research in Vietnam is policy-driven research and donor-driven policy research in particular. In these studies, politics are off limits.

Perhaps the most important explanation for the relative thinness of the literature on politics in Vietnam is the practical challenges it poses. Though Vietnam has become more accessible, independent research on politics remains difficult. The Communist Party of Vietnam (CPV) remains a secretive organization and the country's political institutions and processes remain opaque. Indeed, a great deal of politics in Vietnam is indecipherable. Yet it is equally clear that the usefulness of a "black box" approach to Vietnam's politics has its limits.

Party, state, and formal representative institutions

Authoritarian regimes are organizational complexes built by parties around a set of interests, are maintained by vast administrative apparatuses, and

4 *Jonathan D. London*

are legitimated through more or less elaborate ideational, procedural, and coercive means. Older and more recent debates on authoritarian regimes have centered on their relative durability, the character of their internal and external relations, and the processes by which such regimes seek to buttress, legitimate, and consolidate their domination. In Vietnam the sate comprises the Communist Party of Vietnam (CPV), the state administrative apparatus along with its executive and functional agencies, formal representative institutions, state-controlled mass organizations, as well as the armed forces, police, and a multitude of security agencies organized on a variety of jurisdictional levels. Analysis of these elements and their interrelation generates important insights into contemporary Vietnam's politics and raises important questions for theoretical literature on authoritarianism.

The party

Recent literature on authoritarian regimes has recast attention on one-party states and the conditions under which they rise and fall (Magaloni and Kricheli 2010). Among others, one-party states are said to persist due to their ability to co-opt and to serve as a mechanism for elite bargaining between elites and the masses. Svolik (2012) has likened recruitment into party structures to the illusion of a tournament-like structure, in that those who initially seized power enjoy great gains and retain status whereas later entrants join on the promise of opportunities that relatively few can realize. Single-party regimes retain members by using institutions like mandatory retirement to clear space at the top, thereby allowing lower-level members to believe they have something to gain through continued support.

Politics in Vietnam is not reducible to the CPV but cannot be understood in isolation from the operations of the party and its metamorphosis over time. Put simply, the CPV has been and remains dominant in Vietnam's politics. Founded between 1925 and 1930 and with roots in the Communist International, the CPV developed in the context of a protracted anticolonial struggle. Founded by a small number of youths, the Party gradually expanded its activities and numbers and managed to withstand French efforts to eliminate it. In the so-called August Revolution of 1945, the Indochina Communist Party (as it was then known) seized power in the vacuum created by Japanese surrender. It swiftly assumed a position of leadership and dominance, a position which it maintains to this day.

Arguably, three aspects of CPV rule have been most consequential: its ability to secure national independence and unification in the face of immense and highly destructive external pressure; its ability to maintain its position of dominance in politics in the context of war and post war adversity and the subsequent disintegration of the state-socialism;

and, more recently, its role in promoting unprecedented economic expansions and associated gains in living standards.

Founded on the principles of national independence and socialist revolution, the CPV today governs a rapidly transforming market economy that is increasingly enmeshed in the processes and institutions of global capitalism. The Party's survival is remarkable in its own right. Though the fate of authoritarian regimes is notoriously difficult to predict, the CPV has proven to be a durable force.

Perhaps unsurprisingly, scholarship on the CPV is among the most developed segments of the relatively small literature on politics in Vietnam. (Though there are probably more books on Ho Chi Minh than the party.) On the whole, the literature on the CPV has tended to fall into one of four categories: historical analysis of party origins and development, broad overview of the Party's recent past, polemical indictments by political opponents, and detailed analyses of twists and turns in party politics, sometimes (derisively) referred to as "Kremlinology." The best single study of the Party's early development remains Huỳnh Kim Khánh's *Vietnamese Communism, 1925–1945* (Khánh 1982), followed by the publication of numerous studies of the Party during the long war years (e.g. Turner 1975). There have been several analyses of the Party during the reform era (i.e. post-1986 era) (e.g. Stern 1993; Porter 1993; Abuza 2001). Though sophisticated in respects, these analyses tended to be broad overviews based on close readings of largely translated secondary sources, and they exhibited an uneven grasp of the character and significance of Vietnam's social and cultural institutions.

A number of Vietnamese language analyses have shed considerable light on the party's workings, with the most famous among these being the memoirs of the exiled former Party member and *Nhân Dân* editor Bui Tin (1995). More recent scholarship has sought to assess in broad strokes the development of the party and its behavior in the context of Vietnam's market transition (e.g. London 2009).

The most prolific analyst of Vietnam's politics and by extension of the Party has undoubtedly been Carl Thayer, who has written extensively on developments in the Party since the 1970s (see, for example, Thayer 1979, 1987, 1988, 1995, 2007, 2010). The most prominent emerging scholar of the CPV is Tuong Vu, who in this volume develops a detailed and up-to-date analysis of processes of institutionalization and deinstitutionalization of party rule in Vietnam. This brings us to the fundamental if familiar question about the CPV.

Now, as in the past, a central question concerning the party is its vitality. The Party's significance stems from its formal and real position of supremacy in politics. The CPV's Politburo and its standing committee remain the preeminent decisional bodies. The party's branches and cells are interpenetrated with all parts of the state and are present in all segments of society. But the vitality of the Party is in question. How, in essence, have de-totalitarianization and marketization affected the CPV?

Huntington's seminal notion of "institutionalization" (Huntington 1968) has been favored in the analysis of party systems democratic and otherwise, but has not been obviously helpful in understanding the maintenance or decay of authoritarian regimes. Thus, varieties of authoritarianism in East Asia invite us to reconsider received wisdom.

In a cogently argued chapter that situates Vietnam in theoretical literature on comparative politics, Vu explores the roles of elite politics, violence, war, and rents in the evolution of the CPV and its implications for the party's future. One of the issues raised in Vu's analysis is why or under what conditions people join communist parties. His detailed case studies offer an important challenge to the predictions of the Svolik tournament model.

The state administrative apparatus

Beyond the party lies the rest of the state apparatus. We can begin with the sprawling administrative state, frequently referred to as "the state" (nhà nước) in Vietnamese, and which comprises a full complement of executive and functional agencies designed to govern the affairs of the country. It is helpful to have an understanding not only of the operations of the state but also its organization and its relation to the Party. This can provide a better understanding of the scholarship on the state.

The state (like the Party) extends its organization vertically across four separate levels of authority, from the level of the central government, to that of provinces and major cities, down to (rural) districts and (urban) wards, and finally (rural) communes and (urban) precincts. At still lower levels (e.g. villages and hamlets) lie a variety of party and state officials who contribute in various ways to the governance of social activity. The functional agencies of the state are organized vertically. At local levels, these functional agencies are doubly accountable, to local executive bodies (i.e. People's Committees) on the one hand and to higher-level functional agencies on the other.

The executive agencies of the national state are referred to as the government, led by the prime minister, his deputies, and government ministers. At lower levels of authority (e.g. provinces, districts, and communes), People's Committees serve as the executive agency of local authorities. People's Committees are appointed by formally representative bodies, called People's Councils (see later). Functional agencies of the state (e.g. internal affairs, education, and agriculture) are organized horizontally at different levels of authority and governed vertically, from the central level, through the provinces, districts, and communes.

An important feature of this political administrative system is that local state agencies are doubly accountable (or subordinate) – to their local people's committee on the one hand and to their higher-level functional organization on the other. Once again, all state agencies are penetrated by the Party apparatus, which represents a third dimension of accountability. Typically, and arguably increasingly, local executive authorities – particularly at the provincial level – exert greater power than functional agencies and even local party bodies.

The relationship between the Party and state is interesting in this regard. The state administrative apparatus may be reasonably construed as an instrument of the Party, as is encapsulated in the CPV slogan, "The Party Leads, the state implements, and the people inspect." Nonetheless, it is also the case (again, perhaps increasingly) that state executives and administrative agencies – though they are penetrated by Party structures – are not the same as the Party and have relative autonomy from the Party. But nor should this be exaggerated; the state administrative apparatus is interpenetrated by the Party apparatus at all levels of governance.

The historical development of the state administrative apparatus under the CPV has been the subject of several books, with Phong and Beresford's (1998) analysis of authority and economic decision making and Kim B. Ninh's analysis of education and cultural administration being among the best (Ninh 2002). Hardy's recent analysis of migration policies has drawn praise for its ability to elucidate the lived experience of state administrators and those whose migration they sought to govern (Hardy 2005).

Studies on the state and its administrative apparatus in contemporary Vietnam have provided some of the most outstanding scholarship on the country's politics. Thaveeporn Vasavakul's work on state formation (Vasavakul 1997, 1999) is exemplary in this regard, as it traces three "waves" of state building, in the 1950s, the postwar 1970s, and in the wake of the transition to a market economy. Literature on Vietnam's legal institutions arguably represents a substrata of literature on the state. Analyses by Mark Sidel (Sidel 2008) and John Gillespie (2007) have highlighted the development and transformation of legal institutions and "legality" in the context of Vietnam's market transition (one of the first considerations of the role of law may be found in Thayer and Marr 1993).

Vietnam's economic transformation has affected all aspects of social life, and the political aspects of this transformation have been the subject of numerous studies. The scope of the changes is impressive. During the 1970s and 1980s Vietnam was among the poorest countries in the world. Today Vietnam is listed among the world's lower middle-income countries. Economic organization has changed fundamentally. Living standards have improved significantly, if unevenly, and from a very low base. Even in the context of a likely global recession, Vietnam's economy is likely to experience continued growth over the decades ahead.

The political analysis of economic change in Vietnam is essential and the relation between the state and the economy is itself a major focus of literature on the state in Vietnam. Melanie Beresford (2008) provides an excellent and recent overview. Numerous analyses have examined the interplay between state agencies and foreign investors (e.g. Malesky 2004, 2008). Writing in this volume, Thomas Jandl sheds new light on the increasing autonomy of provincial leaders in wealthy Vietnamese provinces, and on the convergence of interest among central and domestic elites. Jandl's analysis highlights differences in this regard between Vietnam and China, by demonstrating that while provincial officials in Vietnam do indeed gain independence from the center through economic success, such economic success often depends on a breach of central doctrine. Nonetheless, success in economic terms allows elites to advance their stature and influence within networks of national and international elite; economic success trumps coercive power. His analysis raises questions for existing research on the economic aspects of elite factions in other settings, notably China (e.g. Shih 2008).

The study of local politics and administration in Vietnam has also gained momentum. Kerkvliet and Marr's edited volume on local government in Vietnam, *Beyond Hanoi* (Kerkvliet and Marr 2004), includes several excellent analyses of the workings of the state at the local level, including fascinating accounts of local government in the Red River Delta (Pham 2004; Truong 2004), northern mountainous region (Sikor 2004), Mekong Delta (Hicks 2004), as well as Hanoi (Koh 2004) and Ho Chi Minh City (Gainsborough 2004).

The recent growth of literature on administrative aspects of politics in Vietnam has been stimulated by a large program of Public Administration Reform that international organizations such as the World Bank and United Nations have undertaken in partnership with the Vietnamese government (e.g. Painter 2003). The Vietnamese state's adoption of decentralization policies has been the subject of a number of analyses (Fritzen 2006), as have changes in the principles and institutions governing the provision and payment for essential social services, such as education and health (London 2003, 2009, 2011).

What the best of these analyses do is advance beyond a preoccupation with formal institutions to the informal aspects of state administration that animate state administration and the difficulties experienced in attempts to regulate it. In Chapter 3, Thaveeporn Vasavakul presents a nuanced analysis of efforts to introduce accountability mechanisms in the operations of the state and highlights the role of intra-state institutional competition and conflict as driving factors in the evolution of Vietnam's regime. It bears emphasis that while local administration is an analytically distinct category, it is empirically interpenetrated with the CPV. As Jandl's chapter in this volume aptly demonstrates, the Party controls its agents through promotion and demotion, and Party politics ultimately condition the politics of the state.

Representative institutions and mass organizations

As described earlier, one of the more lively debates in comparative politics concerns the significance of formal representative institutions and processes, such as legislatures and elections. Vietnam is according to its constitution a democracy in which representative institutions determine government appointments. In practice, Vietnam fails to meet accepted understandings of democracy (see, for example, Schmitter and Karl 1991). Nonetheless, representative institutions (regardless of whether they are representative in a democratic sense) form an important part of Vietnam's political institutions.

The National Assembly (NA) is the central-level body whose representatives are elected for five-year terms. At local levels of authority (i.e. province and below), People's Councils elect executive People's Committees, which handle affairs of state in their respective localities. Since the early 1990s, many Vietnam observers wistfully held out the possibility that the NA would represent an incipient force for democracy, but there has been little discernible movement in this direction. Though the NA has undoubtedly modernized and has achieved a higher profile, it is still at the end of the day a deliberative body that is subordinate to the Politburo.

There are several features of the NA that deserve mention. The NA comprises representatives of different localities, although some centrally nominated representatives do not reside in those localities. The NA has a tiny number of representatives who are not Party members, and the

number has actually declined in recent years. A vast majority of new
NA representatives are also first-term representatives and are not professional representatives in that their duties are only part-time. Lastly,
all candidates for NA and local people's councils must be vetted and
approved by local election boards, which are managed by the Vietnam
Fatherland Front, and which can effectively bar undesired candidates.

Scholarship on representative institutions in Vietnam has developed
only within the last two decades (Thayer 1993). The clearest analysis
of the organization and operation of representative institutions is
MacElwee's 2006 study (UNDP 2006). Although the democratic credentials of the NA are questionable, the NA has played an increasingly high-
profile role in national politics. One of the more interesting aspects of
the NA concerns the processes by which it is elected.

This is a subject of special interest to Edmund Malesky and Paul
Schuler, who have written a number of pieces exploring the NA. They
have studied electoral institutions, demonstrating how elections tend
to be relatively free of ex-post manipulation, but also show that ex-ante
manipulation is widespread with favored regime candidates benefitting
from districts with lower candidate-to-seat ratios and weaker competition (Malesky and Schuler 2010, 2012). Despite this assistance, every
election a large number of centrally nominated candidates still manage
to lose. These losses are heavily concentrated in rich, southern provinces that tend to be net contributors to the Vietnamese budget, demonstrating a salient political cleavage that has been underexplored. Finally,
the authors have studied what Vietnamese delegates do upon election,
taking advantage of the biannual query sessions, where delegates are
allowed to quiz ministers on important political issues of the data. The
authors find that the most active and critical delegates tend to be full-
time delegates who are locally nominated. These delegates manage the
provincial delegations and often have the most interaction with local
leaders and constituents. Most provocatively, Malesky and Schuler
(2011) find that delegates who survived close elections are also likely to
be more active in query, offering tentative evidence that their behavior is
meant to win the support of local leaders or perhaps even local voters.

In his chapter in this volume, Malesky trains his analysis on the
implications of election for NA representatives, seeking to penetrate
the opaque political maneuvering that governs the selection of candidates and the trajectory of their political careers. Arguing against a
widely hypothesized idea about elections in authoritarian regimes –
that such elections are used to help identify young political talent for
further grooming, Malesky finds that in Vietnam, leaders are largely

determined prior to elections, suggesting that elections for the NA are used for information acquisition and co-optation. Like Vu and Jandl's chapters, Malesky situates Vietnam in the broader literature on comparative politics.

Beyond the Party, State, and representative institutions, lies a number of other important state actors. These include mass organizations, the military, police, and public security forces, secondary associations, and regime dissidents. Mass organizations include the Vietnam Fatherland Front, the Vietnam women's union, the Communist Youth League, Peasants Union, and so on. These organizations play explicitly political roles as they are charged with promoting and ensuring faithfulness to the Party line in word and action across a variety of sectors. While none of the chapters in this volume subjects mass organizations to direct analysis, their significance is explained through various references found across the chapters.

State repression, regime dissents, and secondary associations

A common theme of literature on comparative politics is the mutually constitutive relation between state and society, often problematically termed "state-society relations." Gainsborough (2010) suggests a good way to study the state is to not focus on the state itself, but rather what it does in its external relations. His analysis illustrates the role of the patronage networks that state and party leaders use to cultivate influence, promote upward mobility within the state, and use for protection (Gainsborough ibid.). Kerkvliet's historical analysis of agricultural policy is a good illustration of the complexities of this mutually constitutive relationship, as it demonstrates how tensions between the state and citizens can transform state action (Kerkvliet 2005). The last chapters of this volume contribute to this stream of literature through analyses of regime dissidents, state repression, and "civil society."

Carl Thayer has rightly chided scholars of Vietnam for ignoring the important role of the military, police, and public security forces, who are routinely left out of analyses of politics in Vietnam even as they play an indispensible role in the functioning and maintenance of the regime. As we notedearlier, Thayer's critique can be applied to work on authoritarian regimes more generally. As Thayer and various collaborators have shown, the military and police are important political and economic forces in their own right (see, for example, Thayer 2008 and 2011). In this volume, Thayer presents the first scholarly analysis of Vietnam's institutions of state repression. His chapter details the agencies and individuals involved and the tactics they deploy in their efforts to detect, discourage, and punish dissent. Thayer's chapter examines the repressive role of key state organs in buttressing Vietnam's one-party state: the chapter analyzes how authoritarian rule is actually implemented by examining the methods and tactics used to repress pro-democracy activists, bloggers, journalists, and religious leaders. He concludes that Vietnam's one-party state is a divided entity and that its organs of repression are sometimes manipulated by Party leaders engaged in factional in-fighting.

Thayer's analysis is timely in two respects. First, there has been a great deal of interest among Vietnam scholars in the formation of autonomous secondary associations (i.e. civil society groups). Indeed, there have been several recent analyses of "civil society" and "political civil society" activities in Vietnam (Thayer and Marr 1993 were among the first to appear, see also for example: Kerkvliet et al. 2003; Thayer 2009a, 2009b; Wells-Dang 2010a, 2011). And while there is universal agreement that such organizations operate in a restrictive environment, there has until now been no serious attention to the organizations that monitor and suppress such activity.

The question of civil society is not interesting solely from the perspective of state repression. As Andrew Wells-Dang's contribution to this volume shows, Vietnam has in recent years seen the emergence of new forms of social organization akin to what some people might call "civil society." In a recent comparative analysis of Vietnam and China, Wells-Dang analyzes how the CPV selectively allows NGOs and other actors to shape policy (and even oppose Party decisions) as long as it is done within certain paths – essentially calling for different policies without challenging the supremacy of the Party itself, and by individuals, not organized political groupings. He analyzes opposition to the re-development of Hanoi's Lenin Park and also how the Party uses NGOs in trying out development policies or for environmental policymaking. Writing in this volume, Wells-Dang questions the tendency to view civil society in Vietnam as weak. Through case studies, Wells-Dang suggests that Vietnam possesses a civil society that exercises significant political influence, whether this is achieved through or in spite of the formal political system.

Let us first consider regime dissidents. While Vietnam's political culture appears to have changed, the CPV's treatment of political dissidents exhibits no clear pattern of evolution. If anything, the past several years has seen an uptick in the number of cases against dissidents and in the severity of penalties against them. No doubt, the recent intensification of repression is a reflection of heightened dissident activity, which has been notably enabled by electronic media. What is less clear is who these dissidents are, and why the phenomenon of resistance persists. Within the past years, several scholars have analyzed dissident behavior and the fate of several high-profile dissents (e.g. Abuza ibid.; Thayer 2006). In the present collection, Benedict Kerkvliet takes such analysis further, as he seeks to understand underlying patterns in dissident activity and the state's repressive responses.

Vietnam is frequently characterized as a highly repressive regime. In his chapter in this collection, Kerkvliet moves toward a more nuanced understanding of different types of dissident behavior and how the Communist Party regime deals with the increasing incidence of dissent in recent decades. Arguing against prevailing characterizations, Kerkvliet observes a degree of toleration of dissent by authorities and a lack of uniformity in their repression. He argues provocatively that the claim that authorities in Vietnam tolerate little or no dissent or opposition is off the mark.

The big questions in Vietnam concern the future of the one-party state in the context of a market economy. Some observers believe they detect signs of deep rot. Others readily accept the presence of tensions and contradictions in Vietnam's politics, but also note the authorities' effectiveness in co-opting, deterring, or crushing nodes of opposition. At present, the maintenance of one-party rule in Vietnam remains dependent on the intimidation and punishment of individuals. Recent transgressions by China in the Southeast Asia Sea show that Vietnamese are as politically engaged as ever. Whether sustained collective opposition to repressive rule can materialize is a question time will tell.

Overall, this collection of chapters marks a substantial contribution to existing literature. On the one hand, the chapters elucidate ideographic nuance. On the other hand, they situate Vietnam in relation to wider comparative historical research and their theoretical debates. In this respect, the chapters suggest the studies of Vietnamese politics might avoid a shortcoming of much of the literature on China, which has tended to treat China as a world unto itself. Vietnam is important in its own right. But its analysis has much to contribute to ongoing debates about broader historical experience and attendant social theory.

Authoritarianism and comparative politics

The chapters in this collection, though they are not all explicitly comparative or theoretical, raise significant questions for the broader theoretical literature on comparative politics and authoritarianism. How do one-party states sustain themselves? How and why do such states seek to improve internal accountability and does it matter? How does localities' interplay with a global market economy affect regime coherence? Why do authoritarian regimes invest great energies in electoral processes? And, how does repression and contestation operate? Vietnam offers insights for each of these debates and as such contributes to the development of the broader theoretical literature.

That theoretical literature on authoritarianism is undergoing a revival stems not only from the persistence of such regimes but also from the novel features of their institutional evolution and the debates to which these adaptations have given rise. Questions about regime institutionalization, legitimization, economic governance, repression, and contestation remain as relevant as ever. But the particular metamorphoses of today's authoritarian regimes have raised new questions about the character, determinants, and effects of the processes and institutions that sustain them, and not least the significance of these developments for existing social theory. Many of the leading questions in these debates have been over how, in a supposed "age of democracy," authoritarian regimes have modified their rule in ways that have enabled them not only to survive and be resilient but also to reproduce and even deepen conditions for domination. Given the rapid economic growth in China and other countries, there is also great interest in the relation between politics and economy under authoritarian regimes.

Many of the most important debates in current scholarship on authoritarianism have emerged through ideographic and comparative studies of authoritarian regimes in Asia, and indeed studies of authoritarianism have contributed to the development of Asian studies. The unforeseen and historically unparalleled course of developments in China, for example, has led to a reconsideration of basic questions concerning authoritarian regimes' character and durability. With its rapid and sustained economic growth China and Vietnam, too, have invited a new round of questioning about whether or under what conditions authoritarian regimes are more able to foster "development" and industrialization than their democratic counterparts. In light of the recent histories of Taiwan and the Republic of Korea, we also ponder political effects of economic change.

Analyses of the so-called "hybrid regimes" of Southeast Asia has been another center of debate. Larry Diamond (2002) has distinguished among different types of authoritarian regimes across world regions. William Case (2009), among others, has discussed features of such regimes in Southeast Asia, including electoral authoritarian regimes, liberal authoritarian regimes, and so on. The analysis of hybrid forms has been concerned not merely with how regimes ought to be categorized; they also seek to explain processes and institutions of regime maintenance and transformation and why conditions for democratic transition do not obtain. This, in turn, has invited an engagement with theoretical debates in comparative politics about the mechanisms that underlie different varieties of authoritarian rule (Snyder 2006; Geddes 2005) and about the essential nature of authoritarian regimes. Indeed, the value of the authoritarian designation has been subject to question on both conceptual and theoretical grounds.

Conceptually, authoritarianism has been derided as a "residual" category ascribed to a wide spectrum of regimes that are neither democratic nor totalitarian (Brachet-Márquez 2010). Linz's original definition of authoritarian political systems, for example, refers to

> political systems with limited, not responsible, political pluralism, without elaborate and guiding ideology, but with distinctive mentalities, without extensive nor intensive political mobilization, except at some points in their development, and in which a leader or occasionally a small group exercises power within formally ill-defined limits but actually quite predictable ones. (Linz 1964: 255)

No doubt the unwieldiness of the above speaks to enormous variation in the political systems or regimes that fit this description (Linz 2000: 160). Indeed Linz later followed up with a painstaking conceptual unpacking of six distinctive types of authoritarian rule. Efforts to theorize more precisely the origins and development of different varieties of authoritarianism have produced rich analyses. O'Donnell's notion of "bureaucratic authoritarianism" is perhaps the most classic example in this regard (O'Donnell 1973). Though conceived in the analysis of Latin American regimes, O'Donnell's ideas have been invoked in studies of politics in other world regions. In the face of recent changes, do these studies retain relevance?

Yes and no. Though older literature on authoritarianism remains relevant, it is apparent that it suffers from three principal limitations. The first is its tendency to view regime characteristics through the prism of normative theories of democracy (Snyder ibid.). Second, in much of the older literature, ascription of the term authoritarian tends to lend to a static perspective that directs attention away from how regimes evolve over time (Brachet-Márquez ibid.). Third, earlier understandings of authoritarianism do not offer an adequate analysis of today's nondemocratic post-totalitarian regimes, including but not limited to China and Vietnam.

Indeed, the regimes in contemporary China and Vietnam expose the limits of earlier treatments of authoritarianism in these respects; neither regime exhibits even limited political pluralism, except of the intra-party sort. While interest groups and factions exist, none constitutes a political opposition, at least as it is conventionally understood. In both regimes the nature of authoritarianism has proven dynamic indeed; limited personal freedoms tied especially to consumption and (less) to accumulation have, along with a battery of new forms of surveillance, replaced overt political mobilizations. Nonetheless, groups and leaders within both countries exercise power within reasonably well-defined limits. Though ideology has waned and is at times incoherent (though perhaps especially to foreign critics), ideology plays a nontrivial role in regime maintenance. No doubt China and Vietnam are clear instances of post-totalitarian authoritarianisms, which is consistent with earlier claims (e.g. Brzezinski 1989). Yet at some point the use of such abstract labels as "post-totalitarian" draws us away from the empirical analysis that is necessary for the further development of theory (London 2012).

If older literature on authoritarianism has certain limits, more recent literature poses important new questions and directions for research. In general, the recent revival in the study of authoritarian regimes differs from its predecessors in important ways. Theoretically, the work has placed greater emphasis on the institutional features of authoritarian countries (legislatures, elections, local-central relations). Scholars have argued that such institutions are too costly to be mere democratic window dressing, and must therefore serve other authoritarian goals, such as promoting legitimacy, co-opting opposition, or signaling regime strength.

Empirically, the new literature has operated at a higher level of abstraction, predominantly testing theories using large-n analysis of authoritarian countries over time. This work has delivered several important findings, pointing to an increase in the prevalence and durability of authoritarian regimes (Puddington 2010), especially single-party systems, throughout the world (Magaloni and Kricheli 2010; Geddes 2005). Dovetailing with this finding, a separate sub-literature has emphasized that the successful authoritarian regimes are those that make use of nominally democratic institutions. Contributors to this literature have demonstrated a strong association between having a national legislature and regime longevity, political stability, and economic growth, particularly in single-party systems (Geddes 2005; Gandhi and Przeworski 2007; Gandhi 2009; Wright 2008).

While this literature has been fruitful, these contributions are only the first step. There is a need to build and expand on this work in three principal ways. First, most work that seeks to differentiate between authoritarian regime uses a typological approach, classifying states as single-party, personalist, military junta, or monarchy. These accounts are less useful, however, when it comes to intermediate cases or variation within subtypes. This is unfortunate, because as Malesky et al. (2011) show there is tremendous variation in institutional design and important economic outcomes (e.g. economic growth and inequality) within Vietnam and China, two countries which are always coded exactly the same way.

Second, the new authoritarian institutions literature has tended to overemphasize the transplantation of nominally democratic institutions into authoritarian countries, but has not paid nearly as much attention to the authoritarian institutions that do not have democratic analogues. For instance, the literature's focus on national assemblies and elections overlooks the fact that the official government legislature in single-party regimes is far less influential than the Party legislature, often called the Central Committee. While Shih (2012) has begun to make headway on these issues in China, we still have very little comparative analysis of: (1) election/selection to the Central Committee; (2) the relationship between the Central Committee and the Party Executive (the Political Bureau); (3) accountability mechanisms within the Central Committee; and (4) the responsiveness of Central Committee delegates to the underlying constituencies they titularly represent. Moreover, we still have limited understanding between institutional variation and outcomes we care about (economic growth, public goods provision, inequality, social stability).

Third, the theoretical thrust of the literature has strongly emphasized the role of authoritarian institutions co-opting potential opposition or enabling power-sharing among political elites. According to the co-optation argument, rulers, especially in countries with fewer natural resources, need cooperation from broader swaths of society and will thus use elections and assemblies to give these groups a formal say in the policy-making process (Wright 2008; Gandhi and Przeworski 2007; Malesky and Schuler 2011). The elections may be used to incorporate elites, Party members, or societal interests groups (Gandhi and Lust-Okar 2009), but critically these groups must be outside of the ruling inner circle. Gandhi and Przeworski (2007: 1283) summarize the co-optation argument in this manner: "Authoritarian rulers may need cooperation and may fear a threat from various segments of society. Cooperation can be induced and the threat can be reduced by sharing spoils or by making policy compromises." They conclude that legislatures are well suited for this role.

A related alternative to the co-optation theory argues that the goal of institutions, such as strong parties and legislatures in authoritarian settings, is not about co-opting potential opposition but instead providing a mechanism for power sharing with regime supporters that allows collective action against a regime leader (Gehlbach and Keefer 2010). All authoritarian leaders rely to some extent on allies to provide security and perform the basic functions of the government. To win their cooperation, a regime leader shares power and the spoils of rule with these allies. Critically, however, the arrangement hinges on the ability of the supporters to credibly rebel or oust the leader if he violates his side of the bargain. Because of the secrecy of regimes, it is difficult to monitor the leaders' actions; as a result, authoritarian leaders erect institutions that improve transparency, allowing supporters to better monitor the activities of their leaders (Gehlbach and Keefer 2010; Boix and Svolik 2013) and the regularized participation of all players.

Although the co-optation and power-sharing theories represent important advances in our understanding of why regime's select particular institutional constellations, they underemphasize the coercive nature of authoritarian regimes, neglecting the equally important public security and legal institutions. Institutions, like judiciaries and legislatures, can be used to further authoritarian control (Slater 2008); elections can signal and project regime strength (Magaloni 2006); and regime party promotional mechanisms offer a delicate balance of punishment and power sharing, which furthers party strength (Svolik 2008). In this volume, the work of Thayer and Kerkvliet more deeply explores the coercive nature of authoritarian regimes, by illustrating how public security systems operate and how judicial institutions address political dissidents. Although these repressive institutions are prevalent in every authoritarian setting, obtaining detailed data on them has been difficult, and as a result, scholarship has been skewed toward the normatively positive features of authoritarian rule.

Situating Vietnam in asian politics

The wide variance of authoritarian regimes in Asia has been an important source of theoretical inspiration and debate in the new scholarship. Authoritarian models range from the market-Leninist states of China and Vietnam (London 2012) to the totalitarian cultism of the Democratic People's Republic of Korea; from the unstable "liberal authoritarianism" of Hong Kong to the electoral authoritarianism characteristic of the

regimes in Malaysia and Singapore. What unites these cases is a relatively simple set of authoritarian traits: concentrated power and durable
limits on political expression and or and/or competition. Analysis of
these traits has contributed to the development of theory.

Studies of authoritarianism in China have improved our understanding of "middle range" processes, such as authoritarian regimes'
internal operations and incentive systems (Shirk 1996; Jing Huang
2006; Yumin Sheng 2009), elite politics (Shih 2008; Cheng Li 2001),
local politics and economic governance (Landry 2008), and the politics
of accountability (Tsai 2007) and contestation. As the above citations
indicate, the literature on China has been a growth area, and one that
has generated a tremendous volume of literature. But the literature on
China is insular. Though much of it is theoretically grounded and meth-
odologically sophisticated, it is a literature that has not been particularly
geared to comparison or, by extension, to the development of theory
beyond China. Though there have been exceptions it is arguable that
China studies has in particular become something of a stand-alone
academic industry, in which international comparisons are by and large
not sought out. The same can be said of the much smaller literatures on
politics in Vietnam and the DPRK.

Debates, tensions, and controversies

As this volume has taken shape, authors have been encouraged not
only to situate Vietnam within broader debates in comparative politics,
but also to directly discuss their arguments in light of those advanced
by others. The result is a cohesive and lively discussion that coalesces
around a set of common themes and a number of important controversies. All of the chapters in this volume examine the ways power and
domination in Vietnam is constituted, structured, and maintained. Yet
while the contributors find agreement on many basic questions, they
diverge in other respects. At other moments, authors appear to diverge
from conclusions they previously held dear.

Where Tuong Vu sees a Party-State undergoing decay and ossification,
others suggest the Party and State retain certain dynamism. Malesky's
claim that patterns of elite recruitment in formally representative
institutions facilitate co-optation appears raises questions about his
other work, which has emphasized the independence of the National
Assembly. Jandl's claims that unlike China, where the principal (central
Party) controls the agents through the power of promotion, in Vietnam
the agents have captured the principal and are becoming the principals

as they get promoted as a result of success. This claim raises interesting questions for Vu's contribution as well as for comparative work on China and Vietnam, such as Malesky et al.'s comparison of China and Vietnam referenced earlier. Thayer's analysis of state-repressive institutions, which emphasizes their efficacy and harshness, is contradicted by Wells-Dang and Kerkvliet's assessment, that the Party-State is essentially or significantly "tolerant." Yet Wells-Dang and Kerkvliet's suggestion is itself contradicted by the constant stream of arrests and incidences of dissident persecution of the last two years. The tensions among the conclusions of the various authors makes for a lively volume and provides fertile ground for the concluding chapter, which takes stock of the arguments advanced in the various chapters and its implications for evolving understandings of politics in Vietnam. Having laid this groundwork, we can now turn to the individual chapters and dig deeper into power and politics in contemporary Vietnam. In the book's concluding chapter we will return to these questions and raise additional questions about Vietnam's politics moving forward.

2
Persistence Amid Decay: The Communist Party of Vietnam at 83

Tuong Vu

In the last few decades the theoretical literature on communist regimes has closely followed the rise and demise of the communist camp. In the early 1970s when those regimes were at their peaks, analysts were preoccupied with the question of how they had successfully evolved and adapted after seizing power (Huntington 1968; Huntington and Moore 1970). Strongly influenced by modernization theories, this scholarship assumed that, as vanguard forces of modernization, communist parties were born to last. While most scholars failed to predict the collapse of the Soviet bloc in the late 1980s, theoretical attempts have since shed much insight into the causes of that collapse (Kalyvas 1999; Ekiert 1996; Solnick 1998; Bunce 1999; Goodwin 2001). However, the literature remains limited for the surviving communist systems in China, Vietnam, Laos, North Korea, and Cuba. There, communist parties still dominate and, for China and Vietnam, have overseen successful economic reforms. Among analysts of China, a sharp debate exists between "optimists" (Shambaugh 2008; Nathan 2003),[1] who view the communist dictatorship as viable, and "pessimists" (Pei 2006), who emphasize decay and possible collapse. There is no such well-positioned debate in Vietnam, although similar questions have certainly been raised and have even gained salience in the context of developments in 2012 and 2013. This chapter addresses part of this gap through a historical analysis of the Communist Party of Vietnam (CPV)'s evolution and the causes of its persistence. There have been relatively few studies of this party, not only its current situation but also its historical evolution (Pike 1978; Huynh Kim Khanh 1982; Thayer 1988; Stern 1993; Vasavakul 1997; Gainsborough 2007; Koh 2008). Early scholarship is generally descriptive and woefully dated. More recent scholarship, including my own, has taken advantage of newly released archival documents from Vietnam and the former Soviet bloc (Quinn-Judge 2005; Vu 2010).

A major goal of this chapter is to place Vietnam in comparative perspective and to draw out implications for theories on the persistence of single-party dictatorships. Most scholarship on Vietnam does not engage the comparative literature. On the other hand, comparativists often mention Vietnam only in passing and do not even get their facts right.[2] In this chapter, I extend concepts developed by Huntington, but examine both the institutionalization of the CPV in the 1950s *and* its decay in recent decades. I reject the teleology in much scholarship on authoritarian regimes that assumes their eventual transition to democracy. Mindful of the abrupt breakdown of the Soviet bloc, neither do I assume the eternal persistence of communist regimes as Huntington did. In particular, I will show that the CPV has evolved through three phases: expansion and institutionalization (1945–60), ossification and decay (1970–86), and reform and continuing decay (1986–present). It is facing a combination of threats and opportunities, and its continuing domination is in grave danger.

As will be argued here, the Vietnamese case contributes to theories of single-party dictatorships by illustrating the role of elite politics, violence, war, and rents in the evolution of these systems. Huntington's observation that revolutionary violence is crucial for the durability of communist systems appears to be borne out in the Vietnamese case.[3] While the wars led by the CPV have been viewed by some as catalytic of a durable single-party dictatorship (Smith 2005: 449), my analysis suggests wars have played an ambiguous role. The same is true regarding "rents" (external assistance), which have had both favorable and adverse effects on regime persistence in Vietnam. Finally, an important source of persistence for the Vietnamese dictatorship, as for other communist dictatorships, was its near-total grip on society. Studies that lump communist with other single-party dictatorships naturally overlook this factor.

The evolution of the Communist Party of Vietnam[4]

Huntington defines party institutionalization as "the process by which organizations and procedures acquire value and stability," and which involves four aspects, namely, adaptability, complexity, autonomy, and coherence (Huntington 1968: 18–24). Adaptability refers to a party's ability to adjust over time as its founders pass away from the scene and as the political environment changes. Complexity refers to the development of subunits and the differentiation of functions within a party. Autonomy means a party has the capacity to make decisions independent from the pressure and control of social groups, while coherence refers to members' substantial consensus on the party's goals and procedures. Since seizing power in 1945, the CPV has evolved through three phases. It experienced rapid growth in the first few years and became institutionalized during 1948–60. In the next phase (1970–86), it became ossified at the top and decayed at the bottom. Since 1986, the party has continued to experience a slow decay even while its leaders have sought to reform and rejuvenate it.

Expansion and institutionalization (1930–60)

The CPV was founded in 1930 in Kowloon with guidance from the Comintern in Moscow.[5] First leaders of the party were trained in Moscow and sought to organize it in the Leninist mold. In their views, the tasks of their revolution involved two interlocking steps: the overthrowing of colonial rule and the construction of socialism. The party's strategy was to build an alliance of workers and peasants, but tactically other groups such as intellectuals and landlords were to be mobilized if necessary for short-term collaboration.

The party operated in secret from both inside and outside Vietnam. It led two failed rebellions (1931–32 and 1940) and suffered brutal repression by the colonial regime. Its first five general secretaries died young, either in prison or from execution. In 1941, a small group of surviving leaders set up Viet Minh, a front to unite all Vietnamese, regardless of their social class, to fight for independence. Viet Minh operated out of the jungle near the border of Vietnam and China. At the time, the party had a small following of a few thousands and little formal structure. In fact, in early 1945 most members were still locked up somewhere in colonial prisons, where many had spent a decade or more.

When the Japanese surrendered to the Allies in August 1945, communist cadres, groups of Viet Minh sympathizers, and other political groups rode on the back of mass riots and took power (Tonnesson 1991; Marr 1995; Vu 2010: ch. 5). Failing to obtain Soviet support but forced to confront anticommunist groups and their foreign backers, the CPV sought to build as broad a coalition as possible. The new government reflected this effort and was composed of an amalgam of political groups. The CPV had control over the major ministries and its own militia but not the entire state apparatus. Territorially, government authority was established only in larger towns but not over the entire country.

This amalgam also was reflected in party membership. Over the next few years, the CPV attracted many new members. It grew from a few thousands in late 1945 to 20,000 in late 1946. By late 1949, membership stood at 430,000 (Vu 2010: ch. 6). The rapid growth in membership indicated party policy during this period not to be strict about the class background or ideological loyalty of new members. Central leaders also had little effective control over local party branches. This resulted in fast but unfocused growth as the party sought to broaden membership without much emphasis on quality. Most new members came from more privileged social groups, such as educated urban elites, landlords, and rich and middle peasants. The absolute majority of members came from north and north central Vietnam with comparatively few from southern Vietnam, where the French had taken effective control.

In 1948, CPV leaders were anticipating the victory of Chinese communists on mainland China and the opportunity of joining forces with the Chinese to fight the French. Radical leaders led by General Secretary Truong Chinh feared the "contamination" of the party by the admission of upper-class members and called for tightening the criteria for membership and for other measures to strengthen central control. The party thus began the policy to restrict the growth of membership, to expel members who came from privileged backgrounds, and to intensify ideological indoctrination for all members.

The new policy ended the period of expansion and launched the institutionalization of the party. This coincided with the Viet Minh government's formally joining the Soviet camp and the arrival of massive Chinese aid and advisors (Chen Jian 1993). These advisors were embedded in many party organizations from district level up, and trained Vietnamese cadres in the Maoist methods of thought reform, land reform, and mass mobilization in general. While Chinese military aid helped the CPV lead the anti-French resistance to its successful outcome, Chinese guidance on mass mobilization was critical for remolding the CPV into a Maoist form.

By about 1960, the CPV had become more or less institutionalized if we use Huntington's four criteria of adaptability, complexity, autonomy, and coherence. First, by then the CPV could show that it had overcome numerous challenges and successfully adapted its functions to great changes in its operational environment. The party began as a revolutionary group on the fringe of the colonial society, acquired leadership of the nationalist movement, led the struggle against France for independence until winning control over North Vietnam, and successfully established its rule there. Measured by generational age, however, it is less clear that the party was fully adaptable.[6] While by 1960 the party had adapted to successive leadership changes from Ho Chi Minh (1941–50) to Truong Chinh (1950–56) to Le Duan (since 1958),[7] Le Duan and Truong Chinh were of the same generation, and both Ho Chi Minh and Truong Chinh remained influential in the Politburo after Duan had risen to the top.

Second, through successful adaptation to changing roles the CPV had become a complex organization by 1960. The CPV now formed the core of the state and its cadres held most public offices with differentiated roles in administration and in economic and cultural management. The party controlled a powerful military which had earlier defeated the French at Dien Bien Phu. It had nationalized most private property, including land and factories; had taken over the markets of key products; and had brought most social means of communication (newspapers and publishing houses) under state ownership. The party now had branches in most villages and urban neighborhoods in North Vietnam. The land reform (1953–56), during which about 15,000 landlords or 0.1 percent of the population were executed, had allowed the party to overthrow the old power structure in the village and to promote loyal party cadres to positions of leadership (Vo Nhan Tri 1990: 3; Vu 2010: 103). Party control now encompassed most aspects of social life in North Vietnam, as one would expect in a communist totalitarian system.

Third, Marxism-Leninism allowed the party to claim a vanguard position above and autonomous from society. In particular, the CPV claimed to fight against feudalism and imperialism. Even before being firmly established in power, communist leaders had challenged powerful social forces such as landlords, first with laws to limit land rent and later with the land reform campaign. Yet the party was not beholden to peasants for very long: land reform was only a tactic to mobilize them. As soon as the party felt secure, it took away land, draught animals, and tools from peasants in the collectivization campaign (1958–60). Besides ideology, material support from the Soviet bloc also enabled the CPV to be autonomous from society. In a society threatened by famine and exhausted after a long war, foreign aid gave the party a crucial leverage against social forces.

Finally, the "organizational rectification" campaign (1952–56) that was implemented in most party organizations from provincial level down helped strengthen the coherence of the party, the fourth criterion according to Huntington. During this campaign, which was essentially a brutal purge, most members who came from "bad" class backgrounds were expelled to be replaced by poor peasants. Previously, party members who came from upper and middle classes and who made up as much as two-thirds of membership did not wholly support the party's goal of building socialism. They had rallied to the party only as far as national independence was concerned. After the purge, the poor peasants who owed the party for their lands, houses, and positions could be trusted to follow the party to their deaths if necessary. The cohesion of the CPV was also aided by its leaders' tireless efforts at carrying out a cultural revolution, including the systematic propagation of Marxist-Leninist-Stalinist-Maoist thoughts, values, and methods throughout the ranks of the party and in the broader society (Ninh 2002; Vu 2008, 2009b).

Ossification and decay (1970–86)

By Huntington's four criteria, the CPV seemed well-institutionalized by 1960. Yet in the following decade the party became ossified under the leadership of Le Duan (1960–86). Duan was from central Vietnam and had spent his career mostly in the Mekong delta until he replaced Truong Chinh in 1958 (officially in 1960). Duan advocated the use of violence to unify Vietnam early on, but the party adopted his views only after he rose to the top. Under his leadership, the CPV led a protracted war to defeat the government of South Vietnam backed by the United States. The war ended in victory for North Vietnam, but the CPV emerged from victory a less cohesive and dynamic organization. Evidence is still some-what sketchy, but the general trend is clear.

First, the CPV under Le Duan (1960–86) adapted successfully to changing circumstances in the first half of this period but later became ossified. Measured by chronological age, not only did the party survive but it also won the civil war and emerged as the unchallenged ruler over all of Vietnam by 1975. Measured by generational age, the score is mixed. The size of the Central Committee elected in 1976 tripled, allowing new blood in the top leadership.[8] At the very top, however, not until 1986 when Le Duan died was the party able to arrange for a new leadership to succeed first-generation leaders. From 1960 to 1976, the same eleven Politburo members of the first-generation ran the party.[9] All the surviving members of the previous Politburo were retained except one.[10] New faces made up less than half of the new Politburo. Among these new members, all had been of high ranks in 1960 – in other words, no surprises.[11] First-generation leaders who were in their seventies continued to dominate the Politburo in the 1970s. Several of them would die one by one while in office,[12] and the other Politburo members of this cohort would retire by the mid-1980s but most still wielded tremendous influence even after they had formally retired.[13]

Measured by functional adaptability, the record is also mixed. On the one hand, the party was able to adapt to new challenges as the war against the Republic of Vietnam (South Vietnam) and the United States escalated in the 1960s. This war required the total mobilization of the North Vietnamese population and the enlistment of full support from the Soviet bloc. The CPV performed these tasks brilliantly over the fifteen years that led to its victory. On the other hand, this war was not the first war led by the party, which had accumulated nearly a decade of war-making just a few years earlier fighting the French. Peace but not war was the real litmus test of the party's functional adaptability, and here the CPV failed miserably. There was little new thinking in the policy agenda of socialist construction between the 1950s and the 1970s. Despite the failure of collectivization in North Vietnam prior to unification, the party sought to replicate it in South Vietnam in the late 1970s – to the detriment of the Southern rich and vibrant economy.[14] The CPV also failed to notice changes in the international environment. Proud of their victory, party leaders expected world powers to bid for their favors.[15] Subsequent decisions to invade Cambodia and ally with the Soviet Union against China (1978–88) indicated that the party had been addicted to making war and failed to understand the need for peace after three decades of nearly continuous warfare.

On complexity, the CPV displayed a similarly mixed performance as with adaptability. The party underwent tremendous expansion during the war years. Between 1960 and 1976, party membership tripled from 0.5 to 1.5 million (Dang Cong San Viet Nam: v. 21, 491; v. 37, 705). The number of party cells also tripled, and that of party committees doubled in the same period (ibid.: v. 37, 764). At the same time, party organizations became less differentiated. As the entire society of North Vietnam was mobilized for war, economic, social, and cultural spheres of activity shrank tremendously. Most party and state organizations were geared toward wartime demands. Cadres acquired substantial experiences in military affairs but little else. Tens of thousands of young men and women were conscripted and thrown into the battlefield every year, including fresh college graduates and boys in their teens.[16] The slogan of the time "All for the front, all for victory" indicated that uniformity but not differentiation was favored as an organizational goal.[17] Uniformity helped the CPV lead the war to a successful outcome but sacrificed its complexity in the process.

After the war, the party expanded its organization to all of Vietnam and made economic development its top priority – so its complexity increased somewhat. However, war would resume shortly and last for another decade, meaning that any gains in complexity were limited. By 1986 – 11 years after unification – the CPV still maintained a large army of more than one million soldiers even though the percentage of military leaders in the Central Committee had reduced and some units were assigned to economic development tasks (Turley 1988). Nearly two-thirds of new party members recruited between 1976 and 1982 came from the army (ibid.: 200). Seventy six percent of party members were still from North Vietnam, indicating the party's failure to expand its territorial base to the south after unification (Thayer 1991: 21).

Turning to autonomy, the CPV continued to dominate and be autonomous from society throughout this period. Yet there were many cracks in the edifice after 1975. First, the Marxist-Leninist ideology sounded increasingly hollow in the face of a severe economic crisis that began soon after victory in the civil war. Second, a remarkable trend had occurred since 1976, namely the expansion of the Central Committee to include representatives from state organs and provincial party branches (Thayer 1988: 177–93). This expansion reflected the party leadership's desire to adapt to new circumstances, but the change opened up the potential that the Central Committee could be made to serve the interests of sectoral and local groups rather than those of the central party leadership.[18] As will be seen below, this potential was realized after the dominant figures of the first generation passed away from the scene and their successors in the Politburo could not command the same level of prestige and power.

The coherence of the CPV also declined under Le Duan. Duan formed a powerful alliance with Le Duc Tho, who was the head of the Central Organizational Commission with the power to groom and appoint party members to provincial and central leadership positions, including the Central Committee and the Politburo.[19] While Duan and Tho were never powerful enough to remove the other senior leaders,[20] they monopolized power to an unprecedented extent. Duan and Tho worked closely together in the late 1940s in the Mekong Delta. Both were long-term Politburo members but became close after Duan assumed the position of general secretary in 1958. Their ascendancy in the mid-1960s was helped by the split in the Soviet bloc that had tremendous repercussions for all communist parties worldwide. The split pitted the Soviet Union against China, resulting in intense debates in the CPV about which side it should take in the split (Grossheim 2005; Quinn-Judge 2005; Bui Tin 1995). Duan and Tho placed their bet with Mao, with the support or acquiescence of most Central Committee members. Based on this support, Duan and Tho carried out arrests of many high-ranking party and military leaders who did not agree with them. The arrests reportedly targeted Vo Nguyen Giap, the minister of defense, and even though the general emerged unharmed, his power was severely curbed. Although factionalism in Vietnam never approached the scale of Maoist China, it was significant under Le Duan and made a dent in the coherence of the CPV. As Duan's faction consolidated its grip, fear more than consensus governed intra-party relations.

While factional struggles played out secretly at the top, the base of the party showed signs of decay by the early 1970s. Two trends joined to create this situation. First, party leaders launched two main drives during the civil war to recruit new members – one in the early 1960s and the other in the early 1970s.[21] These two drives primarily accounted for the tripling of membership mentioned earlier, but similar to many campaigns in communist Vietnam, quantity ended up trumping quality in this field. An internal report written in 1966 raised many concerns about the quality of about 300,000 new members who had entered the CPV since 1960. In 1971, an examination of 74 factories discovered that nearly 15 percent of new members admitted since 1970 were "below the standards" set out in the Party Code, and another 19 percent were clearly "of poor quality" (Dang Cong San Viet Nam: v. 32, 303).[22] Party leaders subsequently launched several measures to improve the situation but found that expelling "low-quality" party members was difficult (as it was for any state bureaucrats) (ibid.: v. 443).

The second trend responsible for the decay was the emergence of a massive informal economy in the late 1960s. As Soviet and Chinese aid streamed into North Vietnam just when living standards sharply deteriorated due to war and poor economic management, an increasing number of party members engaged in corruption by stealing state property and selling rationed imported goods and materials on the thriving black market (ibid.: v. 34, 265 and v. 35, 1, 102, 106, 112; Vu 2005: 329–56). The rapid expansion of the party, the poor quality of many new recruits, and the spread of corruption eroded the coherence of the party as war protracted. A significant number of party members by the early 1970s was perhaps more interested in war profiteering or in social and political status than in making sacrifices for the revolution championed by the top leadership.

Reform and continuing decay (1986–present)

After Duan died in 1986 and Tho retired in the same year, new CPV leaders sought to reform and rejuvenate the party. This process has continued for the last two decades and brought many achievements. Yet the decay that began under Le Duan continued at a much faster rate and on many dimensions. Party reform has made the most progress in the criterion of adaptability. The party survived the collapse of the Soviet bloc and has achieved impressive results in economic reform. In the Politburo, the first generation and the transition generation have passed the baton to the second generation.[23] Succession has taken place, often following intense factional struggles, in now regularly held national party congresses. About one-third of Politburo and Central Committee members were replaced in each of the last six congresses. A mechanism perhaps designed to smooth out the process of succession is to allow key leaders who have retired to maintain some influence as "advisors" to the Politburo. On rejuvenating, Central Committee members have become younger and more educated, enabling the party to lead economic development more effectively. Perhaps in response to a more complex society, greater balance of representation among various sectors, gender, age groups, party, military, economic, state, and mass mobilization organizations have been sought in the composition of the Central Committee (Vasavakul 1997).

Adaptability can also be observed in ideological orientations. Party Congresses have dropped Marxist-Leninist principles one by one, such as the dictatorship of the proletariat and the alliance of workers and peasants (Lai 2006). Since 1991 "Ho Chi Minh Thought" has appeared besides Marxism-Leninism as part of an official ideology. After two decades promoting a market economy, the party has recently allowed its members to engage in private businesses, which were once deemed exploitative. From organizational to ideological matters, the CPV has veered far away from the rigidity of Le Duan's era. Still, the fundamental disposition of adaptability has been gradualism by which changes were incremental and lacked clear direction.

It is precisely this incremental adaptability that has not (yet) helped to create a more complex CPV. While the party has recovered from a membership fall in the late 1980s, most new recruits still come from state employees and military personnel.[24] Despite many efforts, the party has failed to penetrate new urban areas and private enterprises.[25] Party members can own businesses now, but owners of private businesses who want to join the party are still rarely admitted.[26] Not development but involution seems to be the trend, as the party can grow only by sucking from the state sector and the military already under its control but not by expanding its roots into a rapidly changing society. Parallel to limited reforms in administration to increase bureaucratic accountability as analyzed by Thaveeporn Vasavakul in this volume, party leaders have launched numerous programs to rationalize the party structure so that the CPV remains relevant and effective. Current initiatives include the formation of huge blocks of party organizations based on similar functions, and a pilot project to have party secretaries doubling as government executives at the local level. We know few specifics about the outcome of these recent institutional reforms, but available party reports suggest that they have brought only limited results (*Tap chi Xay Dung Dang* 1–2/2008).

Incremental adaptability was also insufficient to stem the erosion of the CPV's autonomy as it became increasingly vulnerable to corrupting social influences. We have seen earlier how corruption tied to a thriving black market became widespread among cadres in North Vietnam in the last years of the civil war. Corruption did not abate when that black market was legalized in the late 1980s. New forms of corruption have since emerged, and one particularly serious form involves the selling of office. With state agencies generating lucrative rents, party secretaries can now make fortunes by selling state positions to the highest bidders. Recently the party secretary of Ca Mau province was sacked after it was reported that he accepted money in return for appointments to top positions in the provincial government. His case was never made public, but he turned in 100 million dong ($6,000) that someone tried to bribe him. The said party secretary also claimed that he could have collected 1 billion dong ($60,000) for several appointments if he had wanted.[27]

This is not an isolated case. Le Kha Phieu, a former general secretary, revealed that people had tried to bribe him many times with thousands of dollars, perhaps to receive favorable appointments in return.[28] The power of appointment has turned party congresses into occasions for patronage networks to compete intensively for positions in the Central Committee, as Gainsborough describes:

> For Vietnamese officials, the key question at a congress is whether someone you are connected to personally or through your workplace moves up or out as a result of the circulation of positions, and what this means for you, your institutions, or your family in terms of the provision or loss of protection and access to patronage. In Vietnam, holding public office gives you access to patronage which can range from access to the state budget and the ability to make decisions about how to spend public money, to the authority to issue licenses or other forms of permissions, to carry out inspections, or to levy fines. (Gainsborough 2007)

I have mentioned above that sectoral and provincial interests have gained greater representation in the Central Committee since 1976. In the last two decades, those interests have gained substantial power at the expense of the Politburo.[29] Provincial leaders now form the largest bloc in the Central Committee (every province is entitled to at least one seat and each of the two largest cities send at least two). Provincial officials also enjoy many informal channels of influence through dense patronage networks based on places of origin, family relations, or other informal ties. It is not uncommon that local governments interpret central policies any way they like, ignore central policy with impunity, or comply only when subsidies are provided. After provinces were recently authorized to approve foreign investment projects up to a certain limit, they have scrambled for those projects on top of the regular contests for a share of the central budget.[30] The central party leadership may be more responsive to local demands than previously, but the autonomy of the party as an organization has declined.

CPV leaders see corruption as a major threat to the regime but evidence suggests corruption now involves the highest level, often through family links and crony networks.[31] Patronage and corruption are eroding the party's coherence. The occasional dismissal of a Politburo member (Nguyen Ha Phan), the premature end to the term of a general secretary (Le Kha Phieu), the sudden publicity of numerous corruption charges targeted at certain candidates for the Central Committee before a party congress (e.g. Nguyen Viet Tien) – these cases are clear evidence of patronage rivalries at work (Gainsborough 2007). As a retired high-ranking official in the Central Commission on Party Organization who must be well-informed about the party's internal problems recently lamented: "The [party] bureaucracy has increased greatly in size, while quality and effectiveness of policy decline. Red tape and corruption have not lessened but in fact become more serious. The danger is increasingly apparent that [emerging] special interest groups collude with each other to accumulate power, influence policy, and expropriate public property" (Lai 2010).

In sum, Huntington's concept of party institutionalization has been helpful in understanding the evolution of the CPV since 1945. The party has undergone expansion and institutionalization (1945–60), and ossification and decay (1970–86). Since 1986, CPV leaders have launched numerous initiatives to reform the party, but the results have been limited. The party displays an extraordinary ability to adapt, but has tended to react to challenges when they came. This reactive mentality has not helped the party to stem corruption and decay, which now reach the top level.

Origins of persistence

Studies of single-party dictatorships have shown that the origins of their persistence can be traced back to regime-founding moments. If rulers who come to power face a strong and well-organized opposition, and if no external assistance ("rents") is available, they are likely to build strong party organizations to maintain alliances with powerful social groups (Smith 2005: 430). The struggle against a strong opposition often entails civil wars or the mobilization of large-scale revolutionary violence, which eliminates potential enemies and creates a durable foundation for dictatorship (ibid.: 449– 50).

The case of the CPV confirms some of the above hypotheses but disconfirms others. First, it is clear that the party faced strong opposition when it seized power in 1945. As mentioned above, the CPV was not able to seize power on its own or to monopolize power when it set up the Viet Minh government in late 1945. This government relied heavily on the colonial elites and bureaucracy in its first years (Vu 2010: ch. 5). In southern Vietnam, various religious and political groups challenged Viet Minh, and the returning French quickly retook control of government. In northern Vietnam, anticommunist groups such as the Vietnam Nationalist Party (VNP) and the Vietnam Revolutionary League (VRL) had some popular following and the backing of *Guomindang* occupying forces. These groups attacked Viet Minh authorities in many provinces, and posed a real threat to the survival of Ho Chi Minh's government. The communists defeated the VNP and VRL by negotiating for French forces to replace *Guomindang* troops in mid-1946, only to start a war with the French six months later. On the one hand, their strong and well-organized enemies forced the communists to build a broad coalition, as Smith correctly argues (Smith 2005). On the other hand, it is not this broad coalition that helped the communist regime to persist. While the CPV grew a hundred times in size in just a few years, it lacked centralized control and internal cohesion, and fought the war with the French from a precarious position (Vu 2009a).

It was the campaigns of land reform and organizational rectification in the early 1950s that solidified the communist dictatorship. As discussed earlier, these campaigns were implemented under Chinese supervision and unleashed massive and systematic revolutionary violence. This violence not only reconstructed the party in the Maoist mold but also eliminated the economic and social basis of any potential opposition. It not only destroyed the landlord class, but also drove away nearly a million northern Catholics, who sought refuge in South Vietnam in 1954

(Hansen 2009: 173–211; Huy Duc 2012: 265). Unlike what Smith argues for other cases, "rents" contributed significantly to the lasting domination of the CPV since 1950. While communist China's material assistance was crucial for Ho's forces to defeat the French (and later the Americans and the Republic of Vietnam), Maoist techniques of thought reform and class warfare were key to uprooting social opposition and establishing a communist dictatorship penetrating deeply into village society.

While revolutionary violence contributed decisively to the durability of Vietnam's communist system, the war against the Republic of Vietnam and the United States during 1960–75 had mixed effects. This war necessitated the total mobilization of the northern population. As the economy stagnated, the war helped the CPV channel popular participation through total mobilization. Millions of young soldiers were sent to fight in the South or deployed to defend the North. Participation rate was extremely high: about 70 percent of youth in their late teens and early 20s were conscripted to serve in the military until the end of the war (Teerawichitchainan 2009: 74). US bombing campaigns that created extreme hardship and suffering for ordinary North Vietnamese helped increase regime legitimacy. US crude intervention (compared to discreet Soviet and Chinese support for communist Vietnam) inflamed nationalist anger among many Vietnamese, which the regime successfully exploited.

Yet war was as harmful to the communist dictatorship as it was helpful. I have discussed earlier how the civil war eroded the CPV's organizational complexity with its preoccupation with war. Furthermore, the Politburo dominated by Le Duan's faction used war as an excuse to delay holding a national party congress for more than ten years. In the meantime, the top party leadership aged and party organizations above the middle level ossified.

While the civil war had both positive and negative impacts on the communist dictatorship, the wars with Cambodia and China during 1978–89 came close to unraveling it. These conflicts did not provide upward mobility for youth because they never reached the level of casualties nor required total mobilization as did the earlier war. Military careers were far more limited now that most mobilized soldiers would be released from service in a few years. Vietnam also failed to attract as much foreign aid for these wars as in the civil war, which contributed to a severe economic crisis in the 1980s.

An important factor that has been overlooked in the comparative literature but helped the CPV to persist was its near-total grip of public life until the late 1980s. This is a feature that Vietnam shared with countries in the former Soviet bloc. Organizations created by the CPV for mass mobilization purposes, such as Women's Association, Writers' Association, and Trade Union, maintained branches in most economic, social, and cultural activities. Managers of collective farms were an integrated part of local governments, involving not only in production but also in social surveillance and control. The Communist Youth League and Pioneer Children's Union monitored youth and kept them busy. These organizations lengthened the party's arms to reach most individuals in society, distributing exclusive benefits of the planned economy to their members, offering upward mobility to motivated individuals, and generating a sense of symbolic participation.[32] At the same time, they could be mobilized to completely isolate political dissidents from society and effectively deny them alternative means of livelihood.[33]

Implications for the party's future

This chapter has analyzed the evolution of the CPV, using the concepts developed by Huntington while exploiting newly available archival sources and recently published studies. The CPV has undergone three phases in its history since assuming power: expansion and institutionalization (1945–60), ossification and decay (1970–86), reform and continuing decay (1986–present). The Vietnamese case offers a useful test for hypotheses about the persistence of single-party dictatorships. In particular, revolutionary violence was found to contribute decisively to the strength of the system, while war had ambiguous impact. Fighting war successfully necessitated military effectiveness, which in turn contributed to regime durability. Total war provided an important venue of political participation and upward social mobility. At the same time, (protracted) war facilitated the personal or factional monopoly of power, weakening the cohesion of the revolutionary party and causing it to ossify.

Contrary to theoretical expectations, rents had mixed effects in the Vietnamese case. Existing literature does not distinguish between building broad political coalitions and constructing cohesive organizations. The lack of rents during 1945–50 forced the CPV to build a broad but loose coalition instead of a cohesive organization. Chinese material aid since 1950 was crucial to help the CPV to defeat the French, but perhaps had only marginal effects on organizational building. It was the Maoist techniques of mass mobilization and class warfare imported and implemented under the close supervision of Chinese advisors that transformed the fragile communist party and regime into a cohesive organization and durable dictatorship. Another factor overlooked in the comparative literature is the state's near-total control over social life, a common characteristic of communist systems that is critical for their persistence. This is the most important characteristic that distinguishes totalitarian from authoritarian regimes.

Today the evolutionary path of Vietnam's ruling party is marked by continuing decay, even though decay does not mean immediate or eventual breakdown. Yet understanding the origins of the party's persistence offers some clues about current challenges and opportunities. First, revolutionary violence built a strong base for the party in the countryside, but market reform is destroying it. In the early years of reform, decollectivization was a popular policy that boosted agricultural production and peasants' income. But the regime soon turned its attention to the cities, which have attracted billions of dollars of foreign investment, and neglected agriculture ("So phan cua nong nghiep co phai la dang chet" 2009). While village governments charge peasants hefty fees for public services, provincial governments rush to turn farmland into golf courses and industrial parks to serve foreign investors (*Tuoi Tre* 2006a, 2006b; *Dat Viet* 2008[34]). The peasantry used to be the bedrock of support for the CPV but open rural protests now break out frequently.[35]

As part of the old totalitarian system established through revolutionary violence, the mass organizations led by the CPV have not been able to adjust to the market economy. The official Trade Union has struggled to remain relevant as the government restricts workers' right to strike and keeps the minimum wage low to attract foreign capital. The number of strikes (mostly against foreign employers) has increased tenfold since 2000, and all strikes have occurred spontaneously without the involvement or approval of local unions ("Xu huong lao dong va xa hoi Vietnam 2009/2010" 2010: 24–5; Clarke and Pringle 2009: 85–101). The official Farmers' Association has been criticized for taking the side of polluting foreign companies in disputes involving farmers who wanted to sue those companies for compensation (*Tuoi Tre* 2010). The Communist Youth League is saddled with problems of recruitment and aging leadership as young people lack interest in participating in its programs (*Tuoi Tre* 2006c; *Tien Phong* 2006).

Market reform also shrinks the CPV's monopoly of the cultural sphere. The liberalization of foreign trade and intense pressure from Western countries have forced the party to relax control over religions, which leads to the recent revival of religious activities and a surge of religious protests.[36] At the same time, rising living standards and freedom of travel now allow many families to send their children abroad to study.[37]

These young men and women are being exposed to ideas different from the indoctrination they receive at home. The recent cases of Le Cong Dinh, who came from a solid "revolutionary family," and Nguyen Tien Trung, whose father is a party member and official, attest to the danger of a Western education even for children of the elites.[38] A key challenge to the party's control over culture is the internet, which is not only an indispensable tool of the market but also an effective tool of communication for regime opponents like Dinh and Trung. The internet has provided access to information normally suppressed by the party and has become a virtual gathering place for these dissidents to organize and publicize their anti-government views.

Paradoxically, the current situation also presents opportunities for the CPV to persist. First, rents are now perhaps the strongest glue binding the elites together and keeping the emerging middle class loyal.[39] Rents create massive corruption that is gnawing at the regime's legitimacy, but they give the regime resources to sustain economic growth and maintain its massive coercive apparatus. This apparatus is estimated to employ every one out of six working Vietnamese (Hayton 2010: 73).[40] As long as economic growth continues, the dictatorship should be safe. Second, the mobilization of nationalism in past wars has contributed the recent surge of nationalist sentiments against China (Vu forthcoming). If war breaks out, or if the level of threats from China keeps rising, the CPV may be able to rally popular support while suppressing demands for political liberalization. Unlike the war against the United States in the 1960s, a war with China today may split and destroy the party because the dominant faction in the CPV leadership still views China as a strategically and ideological comrade (Vuving 2010). Opportunities thus exist, but they are not risk free.

Since the 1990s Vietnamese leaders have pondered over the abrupt disintegration of long-standing Soviet and Eastern European brother communist parties. As the CPV turns 83, that fate now hovers over its head. Reckless monetary policy and wasteful state investment into a corrupt and inefficient state-owned sector have led to slower growth, high inflation, and swelling foreign debt since 2006 (Pham Bich San 2013). Street demonstrations are now a common scene, with causes involving not simply land grabbing by local authorities as before, but also national issues such as corruption, police brutalities, abuses of religious freedom and human rights, and the government's timid reactions to Chinese aggressive claims of sovereignty over the Spratlys and Paracels in the South China Sea. Violent police crackdowns on protests and more subtle forms of coercion have not been effective but have earned sharp rebukes from the West.[41] Rising social unrest implies increasing cost to maintain the security apparatus at the very time when state resources is dwindling due to economic difficulties. Yet the party now seems totally beholden to powerful interest groups that block meaningful economic reform.[42] In the context of rapidly accumulating domestic and external challenges, the CPV's continuing domination and even its survival are in grave danger. For decades the party has been able to persist amid decay but one wonders if that is still an option.

Notes

1. Nathan has since revised his view to be less certain about the future prospects of China's authoritarian system. See Nathan, "Authoritarian Impermanence," *Journal of Democracy* 20, no. 3 (2009): 37–40.
2. For example, Smith writes, "In Cuba, the road to power followed a path much like that taken by the Vietcong, in which long-term guerrilla warfare was combined with coalition building in the countryside, but which, unlike in North Vietnam, had no ready source of external revenue from foreign supporters" (Smith 2005: 450). The situation was actually the reverse: the "Vietcong" was under direct supervision of the CPV in North Vietnam and received arms from North Vietnam and the Soviet bloc smuggled in through Cambodian ports and Laotian jungles. In contrast, the government which was set up in Hanoi by Ho Chi Minh in 1945 and which fought a subsequent war with France received no foreign support until 1950 (see below).
3. By "revolutionary violence" I mean systematic violence guided by ideologies and tactics aimed at restructuring the social order. Huntington's term is "class warfare."
4. For simplicity, I am using the name CPV for the entire existence of this party. The CPV had other names in some periods, such as Indochinese Communist Party (1931–45), Association for the Study of Marxism (1945–51), and Vietnamese Workers' Party (1951–76).
5. The best account of the party in its early years is Huynh Kim Khanh (1982).
6. As Huntington explains, "So long as an organization still has its first set of leaders, ... its adaptability is still in doubt" (Huntington 1968: 14).
7. Ho Chi Minh's role in the party weakened in the late 1940s because he failed to obtain diplomatic recognition not only from the United States, but also from the Soviet Union. Ho was criticized by some party leaders for his decision to dissolve the CPV in 1945; this decision led Stalin not to trust the CPV. See Goscha (2006: 59–103); and Quinn-Judge (2005: 33). Truong Chinh resigned from the position of general secretary in 1956 after the party rectification campaign and the land reform went awry under his direction (see Vu 2005: ch. 5). He remained powerful in the Politburo, just as Ho Chi Minh remained influential even after he was gradually removed from the daily management of the state in the early 1950s.
8. The Central Committee had 44 full members and 31 alternate members in 1960 and 133 full members with no alternate members in 1976. Most full

and alternate members in 1960 were retained in 1976 and new members accounted for more than half of the Central Committee in 1976.

9. Two died in office: Nguyen Chi Thanh died in 1968 and Ho Chi Minh in 1969.
10. This was Hoang Van Hoan.
11. These were Tran Quoc Hoan, Van Tien Dung, Le Van Luong, Nguyen Van Linh, Vo Chi Cong, and Chu Huy Man. Le Van Luong was an alternate member of the Politburo since 1951 but lost this position in 1956.
12. These included Le Duan, Nguyen Duy Trinh, Pham Hung, Le Thanh Nghi, and Tran Quoc Hoan.
13. These were Truong Chinh, Le Duc Tho, Pham Van Dong, Vo Nguyen Giap, Le Van Luong, and Van Tien Dung. Vo Nguyen Giap died recently but had lost influence since the late 1960s.
14. For the failure of collectivization in North Vietnam, see Kerkvliet (2005). For the failure of socialist construction in North Vietnam in general, see Fforde and Paine (1987).
15. For an astute analysis of the mindset of party leaders at this time, see Marr (1991: 12–20).
16. The DRV lost about 1.1 million troops in the war out of a population of about 20 million.
17. In Vietnamese, "tat ca cho tien tuyen, tat ca de chien thang."
18. The Central Committee in theory is above the Politburo, but in reality this was not the case until recently.
19. For an astute and most recent analysis of palace politics in Hanoi, see Lien-Hang Nguyen (2012).
20. The only exception was Hoang Van Hoan, who lost his position in the Politburo in 1976 and defected to China in 1978.
21. Party documents referred to members recruited in the first campaign as "the January 6 Cohort" (the campaign was launched on January 6, 1960, the thirtieth birthday of the CPV), and those recruited in the early 1970s as "the Ho Chi Minh Cohort" (the campaign was launched in September 1970 to commemorate the first anniversary of Ho's death).
22. These sources did not reveal the criteria used to rank cadres.
23. Transition generation include such leaders as Nguyen Van Linh, Do Muoi, Vo Van Kiet. Those of the second generation are Le Duc Anh, Nong Duc Manh, Phan Van Khai, Le Kha Phieu, Tran Duc Luong, and Nguyen Tan Dung. For an account of early years of party reform, see Stern (1993).
24. From 1987 to 1991, the annual number of new recruits fell from about 100,000 to 36,000; see Le Phuoc Tho (1982: 24). By 1998, the number for the first time in a decade rebounded to 100,000; see Ha (1999: 44). By 2007, the number was about 170,000; see Phuc Son (2007). Total number of CPV members in 1986 was 1.8 million or 3 percent of the population (Thayer 1991: 21). By 2007, there were 3.2 million members who made up 3.7 percent of the population (Phuc Son 2007).
25. In 2007, 0.55 percent of 20,000 private enterprises in Hanoi had a party cell (*Tien Phong* 2007). In Ho Chi Minh City, the rate was much lower, at about 0.06 percent (*Tap chi Xay Dung Dang* 2008).
26. Interview with Nong Duc Manh, General Secretary of the CPV, *Tuoi Tre*, April 26, 2006.

27. *Ha Noi Moi*, April 22, 2008. See also *Nguoi Lao Dong*, April 28, 2008.
28. Interview with Le Kha Phieu, *Tuoi Tre*, May 26, 2005. He returned the money, but tellingly did not authorize any investigation of those who tried to bribe him even though the law allowed the persecution of bribe-givers.
29. See chapter by Thomas Jandl in this volume on this issue.
30. At least half of provincial governments have been found to violate national investment laws to attract more foreign investment to their provinces (Pham Duy Nghia 2007).
31. No corruption cases involving CPV Politburo members have been reported or disclosed, although their children, spouses, and relatives are widely believed to use family influence for financial gains (Hayton 2010: 20–5). Among ministers and vice ministers disciplined, fired, or jailed for corruption are Ngo Xuan Loc (construction), Vu Ngoc Hai (energy), Bui Thien Ngo (public security), Mai Van Dau (trade), Nguyen Huu Chi and Truong Chi Trung (finance), Nguyen Viet Tien (transportation), Nguyen Thien Luan and Nguyen Quang Ha (agriculture and rural development), and Doan Manh Giao (government office). Other high-ranking officials who have been suspected or accused are Le Duc Thuy (governor of Central Bank), Le Thanh Hai (Politburo member and Ho Chi Minh City party secretary), and Nguyen Ba Thanh (Da Nang party secretary). Numerous provincial leaders are disciplined and dismissed for corruption every year but details have rarely been made public; see for example *VietnamNet* (2009).
32. For the importance of rituals of participation in dictatorships see Wedeen (1999).
33. See memoir by Nguyen Manh Tuong, a French-trained lawyer and scholar who was involved in the *Nhan Van-Giai Pham* Affairs. *Ke bi mat phep thong cong, Hanoi 1954–1991: Ban an cho mot tri thuc* (translated from French by Nguyen Quoc Vy), available at http://viet-studies.info/NMTuong/NMTuong_HoiKy.htm.
34. There were 138 projects to build golf courses in 38 provinces in Vietnam as of May 2008.
35. An example of these protests was those that occurred in Thai Binh in 1997. A woman who lived in a neighboring village of the protests called this event "a coup d'etat" [dao chinh] because the protesting farmers seized a commune chief and held him before marching to the district with their claims against local taxes and corruption. Interview, Dong Hung district, Thai Binh, July 25, 2003.
36. For state efforts to co-opt religions, see Bouquet (2010: 90–108). Recent protests involved the Hmongs in Son La and Catholics in Hanoi, Vinh, and Da Nang.
37. According to a British Council's report titled "Vietnam Market Information," the estimated number of Vietnamese students studying abroad in 2008 was 25,000 and rising. See www.britishcouncil.org/eumd_information_background-vietnam.htm
38. Dinh is a lawyer trained in France and the United States, and Trung received his graduate degree in France. Both were recently tried and sentenced to five and seven years in prison, respectively, for conspiring against the state. For a discussion of their trials, see Forum in the *Journal of Vietnamese Studies* (2010: 192–243).

39. Since the 1990s, Vietnam has become increasingly dependent on Western foreign aid, investment and markets. Public external debt (mostly official development assistance) is currently estimated to be 25 percent of GDP (31.5% if including the private sector); see World Bank (2008a). Annual remittances from abroad are equal to about 10 percent of GDP. In 2008, for example, remittances, official assistance, and foreign direct investment amounted to nearly 34 percent of GDP (World Bank 2008b).
40. See Carlyle Thayer's chapter in this volume for a detailed analysis of this apparatus.
41. See Benedict Kerkvliet's informative chapter in this volume for the treatment of regime critics.
42. At the 4th Plenum of the Central Committee in October 2012, General Secretary Nguyen Phu Trong and the majority of the Politburo tried but failed to discipline Prime Minister Nguyen Tan Dung for policy mistakes and corruption.

3
Authoritarianism Reconfigured: Evolving Accountability Relations within Vietnam's One-Party Rule

Thaveeporn Vasavakul

Between 1986 and 2012 Vietnam undertook institutional reforms aimed at strengthening the external and internal accountability of government. The reforms included measures to improve compliance within the administrative apparatus, strengthen the role of elected bodies, and enhance, if within certain limits, the scope of popular participation in the country's political institutions. These reforms, their implementation, and outcomes have had considerable impacts on the development of Vietnam's political system and its accountability mechanisms in particular. An analysis of these measures and their varied impacts has much to contribute to understandings of politics in contemporary Vietnam.

This chapter probes the development of accountability relations in Vietnam. The first section discusses normative and empirical meanings of accountability and considers their significance with respect to transformation of the Vietnamese state in the era of doi moi. The second section addresses continuity and change in the political economy of accountability networks in Vietnam. The third section focuses attention on a particularly important set of changes in the accountability functions of Vietnam's local representative bodies, People's Councils (PCOs), particularly at the provincial-level. The analysis establishes the nature of these changes and explores their implications for accountability relations and the character of authoritarianism in contemporary Vietnam.

Overall, the chapter argues that the evolution of accountability relations within the Vietnamese state is best understood in relation to the broader structural transformation of the Vietnamese state that has unfolded since the late 1980s. The chapter demonstrates that the development of accountability networks in Vietnam has not entailed a move toward democracy; rather, it reflects the reconfiguration of authoritarianism in response to particular sets of institutional and organizational needs attendant with a bold and not-unproblematic process of administrative decentralization.

Accountability and its significance in the era of doi moi

Accountability is often understood in normative terms as the idea that those with public responsibility should be answerable to "public authorities" as much as to "the people" in the performance of their duties. Yet accountability may also be investigated empirically as a series of related questions about whom is liable or accountable to whom; what they may be called to account for; through what processes accountability is to be assured; by what standards the putatively accountable behavior is to be judged; and what the potential effects are of finding that those standards have been breached (Mashaw in Dowdle 2006: 115–56). From this perspective, an analysis of state accountability has as its central focus state officials within institutions on the one hand, authority relations between particular political institutions, and between state institutions and citizens on the other.

Accountability regimes develop within particular political and social contexts in response to particular conflicts in authority relations (Dowdle 2006). It follows that the analysis of accountability differs under different forms of political economy. Dowdle (ibid.) identifies a wide range of accountability regimes that develop under democratic polities, but notes that such accountability regimes tend to share key features. Free and fair elections, for example, are a key formal mechanism whereby voters can hold politicians accountable, as is the rule of law, which is assumed to place legal constraints on state action. Andreas Schedler sees the development of accountability mechanisms as critical in the consolidation of new democracies. In such contexts, intra-state accountability mechanisms within the state gain force, whereby state agencies become "legally enabled and empowered, and factually willing and able, to take actions that span from routine oversight to criminal sanctions or impeachment in relation to actions or omissions by other agents or agencies of the state that may be qualified as unlawful" (Schedler et al. 1999).

Accountability under nondemocratic regimes differs fundamentally. In such regimes, at least in principle, vertical and horizontal accountability is enforced through rational politico-bureaucratic means. What is lacking in these countries is not formal accountability, but rather the mechanism of formal enforcement. For example, in the absence of elections, the rule of law, and other trappings of democratic regimes, mechanisms to promote and enforce accountability tend to be weak. Still, such mechanisms are not entirely absent. In recent years policymakers in both China and Vietnam increasingly integrated formal participatory elements into state policies (Dowdle 2006: 329–57; World Bank 2010); a phenomenon that is no doubt related to the ongoing diffusion in both countries of various (imported) norms of "good governance." While in China, a diversity of actors intent on promoting greater substantive accountability have employed a discourse of "constitutionalism" (i.e., strict interpretations of formal norms) as a strategy for holding administrative actors' and local governments' to account.

But what has or does accountability mean in the Vietnamese context? Notions similar to "accountability" have traditionally existed in Vietnam and may also be found in the formal institutional makeup of the Soviet Model, which has so profoundly shaped Vietnam's institutional development. Be that as it may, normative and empirical conceptions of "accountability" such as those identified by Mashaw and Schedler's (above) are per se new to the Vietnamese context. Accountability in these senses has been translated into Vietnamese as "trach nhiem giai trinh," or responsibility to explain and present (a case or a justification), that is, answerability. This, we note, is quite different from the more explicitly legalistic understandings of accountability that emphasize, for example, "responsibility before the law."

Indeed, "answerability" in the sense conveyed by Schedler and others implies both a dialogue and a flow of information; elements that, while perhaps emergent in Vietnam (see Malesky's chapter on the National Assembly (NA)), cannot be taken for granted in the Vietnamese context. Be that as it may, in a relatively short time span, understandings of "accountability" as "answerability" have become routine in discussions about politics and public administration in Vietnam. Nor are the changes purely discursive. Accountability relations in Vietnam are indeed evolving.

Holding the administrative state accountable

Theoretical literature on governance makes a distinction between three strands of governance: governance through hierarchies, or public governance, governance through markets, and governance through communities. Accordingly, there are three corresponding regimes of accountability: public, market-based, and social. More narrowly, there are three interrelated forms of public accountability. Political accountability is conventionally construed as accountability to electoral constituents with respect to public policy choices. Administrative or bureaucratic accountability is a hierarchical relationship within which lower-ranking officials are responsible to superiors for their compliance with official instructions. Bureaucratic accountability measures may be enforced through various means, including, but not limited to, merit-based recruitment, tenure, promotion, and reward exercises. More recently, "open government" measures aimed a transparency have gained prominence. Over the last two decades Vietnam's party-state has attempted to strengthen and create accountability institutions and mechanisms along each of these public accountability dimensions, as is discussed in the following.

Elected bodies at national and local levels

National and local elections in Vietnam are noncompetitive in that the process of candidate selection is controlled by party-affiliated organs. Be that as it may, there is "low-intensity" competition among preselected candidates. Moreover, as discussed in Chapter 5 of this volume, the NA has taken on a more prominent governance role and is particularly important with respect to the evolution of accountability institutions in Vietnam. The NA has full-time deputies than in the past and its sessions are longer and take on increasingly substantive deliberations. Increasingly the NA has been given opportunity to vet and approve Cabinet nominations. It has also assumed a role in support of the concept of "rule by law," with its increased attention to the vetting and promulgation of legislation.

It is the NA that oversees the allocation of the state budget among various sectors, programs, and provinces. Be that as it may, the NA public accountability efficacy as a mechanism of accountability is limited. The NA, after all, is a body of, by, and for the Communist Party of Vietnam (CPV) while the establishment of an NA Standing Committee has undermined the influence of individual deputies. At the local level, changes in the role and functions of provincial-, district-, and commune-level elected bodies (i.e., the Provincial People's Councils (PPCOs)) have varied from locality to locality and will be revisited in the final section of this chapter.

Rationalized bureaucracy and performance review

Vietnam's state's ongoing measures to rationalize its public administration system continue to this day and have contributed significantly to the evolution of accountability relations. For example, the Law on Public

Officials and Civil Servants (2008) and the Law on Public Officials and Law on Professional Service Providers (2010), stipulate the introduction of merit-based recruitment and pay, civil service professionalization, and performance management. Contracting arrangements were introduced to encourage competition believed to lead to better performance from professional service providers.

More recently, and perhaps most significantly, the Ministry of Home Affairs (MOHA) has created a first-of-its-kind system for evaluating national and subnational units' performance, the Public Administration Reform (PAR) Index. The stated purposes of the PAR Index are to hold ministries and provinces accountable in implementing PAR measures and to "follow and assess in a concrete and objective manner results of [policy] implementation and PAR measures in government agencies at the central and local levels" (Decision 1294, 2012). The data collected will be published annually. MOHA has developed a two-part system to measure ministerial and provincial compliance first through self-assessment by the ministry and province, and second through social surveys. At the ministerial level, the PAR Index focuses on seven areas of performance measurement: management and leadership in PAR; institutional restructuring within the parameters of the ministry's jurisdiction; procedural streamlining; organizational restructuring; improved professional and civil service capacity in the sector; financial reform; and administrative modernization. Performance measurement areas for the provinces are similar, with an additional item for development of so-called "one-stop shops" to provide convenient public access to an array of local governmental services.

While the effects of PAR Index will remain uncertain for some time, it seems clear that the steady stream of laws and stipulations aimed at rationalizing bureaucracy represent, at the very least, significant changes in the official culture, discourse, and institutions of public administration. Beyond this, they have facilitated an ongoing public discussion within Vietnam's government about how best promote accountability and "what standards" to use in gauging the performance within different government sectors and administrative levels.

Transparency and open government

Vietnam's state has increasingly employed transparency measures as a mechanism for promoting public and social accountability, as can be observed across a full range of state laws and policies governing information about the use of public resources. This includes public notice regarding subcontracting arrangements in which public responsibilities are performed by nonpublic (i.e., "equitized" or "private") entities and (more rarely) cost benefit analyses undertaken by state agencies. Some laws carry regulations requiring publicity and disclosure of various forms of legal, financial, and policy information.

The Law on Anti-Corruption (2005) is particularly important in this regard, as it contains clauses on transparency of information by sector. Clause 12 focuses on methods of release including verbal announce-ment at relevant units; posting at unit offices; announcement in writing to relevant stakeholders; print publication; mass media release; and webpages. Clause 12 additionally requires that construction investment master planning projects receive open public comment; that projects funded from local budgets be reviewed by the PCOs; and that approved projects are presented for public review. Clause 15 focuses on transpar-ency and publication of state finances and budgets. For capital construc-tion projects, the content to be publicized includes the funds allocated to respective projects; project budget estimates and budget allocations; yearly reports on project finances; and final accounting on completed projects. Clauses 31 and 32 address the right of organizations and indi-viduals to request information.

Increasingly, budgetary information is published on government websites. The government discloses online annual budget documenta-tion, in-year budgetary execution reports, and summaries of state audit reports and contract information, while other laws, such as those on "grassroots democracy" (at the commune, workplace, and enterprise levels), mandate the disclosure of information pertinent to the members' rights in any given unit. Vietnam's performance with respect to transpar-ency remains suspect; despite modest improvements, the country ranks among the world's worst-performing countries in the 2012 Open Budget Index, placing above Cambodia and China but below other ASEAN countries. Overall, agreed-upon transparency standards in Vietnam remain deficient while sanctions for noncompliance are nonexistent (http://survey.internationalbudget.org/#rankings).

Inspection and audit agencies

To promote legal accountability, Vietnam's state has created a new auditing agency and revived its inspectorate system (thanh tra), both of which serve to enforce compliance with existing rules and regula-tions in finance and management. The State Audit of Vietnam (SAV) was established by Decree No.70/CP on July 11, 1994, while the SAV Law was approved in 2005. The latter elaborates the formal roles and functions of the SAV and stipulates the appointment of an auditor general by the NA.

Subsequently, the SAV became, in principle, wholly independent from the government and answerable only to the law, even as the general auditor is approved by the NA based on nominations from the standing committee in consultation with the prime minister. Notably, however, the position is equal in rank only with an NA committee chairperson, a minister, or head of province.

The SAV is responsible for the financial, compliance, and performance auditing of agencies and institutions receiving state budgets, funds, or assets. Transparency is a key principle of its functioning. The SAV provides information about the management and implementation of the state budget, funds, and assets for the NA and government; may recommend the abolition, revision, or development of legal documents by the NA, the government, or its members; gives opinions to both audited and state managing agencies for streamlining their financial, accounting, and budgetary administration for the timely prevention of corruption, waste, and loss of state funds and assets; and is entitled to 2 percent of all amounts recovered. Audit results are transparently disclosed to the mass media.

In Vietnam, the inspectorate has a long history in public governance. In the era of doi moi, every ministry and province has its own inspectoral unit. The key function of these units is to review the implementation of policies, laws, and responsibilities by agencies, organizations, and individuals under the respective jurisdiction of their corresponding administrative authority (Luat Thanh tra 2010).

The objective is to prevent, detect, and pursue legal violations, and to discover managerial, policy, and legal loopholes in order to recommend solutions and improvement to the relevant authorities. In addition, Vietnam's inspectorates also process complaints and allegations of wrongdoing, and assist the heads of the relevant agencies in reviewing and resolving them. Under the Law on Anti-Corruption (LAC), the inspectorate conducts inspections to enforce the LAC, develops a national database on preventing and combating corruption, provides assistance to the Government in reporting anti-corruption efforts to the NA, and verifies assets and incomes.

Challenges in the use of inspection to hold the state accountable have been threefold. First, inspection units are dependent; they are attached to government agencies and under the leadership of agency heads. How much inspection is to carry out to hold officials accountable thus depends upon the will and commitment of the agency head. Additionally, there is no framework to enforce compliance with a given inspectorate's findings; more often than not, inspectors' recommendations are not followed. Furthermore, there is a general overlap in the functions and mandates of Vietnam's public accountability mechanisms, as evidenced in the duplication of activities between inspectorates, especially administrative and specialized ones, in addition to the overlap between the inspectorates and state auditing agencies. These weaknesses particularly affected the capacity of the inspectorate system to hold administrative bodies accountable.

Citizen participation

In addition to the above, Vietnam' state has increasingly if selectively integrated participatory mechanisms into its political accountability scheme. At the national and provincial levels, government units drafting legal and policy documents are now required to seek public comment. The Law on Anti-Corruption (2005) includes a clause, later concretized in Decree 47, on popular participation in anti-corruption work. Vietnam has subsequently done comparatively well in promoting a system of grassroots democracy.

In addition to the general framework of grassroots democracy, at the local level the People's Inspectorate and the Committee for the Monitoring of Community Infrastructure Investment are two key institutions that may enforce public accountability. Nonetheless, practices have varied from case to case, and there remains a gap between enforcement and standards. The question of "to whom" these two units are accountable is pertinent. For example, although the People's Inspectorate Unit (PIU) is mandated to scrutinize local authorities' activities on behalf of residents, in practice three models of operation have emerged: the PIU under the influence of the Viet Nam Fatherland Front (VFF), the PIU under the influence of commune administrations, and likewise under the influence of the commune-level party chief (Vasavakul 2012).

In broad terms it is only fair to acknowledge that Vietnam has developed multi-faceted accountability mechanisms under doi moi. Furthermore, each of these mechanisms attempts to address the questions of who is accountable, to whom, for what, through what processes, according to what standards, and under pain of what consequences for violating them. Nonetheless, each of these mechanisms still faces challenges.

Decentralization and accountability: a case study of provincial PCOs

Vietnam's local government structure consists of three levels: provincial or municipal under the central government (called the provincial level); quarter, district, town, and city level under the province (called the district level); and commune and ward (called the commune level). Each level has its own formally representative body, the PCO, whose executive wing is the People's Committee (PC). PCO deputies are elected according to the Law on the Election of PCO deputies. The rise of provincial elected bodies as accountability agencies in a particularly interesting dimension of political decentralization, a process central to the reconfiguration of authoritarianism in Vietnam. Political decentralization in Vietnam is not full-fledged. Rather it is characterized by the decentralization of managerial responsibility or, more precisely, the delegation of certain powers to local authorities – particularly at the province level – in the areas of planning, finance, human resources, and service delivery. It is provincial-level authorities who decide on the management decentralization among the different tiers in the province (Vasavakul 1999).

Within the context of management decentralization, the provincial-level PCs (PPCs) have become the preeminent actors in local governance. The PPCs have become increasingly involved in developing provincial plans within the national strategic framework. Equally crucial is their role in budget allocation for implementing public policy and balancing short- and long-term needs. In addition to planning and budgeting, the provincial-level government has been granted increasing authority in personnel management (Ban cong tac Dai bieu 2009). However, the lack of a clear legal framework and concomitant rise of economic opportunities (not entirely foreseen by national "institutional architects") have prompted PPCs to engage in periodic "fence breaking" policies not in line with the central government's regulations or the national legal framework. This, in turn, has reinforced local autonomy, giving fresh relevance to the old Vietnamese adage that "the emperor's edicts stop at the province gate", or phep vua thua le tinh (Vasavakul 1996, 1999).

As regards finance, for example, in 2003 there were reports of numerous provinces' promulgating regulations to reward businesses that paid taxes – a practice that contravened central government regulations. This practice led to discrepancies in revenue collection between provinces while encouraging imports frowned upon by the central government. To rectify the problem, the central government directly requested that the PCOs should not endorse any PC policies in conflict with central government directives. Cases were also reported in which provinces abandoned financial discipline. In one such case, between 2004 and 2006 Ho Chi Minh City annually overspent its budget. In 2004, it spent VND 6 trillion against a planned budget of VND 2.71

trillion; the following year, the city spent VND 11.5 trillion against a planned budget of only VND 4.3 trillion. This practice continued into 2006, when the discrepancy between the planned budget (VND 4.7 trillion) and actual spending (VND 12.5 trillion) remained egregious (Van phong Quoc Hoi 2008).

In addition to the hierarchical reporting mechanisms imposed by the central government, elected bodies at the provincial level have increasingly played an active role in both appraising the legal validity and supervising the implementation of PPC plans and budgets. The PCOs' accountability role comes close to qualifying as "horizontal accountability," to cite Schedler's term. However, under one-party rule, the rising role of elected bodies serves primarily to consolidate the central–local government management decentralization scheme. The increasingly active role of PCOs in legal appraisal and supervision contrasts with their more moderate roles in representing their constituents' interests. In what follows, this chapter examines the accountability functions of the PPCOs.

Accountability functions of the PPCO

The PPCO is an elected body at the provincial level. Organizationally, it consists of the following components: a chair, a vice-chair, a standing member (uy vien thuong truc), specialized working committees responsible for legal affairs, economics, culture, and society, minority areas (for provinces with a substantial number of minority population), and deputies. The PCO is assisted by an administrative office; most deputies work part-time. The PPCO is granted considerable powers. From the political point of view, council powers include the selection and dismissal of chairs, vice-chairs, and other members of the PC. The Standing Committee of the PPCO coordinates with the PC to decide on the dismissal of elected deputies upon the recommendation of the VFF, which is an umbrella agency of sociopolitical organizations. The Council carries out a vote of confidence for those it has endorsed and also supervises the head of the court and the head of the procurators at the same level.

In the policy arena, the PCO issues resolutions on local master plans and socioeconomic development plans and monitors these plans' implementation. The key master plans include ones for socioeconomic development of the province/city; for sectoral or subregional development; for development of urban and rural centers; and for land use. The short-term plans include annual socioeconomic development plans. In addition, the PCO is also responsible for supervising budgetary allocations.

The Budget Law of 2002 opened up an official space for the PPCO to participate in financial decision-making and approval. Specifically, the

PPCO has been assigned responsibility to allocate budgets for the three levels of government. It decides on collections, spending, including fees, and popular contributions within relevant legal frameworks. It also promulgates the cost norms of the local government. The 2002 State Budget Law grants the PPCO the authority to mobilize capital within the country within the framework stipulated by the central government. The PPCO also determines the decentralization of collection and spending responsibilities among the three governmental levels. Within the framework of budgetary stabilization over the period of three to five years, localities can use their increased budget collections for local purposes, a decision-making area also necessarily involving the local PCO. Within this management decentralization context, the PCO has considerable decision-making and approval power over local finances.

The only main item not under local jurisdiction regards central government budgetary reserves for specific target programs. To carry out its function, the PPCO relies on various work procedures, including the preparation of Council resolutions, legal appraisal of local government documents, monitoring, questioning of government agencies during Council sessions, and public consultation (Ban Cong tac Dai bieu 2009; Luat Ngan sach nha nuoc, Clause 25).

The PCO undertakes a number of work procedures and accountability functions. These include socioeconomic planning (master planning and annual planning), where the Council focuses on identifying the baseline situation, policy directions, and policy options proposed, and the benefits of different options. The objectives are to ensure feasibility, effectiveness, and impacts. They also have accountability for decisions on Council resolutions; decisions on budgetary process; legal appraisal of local government proposals; monitoring; questioning of the local government (chat van); public consultation; and budgetary allocations (the Council identifies equality in budgetary allocations, effectiveness in collections and spending, and impact of the use of budget).

Under one-party rule, there remains a gap between the legal stipulation of powers and authority on the one hand and actual practice on the other. A review of the PPCOs' practical work provides some insight into the way in which the system of one-party rule has been reconfigured at the local level.

Decision-making

The Legal Framework of 2004 grants the PPCOs decision-making authority. Nonetheless, in practice, the PPCOs' decision-making or policy-approval roles are met with institutional challenges related to intra-party relations, relations between PPCOs and the VFF, and rela-tions between the PPCOs and their local governments. Furthermore, provincial-level party committees (Tinh uy) still play an important role in approving the content of local plans. This role hinges first on the fact that PCOs each have a party committee attached to guarantee Party leadership. Technically, to strengthen the role of the PCO in policy discussions, the Party committee for the PCO has to meet before the PCO Standing Committee sets up a schedule with the PC and the VFF; yet, there is still no clear procedure for conducting the PCO Party committee. Nor, secondly, is there any well-defined authority relation-ship between the local governmental unit and the PCO. In many cases, the chair of the PCO is also a member of the party standing committee, while the chair of the PC may be the Party vice-secretary. Within this party-dominated hierarchy, the role of the PCO in holding the local government accountable is compromised.

In addition to their problematic relationship with local party commit-tees and PCs, PPCOs' effectiveness may be diminished by their depend-ence on local VFF branches. In order to succeed in policy areas the PCO needs to coordinate with the VFF, an agency assigned to provide social commentary (phan bien xa hoi) on any policy statements; in practice, however, the local VFF and its affiliated mass organizations have rarely undertaken policy commentaries on their own initiative. Although the VFF organizes voters' meetings and compiles opinions to be presented at PCO sessions, there is no guarantee that these opinions will then be given serious heed.

Budgetary funding approval

Of particular importance among the PPCOs decision-making powers, decentralization has opened up opportunities for local financial discre-tion. The PPCO is responsible for monitoring implementation of local budgets a charge carried out through the appraisal of PC reports on revenue and spending estimates and records. The PPCO intervenes to provide recommendations on revenue collection deficits, inappropriate budgetary allocations, slow disbursement to investment projects, and fee levels imposed on citizens.

In a majority of provinces, the PPCO is active in determining local fee levels and collection practices. A preliminary analysis of the fee system in the provinces as approved by their PCOs indicates that while the prov-inces adhere to the fee ranges stipulated by central government agen-cies, the elected bodies consider the local income level when deciding on the level of fees for the province. One crucial "show case" of this "check and balance" situation is the debate within Ho Chi Minh City's PCO on the PC's proposal to increase school fees. The PCO decided to postpone raising fees pending additional information and justification (Ban cong tac Dai bieu 2009; field interviews 2010).

Despite some opening up of space for such "checks and balances," however, here again there remain institutional limitations on PCO involvement in the budgetary process. PCOs' authority does not extend to overseeing crucial financial areas such as the use of state property by various state agencies. Nor are the Councils involved in making financial decisions on implementation of local, central government-funded projects; the PCO is merely involved in approving final accounting for such projects, not in guiding preparations. The lack of criteria for programs and projects at the local level where PCO approval and guidance are needed further limits the Councils' effectiveness.

Legal appraisal

The PPCOs have played an increasing role in the process of legal appraisal. Their key purpose here is to ensure compatibility of draft documents with the existing national legal framework. The PC submits a "debriefing note" (to trinh), a draft resolution, and plan proposals. These "debriefing notes" and their attendant documents have normally first been "appraised" by the Department of Justice at the same level. The PCO committees are assigned the job of doing another round of appraisal and presenting an appraisal report (bao cao tham tra). The PCO reviews the legal basis of the documents and makes recommendations. The local government drafting committee then amends the documents accordingly.

Current problems focus on the relationship between the PPCO and the local government. Five days in advance of each Council session, government agencies are required to provide deputies with relevant information. In practice, there are often delays in delivering these materials on schedule, and they may in fact remain undelivered until the very day the Council meets. Deputies not affiliated with the executive may thus have difficulty gathering the relevant information. Without this requisite background information, it is impossible to prepare adequately for the meeting (Ban cong tac Dai bieu 2009: 143).

Supervision

Within the current legal framework, different components of the PCO have different supervisory/monitoring (giam sat) roles. Supervision may be exercised by the PCO, its standing committee, or its specialized committees. There are also several methods of supervision. In principle, the parameters for supervision are broad, focusing on supervision of the Standing Committee of the PC, the court, and the procurator at the same level; the implementation of PCO resolutions; and activities of state management agencies, economic organizations, and army units in the locality. The current legal framework designates three units to carry out supervisory responsibilities: the PCO Standing Committee, the PCO committees, and individual PCO deputies. There are three key monitoring areas: specific tasks that have been implemented, fixed supervisory activities during the mid-year and end of year meetings, and unplanned supervisory activities driven by public concerns or press coverage.

Although operating within the same framework, in practice different provincial PCOs have developed their own supervisory activities, with varying procedural details. A study of the system of PCOs in Ninh Thuan province shows that when the PPCO issues a resolution on the socio-economic development plan, the PCO committees set up their respective supervisory plans and integrate them into the general resolution of the PPCO on supervision for the year. The Committee informs agencies under review in advance to coordinate the process and sets up a work team that will finalize a report with recommendations (Resolution 753, Clauses 51 to 66). The PCO Standing Committee carries out supervisory work on multi-sector issues (around one or two missions annually) and prepares reports on PCO activities (mid-year and end of year), itself undergoing supervision by deputies. It assigns the Economic and Budgetary Committee to coordinate the preparation of a supervisory report on the PCO. Supervisory activities carried out by individual deputies are limited. In Ninh Thuan, implementation of post-monitoring recommendations is limited by a lack of overall implementation and sanction mechanisms (Field interviews 2009 and 2010).

Enforcement depends on individuals following up when they attend PC meetings (Vasavakul 2009). A report from Ninh Thuan shows that there has been a move away from the traditional method of reviewing official reports submitted by government agencies to data collection at the site. The PCO relies on its office staff to collect information from the sites to serve as inputs for supervisory activities (Ban cong tac Dai bieu 2009). In terms of supervisory activities, the Ho Chi Minh City's PCO exhibits notable differences from Ninh Thuan's model. According to Huynh Thanh Lap, vice-chair of Ho Chi Minh City PCO and also the vice-chair of the NA delegation in Ho Chi Minh City until 2011, the supervisory role of the PCO is aimed at bringing the law to life (dua phap luat vao cuoc song) and contributes to ensuring order (trat tu ky cuong) while also creating dynamics for the city's development.

For Ho Chi Minh City, as in other provinces, during the second council session at the end of each year, the City PCO approves plans for the year to come. Work will be allocated to PCO committees based on expertise needed. For example, in supervising the use of a capital construction budget, which is a large portion of the city budget, the PCO Standing Committee assigns the Economic and Budget Committee the task of formulating a plan and setting up a supervisory committee consisting of a head and a lieutenant, an Economic and Budgetary Committee, and deputies. It is a practice in Ho Chi Minh City that prior to any supervisory fieldwork, the committee invites specialists for debriefing. Such debriefing is quite unusual as the centrally allocated budget allowance for outside experts is limited. After the supervisory mission, there is a report with recommendations submitted to the Economic and Budgetary Committee, which will then meet to comment on the findings and formulate an official report to send to relevant stakeholders (Huynh: N.D.)

Generally speaking, "check-and-balance" activities have expanded in practice, though they still are restrained by the preexisting one-party rule framework. Supervisory activities have focused mainly on implementation of policies approved or endorsed in PCO resolutions, to review whether the policies have been carried out as planned. In this sense, the focus is on compliance with national policies and laws. The supervisory activities do not question the rationale of the policies per se, nor do they review the effectiveness and efficiency of the policies or the performance of the local state. Furthermore, it is commonly acknowledged that access to information remains a problem, as the PCO still has to rely on information supplied by the government; the current legal framework does not facilitate the collection and use of other sources of information. In the financial domain, the current legal framework mandates coordination between the PCO and the State Audit of Vietnam, the latter supplying audit information to serve as the basis for the former's financial supervision activities. This mandate is not yet commonly observed in practice. Finally, as the current legal framework does not include any detailed stipulation that recommendations actually be implemented, more often than not no serious action is taken to address them in supervisory reports.

Public consultation

Public consultation through constituent meetings is an integral part of the PPCOs' work procedures. According to the existing legal framework, each PCO holds four such sessions annually. In addition, deputies may meet with voters at their workplaces with assistance from the Office of the PCO and the NA Deputy group in the province, or the head of the agency where voters work. Similar to other work procedures, public consultation has met with challenges. A scholarly study conducted to assess the deputies' relationship with voters has indicated several inadequacies in the process (Pham et al. 2008). Not all provincial-level deputies in the study sample had met with voters as regularly as required; there also were times when deputies failed to participate in the meeting sessions owing to official work obligations.

Existing writings as well as field studies provide some insights into limitations in the process of meeting with voters. First and foremost, voter turnout for meeting sessions is small compared with turnout for elections. Secondly, the social composition of voters participating in meetings lacks diversity. Attendees tend to be, in one deputy's words, "professional and full-time meeting-goers" (cu tri chuyen trach), that is, those who are always present at meetings, possibly because of their good relationship with the head of the hamlet; obviously, this composition is less than ideally representative. Thirdly, the meeting sessions are not always effective. A number of deputies do not have a good grasp of the decision-making jurisdiction of state management agencies. Voters have a higher level of education; most of them are concerned with problems related to their locality and individual interests. Fourthly, responses to the voters' concerns and the follow-up on the implementation of their recommendations are unsystematic (Field interviews 2009–10).

The lack of an urgent need to boost the representational role may be explained in two ways. First, under one-party rule, PCO deputies are considered "people's representatives" (dai bieu nhan dan), not representatives for particular groups of citizens or interest groups. Any development concerning the latter, although common on the international scene, is not discussed openly in Vietnam. This peculiarity has, to some extent, limited the content of the dialogue with citizens as well as the way in which solutions to problems are found.

The second explanation is that the constituent meeting is only one among many different channels for citizen-interest articulation and mediation. Under Vietnam's one-party system, there exist a wide range of formal mechanisms for citizens to voice their opinions on issues and concerns. There are also a wide range of mechanisms to allow mediation or conciliation of conflicts among citizens, between them and the state, or with businesses. At the commune level, for example, interest articulation and mediation can be seen in measures falling under the framework of the Ordinance on Grassroots Democracy (2007) which enshrines the maxim that "people know, people discuss, people act, and people inspect."

While public consultation is a crucial element in public accountability and in deputy–citizen relations, challenges have also emerged to
determining whom citizens ought to hold accountable in the context of
changing service delivery functions.

Three accountability disputes illustrate these challenges especially
well. The first deals with administrative accountability in urban service
delivery. At a meeting between the City's PCO deputies and voters, one
voter complained about garbage trucks collecting refuse during peak
hours in disregard of sanitation requirements and residents' complaints.
City Council deputies clarified that garbage collection was managed by
the province, which had contracted the work out to a private company
(Field interviews 2009). The second case deals with health care and health
insurance services. A female patient sought legal advice in a dispute with
a district-level health facility which refused to transfer her to an upper-
tier facility for treatment. The patient contended that the district facility
was not sufficiently equipped to provide her with required services and
thus insisted she be transferred to a provincial-level facility. The district
health facility contended that the treatment fell under its jurisdiction.
Within the framework of Vietnam's health insurance law, insurance
would only partially cover medical costs for a transfer without the lower
tier's authorization (Field interviews 2009).

The third case dealt with entrepreneurship for poverty reduction. In a
minority area with an average per capita income of US$800 per year, one
minority household that had just escaped the US$22 per month poverty
threshold enumerated their obstacles to sustainable poverty reduction.
Highlights included the household's lack of expertise in commercial
planting techniques, their lack of start-up capital, and the wait between
planting and their first harvest. The head of the household commented
that he had no information about any government support in these
areas. Nor had he received support from local community members
engaged in commercial agriculture (Field interviews 2012).

These cases indicate that the question of who is accountable to whom
and for what can be complicated in the context of Vietnam's restructuring. The garbage service case illustrates the effects of service decentralization from the central to the local government, combined with
the gradual distribution of public service work to private contractors.
It involved several relationships within an increasingly complex local
governance structure, the relationships between voters and deputies,
between deputies and government agencies, among different government agencies, and between the government agency and contractors.
The health service case illustrates on the one hand decentralization to a
lower-tier facility, but on the other shows how lower-tier facilities' real

and perceived capacities may vary in practice from one locality to the next. It reflects at least three sets of direct relationships – between the citizen and the health facility, between health facilities and the insurance agencies, and between health insurance and citizens as clients.

As regards poverty reduction, the central government has developed preferential schemes to aid those in poverty. While the locality had managed to reduce the number of poor households, these achievements were not necessarily sustainable. This case reflects the coexistence of disparate accountability regimes to support inclusive growth and poverty reduction and raises questions of what the government, the market, and the community may or may not respectively be responsible for.

Reworking accountability relations

The above account highlights some major developments in the evolution of accountability relations in Vietnam's state administrative apparatus. Additional studies carried out by the present author have examined additional aspects of PPCOs authority accountability relations. These studies note that the accountability role of the PCC itself is affected by the way in which the organization is held accountable. And that the PPCO, as an organization, contains multi-layered accountability networks, which are at times contradictory: PPCOs are under the supervision and guidance of both the NA Standing Committee and the central government. At the same time they are held accountable by the VFF. However, individual components of the PPCO system also have their own multiple accountability relations.

Practical experience from a number of provinces suggests possibilities for developing and consolidating various authority relations. Quang Ninh PCO, for example, has reportedly developed a working procedure between its Standing Member and its specialized committees in order to prepare better for Council meeting sessions. The work procedure involves dividing responsibilities among different committees in order to legally appraise draft resolutions, reports, and proposals submitted by the government and to monitor the implementation of PCO resolutions. After each session, the Standing Member of the PPCO works with the relevant committees on responsibilities that serve as their basis for drafting plans. The Standing Member also meets routinely with the committees (Dai Bieu Nhan Dan 2012). A number of other innovations have emerged in the area of monitoring. Ha Tinh PPCO, for example, has strengthened its role in monitoring budgetary management. Ha Tinh's approach was to select a set of key spearhead areas for monitoring: capital construction; land planning and zoning changes; tax collection; investment in rural transportation; land compensation and resettlement; and the use of overseas development assistance.

Other provinces have taken still different approaches. Bac Ninh PPC (Bac Ninh People's Council) undertook an initiative to design a work procedure for public consultation that involved organization and topic selection of a public consultation, selection of the procedural order, and conducting the session. In Bac Ninh the PCO chose to focus on a rural development topic, namely the implementation of Resolution 132 on rural development and infrastructure. The purpose was to support rural production by assessing whether certain measures approved by the PCO were actually being implemented. The Standing Unit of the People's Council = PCO was in charge upon approval by the Standing Committee of the provincial Party Committee. It set up task forces consisting of key deputies from a specialized committee, the VFF, the Office, and relevant government agencies. The PPC identified consultation methods, including meetings at the hamlet, commune and district levels, social surveys, conferences, public consultation via the internet, and provincial-level review conferences. Based on the information gathered, the Standing Unit of the PCO amended the policy measures that had been put forth.

Pilot to dissolve district- and ward-level PCOs

In 2009 the central government moved toward restructuring the local government system by piloting in several provinces the disbanding of district PCOs in rural areas, urban district (quan) PCOs in urban areas, and ward PCOs in large urban areas. The pilot was justified by the argument that the local government apparatus consisted of too many middle layers and that as a consequence redundant responsibilities were being assigned to different levels. It was also argued that the system did not sufficiently take into account differences between urban and rural governance. For the urban areas, urban government units had organized PCOs and PCs at all three tiers of the administration – a practice resulting in lack of management conformity. Decisions and commands from the upper echelon were dispersed along unclear lines of responsibility from local to upper levels, which also failed to monitor compliance consistently. The pilot aimed to rectify these problems of unnecessary intermediaries and overlapping responsibilities by eliminating elected bodies at the district and quarter levels. It would institute a unified urban management system with decision-making power concentrated in the provincial echelon (Department of Local Government of MOHA 2009).

There are several documents governing the dissolution pilot. In August 2007, the Fifth Plenum of the Central Committee issued Resolution no. 17/NQ-TW on PAR in which it called for a pilot dissolution of PCOs at the district, quarter, and ward level. The results of the pilot would serve as inputs for the revision of the 1992 Constitution. The NA confirmed the pilot in its Resolution no. 26/2008/QH12 and the NA Standing Committee's Resolution no. 725/2009/YUBTVQH12 that adjusted the functions and role of the PCOs, and PCs as well as the re-organization of the district-level and the ward-level administrations where the PCOs were being dissolved. The pilot was carried out in 10 of 63 provinces and cities; 99 of 684 district-level units; and 483 out of 1,300 wards (of 11,774 commune-level units) (Nguyen Hai Long 2011).

From a comparative point of view, this pilot has crucial implications for the transformation of the local government structure in Vietnam as much as for accountability. First, changes, if any, would consolidate the authority of the provincial-level government. At the moment, important issues, especially finance, are already being decided by the provinces, and the degree of decentralization to the district has only been moderate. This change would be a key departure from the legacy of the central planning period, when in rural areas the district was granted a greater decision-making and management role. Second, it is likely that the power of the commune-level government will be reinforced. Thus, important matters regarding the development of the province will be decided by the Provincial PCO, while important issues at the commune level will be decided by the Communal PCO. Finally, this restructuring should allow for differences in local government structure between rural and urban areas.

The pilot raises a number of issues related to accountability. Resolution 725 assigned the Provincial People's Council = PPCO to monitor activities of the district-level PCs, the courts and the procuracy as resolutions of the PCO at the commune level. Only the ward administration is not subjected to any monitoring by the provincial elected bodies. In addition, Resolution 725 does not specify the methods of monitoring of the district-level agencies and their procedures. Of the five methods of monitoring discussed earlier (votes of confidence; reviews of reports; questioning sessions; legal documents; and monitoring reports), the PPCO cannot use the vote of confidence, which can be conducted only against persons appointed by the council at the same level. With the abolition of the district-level PCO, the transfer of its duties to the PPCO within the framework of Resolution 725 will increase. This shift presents a challenge, given the small number of full-time deputies at the provincial level.

Together these changes mean that matters previously carried out by district, quarter, and ward PCOs will probably have to be transferred to provincial-level PCOs. Changes of the local government system along these lines will require the adjustment of the provincial-level PCOs' functions and responsibilities so that the PPCOs can serve as effective agents for accountability under the new system. Successfully achieving such an adjustment would involve strengthening the decision-making and supervisory roles of the PPCO. It is likely that the new system will present a need to set up intra-agency accountability mechanisms for the district, quarter, and ward administrations, answerable to upper echelons. While the PPCOs may not be responsible for the appointment and endorsement of these positions, there may be a need to institute a process allowing the PPCO to hold the provincial government agencies accountable in the appointment of lower-echelon administrators and for the smooth operation of lower-echelon implementation work.

In addition, the NA, the inspectorate sector, and the PPCOs will likely have to take over supervision of the court and the procurator at lower echelons. Finally, the provincial-level PCO will also have to increase its citizen reception activities at the district, quarter, and ward levels. In terms of human resources, the additional required tasks will necessitate an increase of the number of deputies and full-time deputies to represent the quarter, district, and ward and to increase the power of the committee as well as the deputy groups for supervision. The role of the commune-level PCO will depend on the extent to which management decentralization devolves to the grassroots level.

Conclusions

Though Vietnam remains under "one-party rule," reconfiguration of Vietnam's one-party state has been taking place at both the national and local levels. The approaches adopted range from check-and-balance mechanisms and bureaucratic rationalization to transparency, open government, and citizen participation. A key driving force for the promotion of state accountability lies within the need for the one-party system to curb the rising power of the executive state.

Be all of this as it may, there are yet limitations to the effectiveness of Vietnam's accountability project. The accountability landscape in Vietnam is by no means even. Almost as significantly, the notion of accountability has developed mostly within the state institutional sector and for state-related actors. There remains a lack of any legal framework for further institutionalizing formal vertical accountability that would allow non-state actors to hold state officials accountable. In legislation, this absence includes that of any framework allowing associations to engage in public consultation on behalf of their members. Meanwhile, while the rising "checking-and-balancing" role of the PPCOs has undoubtedly been noteworthy, still a redefinition of the multiple authority relations within and among the PPCOs and other political institutions is needed for PPCOs to function fully as agencies of accountability.

Finally, while the seed of the "answerability aspect" of accountability has certainly been planted, the notion of "enforcement" nonetheless remains unaddressed. In both cases under examination, the notion of "enforcement," including who is to be the enforcer and how there can be enforcement without responsiveness and answerability, is unclear. To balance the rising power of the executive state, under one-party rule Vietnam necessarily continues its accountability project to address and clarify the questions of who is accountable to whom, for what, through what processes, by what standards of success, and with what consequences for failure.

4
State versus State: The Principal-Agent Problem in Vietnam's Decentralizing Economic Reforms

Thomas Jandl

The overarching topic of this volume is the exercise of political power in Vietnam. Various chapters illuminate the Communist Party of Vietnam's (CPV) staying power (Vu), dissent and its repression (Kerkvliet, Thayer), selection methods in an authoritarian assembly (Malesky), and civil society (Wells-Dang) and accountability (Vasavakul). All these chapters focus on the CPV's relationship with the rest of society. This chapter adds a different approach by analyzing relationships within the CPV – between central and provincial Party elites. This principal-agent problem emerged after the 1986 *doi moi* market reforms, which gave provincial leaders more influence in Ha Noi, as provincial revenue increasingly paid the bills of the central treasury. Moreover, international economic integration altered dependencies within the state. The economic performance of localities began to depend less on domestic factors than on foreign direct investment (FDI) and international trade; thus local cadres may look to foreign investors and markets as they seek rents from political office. Such a constellation poses a challenge to central authorities, because local leaders can engage in fence breaking – a process of pushing the legal envelope as far as possible, and on occasion intentionally overstepping provincial legal authority during interprovincial competition for foreign investors. Contestation within the CPV at different levels of the Party apparatus is likely to impact forms of dissent and coercion, the development of civil society, and of course the (s)election processes of Party leaders. The findings of this chapter thus complement other research presented in this volume.

The chapter addresses the question how the center maintains control over provincial Party leaders. Are provincial leaders of economically successful provinces re-shaping the Party's discourses and policies, or is the central Party – the principal – capable of imposing itself and keeping its agents in line? The literature on China, after whom Vietnam has modeled its reforms, has addressed this issue in some detail, but has failed to come to a clear conclusion. Some authors find that the principal rules *from the top down* through direct control of local agents, via the positive and negative sanctions of promotion and demotion. Others find that local officials can advance their political careers not by obedience to the Party line, but by being economically successful. In this *bottom-up view*, the central Party's ability to impose discipline is reduced and officials are rewarded for their ability to maintain social peace through economic success.

This chapter suggests that Vietnam pursued a bottom-up strategy. The center warned fence breakers about their actions while letting the experiments go forward. Where they succeeded, the center legalized them ex post. Most importantly, successful fence breakers were elevated to top political positions. Fence breaking is evidence that the CPV considers its own interests best served by economic growth and the resultant social peace. Such behavior conforms to Olson's "stationary bandit" terminology, in which an elite with a long time horizon self-limits its predation in return for future gains (Olson 1993: 567).

In the following, the chapter lays out the principal-agent problem in the era of China's entry into the global economy and discusses a cross-section of the China-related literature on the problem. Then, it explains the Vietnamese decentralizing economic reforms and their impact on center-province power relations and on the political fortunes of provincial leaders. The special focus in both sections is on the question whether obedience to Party doctrine or economic success is a better determinant for career advancement for local officials in China and Vietnam. It concludes by analyzing similarities and differences between the two countries and their impact on principal-agent theory.

The principal-agent problem in the China literature

Scholars who have studied the domestic political changes associated with integration into the global economy have suggested that local leaders whose subunits benefit most from international interactions demand increased local autonomy. Centrifugal forces that reduce the power of the central government come to the fore and can ultimately lead to the disintegration of the state (Alesina and Spolaore 1997; Hiscox 2003). Disintegration is an extreme outcome that is unlikely in a state like China or Vietnam, both of which have developed a national narrative over many centuries. But the principal-agent conflict remains a constant political problem.

Global market integration leads to winners and losers because the cost of being small diminishes with modern communication and transportation technologies (Alesina and Spolaore 1997). Subnational economic units can make use of their natural endowments without the transaction costs that used to make small units inefficient. As a result, regions or provinces with better human capital, beneficial geography, natural resources, and similar advantages will thrive under conditions of international market integration, while the "hinterland" will fall further behind. These hinterland regions will either oppose integration or demand compensation from regions that benefit from these changes, in return for consenting to free trade policies (Arzaghi and Henderson 2005; Garrett and Rodden 2003). This assumption, that the interests of regions in a country begin to diverge as soon as parts of the country gain while others lose, forms the base of the principal-agent conundrum. A government can hold its provinces together and keep the cadres in line as long as they are all in one boat, but faces increased challenges in doing so when some gain more clout than others.

The research conducted on this question in China investigates by what means the principal attempts to stay in control, via bottom-up or top-down strategies. Edin (2003) and Yu Zheng (2009), for example, find evidence in support of the bottom-up assumption. Edin investigates the Chinese central state's extractive capacity after decentralizing reforms and concludes that through a policy achievement evaluation, cadres are incentivized with monetary and career rewards to implement the targets passed down from Beijing to the provinces and townships. Failure to implement these targets, or being subject to a large number of complaint letters, reduces the cadre's chances of moving up in the Party hierarchy and of obtaining a merit bonus. Importantly, Edin finds that the most important criterion for promotion is keeping social peace, measured by absence of violence or mass protests, followed by economic success. This finding suggests that the central Party values its long-term survival above all else, including short-term rent seeking. The Party values economic progress not as an end goal in itself, but as a means to maintain legitimacy through success, which in turn increases its chances for survival.

Along similar lines of research, Maskin et al. (2000) and Montinola et al. (1996) posit that competition among provinces leads to improved economic performance and is thus tolerated by the center. The argument for decentralization is that local authority is closer to the constituents and better positioned to understand local needs, an argument known as *allocative efficiency* (Tiebout 1956; Oates 1972; Buchanan and Tullock 1962). Along this line of argument, Hongbin Li and Li-An Zhou (2005: 1760–61) find that "the likelihood of promotion (termination) of provincial leaders increases (decreases) with their economic performance. The findings support the view that the government uses personnel control to motivate local officials to promote economic growth."

Contrasting these results, two studies by Sheng and Shih et al. support the top-down view of principal-agent relations. Sheng (2009) finds that the center maintains control through its power to promote and demote. In other words, the central government may rely on successful provinces for its fiscal well-being, but provincial officials remain dependent on the center for their careers. In China, a political career opens doors to financial success. The central government's ability to make or break career advancement remains a powerful factor in keeping provincial leaders in line. In Sheng's telling, not only did the center forestall demands for greater autonomy among provincial cadres; it even managed to tighten control over the most successful, coastal provinces. It did so by sending to those provinces governors and other high-ranking officials with a long experience in Beijing, to ensure that provincial leaders would feel closer allegiance to the center than to the province where they temporarily worked. This "bureaucratic integration" focuses on central policies and careers in the central government. Sheng hypothesizes a correlation between bureaucratic and market integration: the greater a province's integration into international markets, the stronger will the bureaucratic integration be. This is to say that Beijing is less concerned that a hinterland province may exhibit secessionist tendencies than a wealthy one, which could more easily afford to chart its own course.

Sheng identifies three groups of actors: the winner and loser provinces and the central government. Winners want to retain more of their gains and are willing to push for increased autonomy. Losers may also push for more autonomy, in order to re-impose the more closed economy whose demise led to the emergence of the wealth gap between winners and losers. All provinces have an interest in carving out autonomous space, albeit for different purposes. The central government, whose claim to legitimacy is based on the common purpose of the nation, counteracts these tendencies and tries to maintain control by opposing demands for increased autonomy by both types of regions. This argument is one of *divergence of interest*, which the center has to counteract. Sheng's results show that bureaucratic integration is negatively correlated with the amount of tax revenue a province retains. These results indicate – in direct contrast to Edin's findings and the hypothesis about Vietnam in this chapter – that agents prefer to make the principal in Beijing happy in hope for a promotion, rather than to serve their local constituents.

Shih et al. (2012) arrive at a similar result from a different angle. Their research uses a biographical database of China's top leaders to identify the causes for promotion into the highest positions of central power. Based on McGuire and Olson (1996), who argue that encompassing political systems (in which the elite represents a large segment of society) exhibit better economic growth performance than fractious ones, Shih et al. hypothesize that if the Chinese Party had a long time horizon, it would favor economic growth for all in order to promote social peace and Party survival. If, by contrast, the Party is afraid of being overthrown, it would focus on short-term predation.

The results of the study indicate that economic performance of local leaders has no impact on promotion to the Central Committee. Relevant factors are personal ties to higher-level officials, provincial revenue collection and transfer to Beijing, and education level of the cadre. The study concludes that factional loyalties and providing immediate rent for the Party outweigh encompassing goals, such as growing the economic pie for all. Careers run through Beijing, not performance at the provincial level – a top-down rather than a bottom-up career path.

Another study adds process to the mix. Zheng's (2009) empirical review of career paths shows how changing conditions alter actors' preferences. Studying how a strong, authoritarian state like China could signal enough commitment to investors' rights, he argues that after the creation and the success of the first industrial zones, the inflow of FDI led to an alignment of interests between provincial and central elites. Initially, some political leaders saw high growth as a legitimation of their rule, while others, the conservatives in the central party structure, were more concerned with loss of ideological purity. Inland politicians did not like the special arrangements benefiting coastal provinces, but over time, the success of the special economic zones aligned interests of the various actors and created an equilibrium among central government, coastal, and inland provinces in which no one had a strong interest in changing the status quo. Simultaneously, the composition of the central party leadership changed in the 1990s. The wealthy coastal provinces began to send more officials to the top positions in Beijing as it became obvious that their economic experiments were successful. Until 1992, officials from Beijing, Shanghai, Tianjing, and Sichuan regularly served in the Politburo. Later, Guangdong and Shandong gained increased access to the halls of power (Yu Zheng 2009: 16–17). This shift,

Zheng argues, empowered liberals and marginalized conservatives in the center, making the center look more like the successful provinces rather than keeping the provinces in line with central policies.

Zheng, then, bridges the two poles. He recognizes the importance of factional politics in the Party, but in his interpretation of the data, the bottom-up faction with its encompassing view ends up winning. Clearly, the China literature is not conclusive. In the following section, we take a close look at Vietnam's approach to reform, internationalization of the economy, decentralization, and the principal-agent problem. Then we return to China and propose a comparative analysis of the China literature and our findings in the Vietnam case.

Decentralization and principal-agent relations in Vietnam

The CPV officialized market reforms in December of 1986. This momentous change was not as much a result of a sudden change of mind within the highest Party strata as it was the accumulation of the lessons of continuous local experimentation and fence breaking. In 1986, foreign investment was nonexistent, more than seven in ten Vietnamese lived below the poverty line, and the economy required support from the Soviet Union (Dang Phong 2004).

Prior to the reforms, the Party tightly controlled allocation of all economic resources, and the flow of goods was strictly limited. Trade across district lines was not allowed for many basic items of daily use. Only the government had the legal right to ship goods across district lines and distribute them according to government plans through ration coupons. Since districts are fairly small political entities below the province level – the number of districts in 2010 was 599 (GSO 2010) – with these restrictions in place, legal trade was essentially limited to the local market in the immediate vicinity of the producer. When the system was abandoned, agriculture exhibited rapid gains in productivity.

Following the liberalization of agriculture, Vietnam's dominant economic sector at the time, the government began to court foreign investors, first to produce goods for which a domestic shortage existed, later for export production. The export-led growth model has taken hold and is the dominant economic policy priority today. Within a decade of *doi moi* reforms, FDI flows increased from nil to $8.6 billion in 1996, making Vietnam the world's second-biggest recipient of FDI by share of gross domestic product (World Bank 1997). Commitments of FDI between 1988 and 1998 totaled $35 billion for over 2,500 projects (Mai 2004: 22). Ho Chi Minh City and neighboring Dong Nai received 60 percent of all approved projects (Malesky 2004a: 287). As a consequence, regional income differences increased. The average difference between the richest region (the Southeast) and the poorest (the Northwest) grew from 2.1 times in 1996 to 2.5 times in 1999 and 3.1 times in 2002 (GSO and UNFPA 2006: 10). The second decade of *doi moi* brought with it a significant acceleration of economic performance. Total committed FDI between 1986 (*doi moi*) and 2008 had grown to some $98 billion, across 9,800 approved projects (Ninh Kieu 2008); 8,600 projects were operational (Chinanet 2008).

In 2008 alone, the country expected $20 billion in new commitments prior to the onset of the global financial crisis. To put these numbers in perspective, 2007 saw more than double the realized investments of 2006, which stood at $4.1 billion (Chinanet 2008). This made Vietnam one of the world's top destinations for FDI. With 85 million people, the country received more FDI than India, and roughly one-third as much as China. When measured in relation to the size of the economy, Vietnam is the world's top FDI recipient among developing or transitional nations (Foreign Investment Advisory Service, in Malesky 2008: 100). The second decade of market opening is associated with export-oriented foreign investment, improved regulations and tax incentives for exporters, and the creation of dozens of export processing zones. At the end of 1999, 14 export processing zone projects had been approved (Mai 2004: 43); in 2012, the Ministry of Planning and Investment counted 283.

The FDI-based development formula is important, as FDI and the pressures brought to bear by investors have altered the relations between political agents in Vietnam. One of the crucial changes since *doi moi* can be found in the altered relationship between central and provincial elites. Economic success, and particularly success in attracting foreign investors, is highly concentrated. Between 1988 and 1998, Ho Chi Minh City in the Southeast region and Ha Noi and the port city of Hai Phong in the Red River Delta region received a cumulative 54.7 percent of committed FDI (Mai 2004: 101). Binh Duong and Dong Nai, two provinces adjacent to Ho Chi Minh City in the Southeast region, were investment poles as well. The other five regions combined received less than 20 percent of FDI (ibid.: 104).

Thanks to their economic prowess, the top provinces find themselves in a position of growing importance for the central government's treasury. Table 4.1 shows that 11 of the 63 provinces contribute to the central treasury; the other provinces are net recipients. The top

Table 4.1 Net contributors to the central budget

Province	Region	Percentage of revenue retained in province
Ho Chi Minh City	Southeast	26% vs. 74% to central treasury
Ha Noi	Red River Delta	31% vs. 69%
Binh Duong	Southeast	40% vs. 60%
Dong Nai	Southeast	45% vs. 55%
Ba Ria-Vung Tau	Southeast	46% vs. 54%
Khanh Hoa	South Central Coast	53% vs. 47%
Vinh Phuc	Red River Delta	67% vs. 33%
Quang Ninh	Northeast	76% vs. 24%
Da Nang	South Central Coast	90% vs. 10%
Hai Phong	Red River Delta	90% vs. 10%
Can Tho	Mekong River Delta	96% vs. 4%

Source: Ministry of Finance 2008.

contributors account for almost all the fence breaking. The central government depends on their continued success to be able to distribute money to poor areas of the country. Since the government has made continuous improvements in living standards its raison d'être, the success of the high-performing provinces finances the government's political promise.

This fiscal prowess has been translated into increasing autonomy – an autonomy that was not given by Ha Noi but taken by provincial leaders. These leaders have wrestled away decision-making powers from the center as their provinces grew and provided more resources to the central state. The early success stories pushed the envelope, with the support of foreign investors, who enjoyed the improving business climate. The argument was that since investors like what they get, any push-back from the center would reduce the attractiveness not only of these particular provinces, but of Vietnam overall. Not surprisingly, there is a clear connection between success in attracting FDI and in paying into the central government's treasury.

All these changes during *doi moi* point to the same questions the China literature posed: With the growing importance of a handful of provinces to the central treasury, did the principal in Vietnam maintain control? Did Vietnam follow the top-down or the bottom-up approach? Does the Party see its fortunes in the long run, which would point toward encompassing goals of legitimacy through growth and increased living standards for all, or will the elite grab what it can and prepare to run?

It is of note that the policy reversal from a collectivist, planned economy to a market system with focus on international investment arose from the dire needs of an extremely poor and malnourished population, not a sudden change of heart by local cadres. Too many of the leaders had spent much of their lives in the jungles fighting capitalism just to turn around and adopt it. It was only through the trickling up of popular demand and satisfaction with the reforms on the ground level that reformers could win their argument. This popular demand came with improved living conditions where market forces were introduced, often in fits and spurts. The new system was sustained and strengthened by the success of the early movers. While officials at the central level may not have appreciated the gradual devolution of power toward the local level, they recognized that it was in their own interest to accept the rise of the province. The most successful provinces provided the treasury in Ha Noi with the funds that permitted the fiscal transfers to poorer parts of the country, thus maintaining social cohesion and the legitimacy of the Party, which could claim that it was making all Vietnamese better off. A *harmony of interests* emerged between the center, which depended on tax revenues from the most successful provinces, the provincial officials in the poorer provinces who received transfer payments that allowed them to stay in their constituents' good graces, and the officials in the successful provinces who benefited from the success of their provinces and the increasing autonomy that made this success possible (Jandl 2011, 2013). Centrifugal forces are kept in check by this harmony of interests rather than by coercive measures.

It is to the mechanisms by which a harmony of interest is established and maintained that we now turn. Fence breaking creates realities on the ground that are difficult to repress as long as they are successful, are viewed positively by a large share of the population, and end up increasing the center's tax take from a province. Interprovincial competition produces pluralistic contestation that creates what federalists call a "commitment device" (Weingast 1995) against elite collusion and excessive rent seeking.

Fence breaking: the push of the market

In stark contrast to the market reforms in Eastern Europe after the fall of communism, Vietnam's institutions stayed intact throughout the reform period. The central government, grudgingly at first, accepted local reforms as a necessary, ideologically questionable evil as long as it fed the people and helped the Party maintain its performance legitimacy. Unlike Gorbachov's simultaneous *glasnost* and *perestroika* – political and economic reforms – Vietnam, as well as China half a decade earlier, focused entirely on improving living standards to stave off any discussion of political change. In that process, they pragmatically learned from historical experiences. Fence-breaking experimentation started prior to 1986, especially when provinces tried to harness market forces to increase food production. As Malesky (2004b: 164) points out:

> These reforms were in response to the economic crisis, so they were not so much improper [with respect to communist doctrine] as necessary behavior that discipline would slow but not stop. If the Party was to retain its relevance it had to allow necessary local reforms to be legitimized and even spread. Therefore pressure from the bottom combined with an accurate sense of urgency resulted in major change of direction for the communist country.

One famous example dates to 1978, when Ho Chi Minh City ran low on food. Officials wondered why nearby An Giang province, a rice basket, could provide so little of Vietnam's staple to the country's biggest city. The Ho Chi Minh City People's Committee Chairman and Politburo member Vo Van Kiet sent a procurement official to An Giang. The official reported that farmers had rice but would not sell it at the legally prevailing price. She could get it only by breaking the law. Kiet reportedly told her to get the rice; should she go to jail, he, Kiet, would bring her rice to her cell. Ho Chi Minh City received the rice, its population was fed, nobody went to jail and Kiet became prime minister. Soon, rice was sold everywhere at the new price paid in An Giang (Dang Phong 2004: 30–1).

In Long An, leaders effectively abolished the state price system. Seeing the positive results of marketization, other provincial leaders visited to study Long An's experience. Because of that interest, even the conservatives had to let the experiment go forward. As hardships increased and problems seemed to be solved by innovative ideas, these ideas took hold and more and more leaders changed their position. The rest were removed (ibid.: 33–5).

These and other incidents of fence breaking set the stage for the 1986 reforms at the central level. As Susan Shirk points out about China, the Communist Party system may not be democratic in terms of national elections, but the principles of contested politics apply within the Party apparatus. Leaders cannot swim against the current of the opinions of rank-and-file officials, at the risk of being pushed out at the next Party Congress (Shirk 1993). In Vietnam, these changes based on intra-Party popular opinion were pushing policy. At the Sixth Party Congress in 1986, key reform policies were now written into national law, including the principle of a multisectoral economy, the acceptance of private and foreign investment, a market economy for a number of commodities, and concentration on certain spearhead sectors of the economy where a great need or competitive advantage existed. Fence breaking did not stop with the victory of early pro-market officials. It continued straight into the new, open economy, now with respect to regulations regarding the investment climate.

Market opening represented an experiment for the Party, and the risks of negative fallout had to be contained. The government tried to restrict this new free-market model geographically to the south, far away from the political center Ha Noi. In the early stages of *doi moi*, the central government licensed all new investments, and placed the vast majority of them in Ho Chi Minh City and adjacent Binh Duong and Dong Nai. Provinces had no say in the matter and could at best lobby the investors to request that their project be located in their province. Seeing the benefits, these three main beneficiaries of FDI began to push the envelope and started to license investors themselves. As the center continued to receive ever-increasing tax revenues, it refrained from cracking down. The "one door – one stop" policy for licensing began as a fence-breaking experiment in Binh Duong province and in Ho Chi Minh City. It was first criticized in the official newspapers, but then legalized. The *New Foreign Investment Law* of 1996 authorized Ho Chi Minh City and Ha Noi to license projects with a value of up to $10 million directly; other provinces could license projects worth up to $5 million – some ignored the limits. Also in the south, some provinces violated customs laws to provide intermediary goods for firms. No leaders were punished (Malesky 2004b: 181–82). An even more obvious indication that success leads to enhanced bargaining power occurred in the early 1990s. Some leaders were punished for selling land to investors illegally, yet all of those punished were from economically less successful provinces, while similar activities by officials from Ho Chi Minh City, Song Be (now Binh Duong), or Dong Nai were not pursued (ibid.: 176). As a consequence of the obvious devolution in power, line ministry officials who, due to dual subordination, reported to both Ha Noi and the provincial People's Committee began to show more loyalty to the province (ibid.: 189–90).

Fence breaking is a bottom-up process. Assuming local cadres are rational actors who have their own best interest in mind (instead of a moral obligation to do what is right regardless of the consequences for them), they disobey the principal only if they are confident that successful policy outcomes will be to their benefit. The history of fence breaking in Vietnam is therefore difficult to reconcile with Shih's and Sheng's findings on China (see earlier) that success through fence breaking leads to punishment.

Since economic reforms in Vietnam started with fence breaking, the province had already established itself as the center of successful experimentation at the time the central government adapted the legal code to reflect the changes on the ground. The next section describes the mechanisms by which competition among provinces is responsible for the harmony of interest among the major interest groups in Vietnam.

The province in Vietnam's economic reforms

The most trade-integrated provinces with the highest FDI levels soon enjoyed a high quality of life. As social indicators improved, Vietnamese voted with their feet by migrating to these high-growth provinces in large numbers. Table 4.2 provides a poverty count and Table 4.3 shows migration flows into the wealthier FDI-receiving regions. For the provincial governments, this means not only an opportunity for rent seeking, but also a good argument for political promotion. For the center, it means that these provinces are at the same time allowing large numbers of Vietnamese to improve their lives *and* paying the bill for the central government as it supports the poorer provinces through transfer payments. For a government that has staked its legitimacy on economic

Table 4.2 Poverty count by province

	Poverty headcount index (%)			
	1993	1998	2002	1993–2002
Nation	58.1	37.4 (–20.7%)	28.9 (–8.5%)	–29.2%
By region				
Red River Delta	62.7	29.3 (–33.4%)	22.4 (–6.9%)	–40.3%
Northeast	86.1	62.0 (–24.1%)	38.4 (–23.6%)	–47.7%
Northwest	81.0	73.4 (–7.6%)	68.0 (–5.4%)	–13.0%
North Central Coast	74.5	48.1 (–26.4%)	43.9 (–4.2%)	–30.6%
South Central Coast	47.2	34.5 (–12.7%)	25.2 (–9.3%)	–22.0%
Central Highlands	70.0	52.4 (–17.6%)	51.8 (–0.6%)	–18.2%
Southeast	37.0	12.2 (–24.8%)	10.6 (–1.6%)	–26.4%
Mekong River Delta	47.1	36.9 (–10.2%)	23.4 (–13.5%)	–23.7%

Source: Headcount calculations by Phan and Coxhead (2007), based on Vietnam Living Standard Survey 1993, 1998, Vietnam Household Living Standard Survey 2002, 2004, Vietnam Development Report 2004. Additional calculations by author.

Table 4.3   Gross inter-provincial migration flows – 2004–09

| | Place of residence, April 1, 2004 | | | | | | | |
Place of residence, April 1, 2009	Northern Mountains	Red River	Central Coast	Central Highlands	South-east	Mekong River	Total in-migration	Net migration
Northern Mountains	–	70	13	3	4	1	91	–180
Red River	160	–	98	9	19	4	298	–42
Central Coast	8	29	–	29	36	9	110	–665
Central Highlands	27	29	79	–	23	7	166	41
Southeast	73	195	570	83	–	713	1635	1510
Mekong River	2	9	15	2	43	–	70	–664
Total out-migration	270	331	775	125	125	734	(2361)	–

Note: Numbers do not add up due to rounding.

Source: Population and housing census 2009.

progress for its citizens, the success of these provinces becomes the backbone of the government's claim to power.

Crucial to the story is that no province could monopolize the recipe for success, because capital, goods, and labor could flow almost freely from province to province. Charles Tilly's argument about Europe's exceptionalism is relevant here. He argued that democracy arose in Europe because after the demise of the Roman Empire, no dominant state emerged, leaving room for a multiplicity of nearby jurisdictions in a constant state of contestation. If a prince did not like a new idea, a new technology, or a new philosophy and oppressed it, people were free to pick up and literally walk across the border to look for a different government (Tilly 2004). In Vietnam's case, if a provincial government cannot provide reasonably good conditions or if government engages in excessive predation, investors, and also workers (who have become a scarce factor in the most economically active provinces), can pick up and go elsewhere. Predation is best checked if regular people have exit options. Economic success stories are credited to a federal organization structure, as prevails in the United States and Switzerland (Parente and Prescott 2000). Where citizens are free to move across jurisdictional borders as well, elites face declining fortunes in the longer run if they make decisions that are immediately utility maximizing for them, while suboptimal from a societal point of view. Competition for these mobile resources – capital and people – shifts bargaining power not only among elites, but also from elites to nonelites.

This ability of local elites to provide good business conditions to induce investors – and also workers, who follow the employment opportunities – to come to their province is key to the shifting bargaining power between interest groups. First, local elites gained significant bargaining power vis-à-vis the central elites in Ha Noi. Second, nonelite workers gained bargaining power because they were needed where the economic growth occurred. In places where a local elite is unable to create employment with decent salaries, or engages in excessive predation or a regulatory race to the bottom by reducing social wages, workers can pick up and leave. As the data show, large numbers of them do.

At this point, the central government is restrained in its actions by the fact that investors have been voting with their money by locating their factories in a small number of preferred provinces, and workers by voting with their feet, as they decided to migrate into these provinces. A mix of remittances from migrant workers and fiscal transfers from rich to poor provinces via the central government also keeps the less successful provinces afloat and allows the government to make a credible claim that the economy is indeed lifting all boats. Imposing central orthodoxy would disrupt the harmony of interests that has emerged among the three actors, winning provinces, losing provinces, and the central authorities (and workers who also benefit from growth). The winning provinces earn significant amounts of money, which offers the opportunity for rent seeking by officials, but also allows them to claim that their good work legitimizes the system and that they should therefore be promoted. The losing provinces may be falling behind in relative terms, but are aware that without the success stories that pay for the fiscal transfers and make large amounts of remittances possible (in addition to reducing the burden of underemployed young people, who can now migrate), they would be worse off. And the center claims legitimacy for distributing shares of the rapidly growing economic pie across the country. In direct contrast to Sheng's hypothesis, it appears that in Vietnam the central government would be more threatened by an economic downturn that leads to less employment and less money to be distributed than by continued success in the high-FDI provinces, even if the latter situation brings with it demands for more policy autonomy.

Autonomy and political careers in Vietnam

In a harmony-of-interest scenario, economic success promotes political careers at both provincial and central levels. As the theory suggests, leaders of successful provinces push for increased autonomy. Since their success also serves the interests of the less successful provinces through fiscal transfers, and the central state through legitimacy-conferring revenue to be distributed, none of the actors has a strong incentive to push for more radical change. Leaders in successful provinces can only engage in fence breaking because they know that the center needs them. Their fence breaking is tolerated because it serves the greater good of all actors; any excessive demands for autonomy would break that harmony of interest and provincial officials would be punished, as were those who broke central rules without concomitant economic success.

Foreign investment works as a bargaining chip for subnational jurisdictions when a convergence of interests exists between the higher and lower levels of administration. Provincial leaders benefit from increased economic activity in their province in a variety of ways. They can extract rents from the growing local economy. They can maintain their positions of power if they are seen as successful administrators of their province. And they can obtain promotions to central-level positions thanks to their performance at the provincial level. The center gains because of its ability to maintain social peace owing to its increased capability to transfer surplus money from the successful provinces into the hinterland. Thus, local success not only strengthens the hand of these reformers in the provinces, but also allows reformers at the center to make their case more forcefully (Malesky 2004b: 9).

Clearly, Vietnam has a strong governing party that ensures that local interests cannot entirely override national ones. On the other hand, the top-down pathways that Sheng and Shih (above) have described do not prevail in Vietnam. The assumption that career advancement will keep local cadres in line with central policy is not observable. Indeed, central government careers depend on local success, but success is defined in terms of maintaining social peace and order and paying into the central government's treasury by growing the revenue base. The most successful risers in the ranks were not those who defended Ha Noi's traditional line while on duty in the provinces, but those who challenged it effectively and achieved results that were in the interest of center and province.

One recent president, Nguyen Minh Triet, started out as Party leader in Song Be province (now Binh Duong), before taking over the same position in Ho Chi Minh City. He was one of the principal fence breakers, turning his rural Song Be into one of Vietnam's economic powerhouses. Vo Van Kiet (prime minister from 1991 to 1997), another key fence breaker, was one of the main supporters of *doi moi*. Gainsborough (2004: 264) points out that of the five Party leaders of Ho Chi Minh City between unification and publication of this book, only one did not move on the positions in the central government. Vo Tran Chi, a conservative critic of market reforms, retired.

The career paths of successful officials in Vietnam follow Edin's and Zheng's view (appointed to central positions of power *after* success in the province), rather than Sheng's and Shih's (sent to the province to enforce central doctrine). Yet with Vietnam's economy sagging in the aftermath of the 2008 global economic crisis, moving up the ranks through economic performance is becoming more difficult. At the 2011 Party Congress, reformist Prime Minister Nguyen Tan Dung had to fight for his re-election. Former Ho Chi Minh City Party chief and market-oriented reformer Truong Tan Sang was elected president. The third power position of general secretary of the Communist Party, however, went to Nguyen Phu Trong, a man who had risen through the Party ranks without a history of economic success or reformist attitudes.

Conclusion: lessons from Vietnam and China

Yumin Sheng (2009) hypothesizes that Vietnam, due to the similarity of its political structures and the way it fashioned its reforms on China's, should behave very similar to China on the question of principal-agent relations. This assumption proved incorrect. One potential reason is that China, with its size, its earlier reforms, and its different history, simply does not easily compare to any other country. But since some of the literature found that China is much more like Vietnam than Sheng and Shih et al. accept, the alternative view is that their studies misinterpret the data.

If Sheng is right about China, then China is a state in which political success results from obedience to doctrine. By contrast, Vietnam's system would be truly pragmatic in comparison, since personal careers are advanced by success, even if this success stems from challenges to doctrine and conventional wisdom. To be sure, China is an economic success story second to none. This makes Sheng's findings all the more puzzling. If provincial elites obeyed Beijing for career considerations, the implication would be that the Chinese leadership was either extraordinarily wise or outstandingly lucky. That a small band of aging, communist leaders, most coming of age during revolutionary, anticapitalist struggle, would be able to make long-term decisions about free-market capitalism so successfully is extremely unlikely. Vietnam's system of local corrections where the principal's wisdom falls flat is much closer to the orthodoxy of economic thought that holds that markets do well because they respond rapidly and efficiently to the innumerable stimuli in the system, and correct mistakes as they arise.

Sheng's work also contains some assumptions that defy the internal logic of his argument. If the center indeed sends Beijing-oriented cadres to the wealthy coastal regions to curb their potential for demands for more autonomy, then one would have to assume that the two openly secessionist provinces, Tibet and Xinjiang, would rate on top of the index. Tibet indeed rates high but still lower than some hinterland regions. Yet Xingjiang rates low on integration. Moreover, early protests against Beijing's policies came from hinterland provinces who resented the special treatment for the coastal ones. Based on the logic of assuring obedience, those provinces should also be governed by Beijing-oriented officials. In fact, there is no reason why any one province should not be, if control is the goal. Therefore, the great divergence in Sheng's integration index itself raises doubts about the theoretical usefulness of the data collected.

Both Sheng and Shih et al. point to provincial revenue retention rates as evidence of central control. If a wealthy province sends a lot of money to the center (Sheng) or if promotions are correlated with having provided a lot of revenue for the center (Shih et al.), the logical conclusion is argued to be that local officials value their careers in the center more than their economic success in the province. What goes unsaid is that revenue retention is a ratio. The higher a province's income, the more it has to send to the center. But the retained *absolute amount* can still be vastly superior to the amount retained in poorer provinces, even if the retention rate there is 100 percent. Table 4.1 has shown that in Vietnam, revenue retention rates in the most integrated provinces are extremely low, yet officials in exactly those provinces are fence breakers who push for better business regulations. Hence Sheng's data are open to a variety of explanations. Senior officials may be sent to the province to maximize tax revenue, which could very well lead to increased bargaining power for these officials. They could – and in Vietnam definitely do – make the argument that they provide the center the money it needs to keep the social peace in return for noninterference and a promotion down the road, and should be left alone with respect to the means to accomplish the task. This explanation, which suggests increased provincial autonomy, is just as consistent with the data as is Sheng's position of more central control. By contrast, the low levels of bureaucratic integration of provinces with high secession risk are clearly inconsistent with Sheng's argument. On balance, Sheng does not appear to have made his case.

The work by Shih et al. addresses some of the problems through rigorous use of control variables, but some of their conclusions remain dubious. It is assumed that leaders have too short a time horizon to focus on encompassing, long-term goals. Instead, they emphasize rent seeking and short-term power retention. To maintain power among the many factions, top officials intentionally promote cadres who have not distinguished themselves in the province, to keep the best qualified competitors at arm's length. A serious logical problem arises: How can one explain the stunning success of China's economy over three decades if each generation of leaders is – by design – less qualified than the previous one?

Another unanswered question is why an authoritarian, but factional political system would have a shorter time horizon than another. The communist parties of China and Vietnam have planned for a long reign. If Shih et al. were correct, why have the parties in China and Vietnam placed so much emphasis on socio-economic development and not on the forms of pillage seen in other parts of the world? It is indicative that Shih et al. base the time horizon argument on McGuire and Olson; yet in their work, time horizon is but an afterthought. Their main aim is to illuminate economic reasons for elites to limit their rent seeking at certain levels that provide an optimal take in a given situation. Given the benefits the principal in China and in Vietnam reaps from the success in the most economically advanced provinces, McGuire and Olson are unlikely to underwrite the conclusions Shih et al. attribute to their theory. In fact, they write:

> Paradoxically, the same self-interest that leads an autocrat to maximize his extraction from the society also gives him an interest in the productivity of his society. ... Thus a rational autocrat always limits his tax theft: he takes care not to increase his rate of taxation above the point where the deadweight losses at the margin are so great that his share of these losses offsets what he gains from taking a higher percentage of income. Second, the rational autocrat spends some of the resources that he could have devoted to his own consumption on public goods for the whole society. He does this because it increases his tax collections. (McGuire and Olson 1996: 76)

The CPV has made development the argument for its legitimacy. In a short-time-horizon-focused political system, it would be hard to explain policies like recent changes in mortgage lending in response to a real estate bubble risk and increases in inflation. The Party made decisions that hurt its own cadres, such as prohibiting the use of stocks as security for mortgages. Very few laborers and peasants have either stocks or mortgages. In this case, the Party is taking the long view.

Statistical analysis, in any case, does not lend itself to making causal claims. Sometimes, the classic method of meticulous process tracing yields more than correlations do. In this light, a recent biography of Deng Xiaoping (Vogel 2011) can add to the debate. In it, the detailed description of the ups and downs of reforms in China paints a picture that indeed indicates that China is different from Vietnam. In China, local officials had to look over their shoulders constantly to gauge which faction – reformers or conservatives – were on the ascent in Beijing. Siding with the wrong one could bring trouble to a provincial leader. In Vietnam, as Malesky (2008, 2004b) has laid out so thoroughly, the center lost control over the reforms early on – arguably even before the reforms were institutionalized during *doi moi*. The Party could not isolate successful reforms. A smaller country with a much more mobile population learned rapidly where there was enough food or better job opportunities. Asking Vo Van Kiet to undergo self-criticism for feeding his hungry people would not have worked in Vietnam. Factor mobility among provinces in this much smaller country makes the top-down approach more difficult.

Vogel's account appears to strengthen Zheng's conclusions. The comrades in Beijing started with a top-down approach, but over time, successful provincial cadres progressively took over the central apparatus and brought their ideas with them. The same appears to be the case in Vietnam, except that the transition was much faster there.

Moving beyond the regional comparison, the principal-agent relations in Vietnam also tell a story about domestic politics. The authors in this volume have come to various conclusions with respect to the dynamism of the Party in Vietnam. The analysis in this chapter does not see decay, but continued adaptation to social realities and challenges to regime survival. As both Kerkvliet and Wells-Dang (this volume) have pointed out, the Party exhibits a mix of toleration and repression. Dissent is generally tolerated when it addresses policies; it is repressed when it affects the Party itself, particularly its monopoly on power inscribed in Article 4 of the Constitution. This is consistent with the harmony-of-interest approach. Provincial leaders who breach a law but end up improving the Party's standing in popular opinion are tolerated and even promoted. It is unlikely that the CPV would brook dissent by even the most successful local cadre if such dissent were to weaken the Party itself. It is not surprising, then, that after all the successful fence breaking in Ho Chi Minh City, Binh Duong, and Dong Nai, these three provinces still send the great majority of their revenues to Ha Noi.

If we accept that repression is the response to a certain set of circumstances, toleration to another, the question arises whether the Party will become less tolerant as the economy slows down. The harmony-of-interest view suggests this to be the case, since the harmony is reflected in the sharing of the benefits that come from autonomy. As these benefits shrink, the principal has less interest to give the agents a longer leash. On the other hand, as the economy slows down, the principal may see it in its interest to allow even more deviation from the rules in an attempt to make up for the loss in revenue. The question is whether the agent can convince the principal that the longer leash will pay off, even in times of higher risk and broader contestation against Party policies. Naturally, success remains the critical factor. The rare intra-Party challenges to the sitting prime minister shortly after the 2011 Party Congress are an indication that Nguyen Tan Dung's credentials for economic success were seriously tarnished by the recent scandals in state conglomerates, which he had pushed.

In a final summary, Riker (1964) and Enikolopov and Zhuravskaya (2007) are correct in pointing out that a strong party is important to provide coordination and enforce the rules of the game. But in the Vietnamese case, the pathways of control between center and province are reversed. Based on the strong sense of nationalism, all politicians must support the nation. But in what way they do so is less controlled by central leaders' disciplining the party cadres than by the most successful reformers, who in the case of Vietnam have resided in just a few provinces. The norms to which officials are held for career advancement are determined much more in the economic growth pole than in the halls of the central government in Ha Noi. It is ironic for a country that has forged such strong rhetoric about the primacy of ideology that in the end, Vietnam appears to be *governed very pragmatically by success.*

5
Understanding the Confidence Vote in Vietnamese National Assembly: An Update on "Adverse Effects of Sunshine"

Edmund J. Malesky

For analysts of Vietnam's politics, the country's representative politics have always been an object of curiosity and controversy. Although the present chapter is the only one that deals specifically with representative politics in virtually all the chapters in the volume, the Vietnamese National Assembly (VNA) appears as specter in the background, quietly shaping and interacting with the actors profiled by the other scholars. To offer but a few examples: The Wells-Dang discussion of Civil Society speculates on a critical question of how advocacy can be converted into legislation. Many of the dissidents analyzed in the extraordinary Kerkvliet chapter interacted with the VNA or were responding explicitly to its activities and, more importantly, to its lack of activity. Vu's study of party membership is critical for understanding how regime leaders exert control despite reforms that have granted the VNA increased prestige and policy-making authority. In these and other chapters, the authors' arguments are explicitly shaped by the unique role the VNA plays in Vietnamese policy making. Despite abundant representation of reforms of political institutions in the extant literature on authoritarian politics, there have been relatively few in-depth studies of representative politics. In this context, this chapter attempts to embed the study of the Vietnamese parliament into the broader literature on authoritarian politics, and provide a road map for future research on Vietnamese politics.

It has now been a year and a half since *Adverse Effects of Sunshine* (Malesky, Schuler, and Tran 2012) was published and nearly three years since we first initiated the online experiment that generated the results. Since we posted information about delegate participation in query sessions and legislative debates on *VietnamNet*, a great deal has happened in Vietnamese politics, with the Vietnamese National Assembly (VNA) often at the center of the action. In this reflection to the article, I reflect on the most high profile of these developments – the confidence vote on high-ranking VNA officials and ministers that took place in June 2013. The results suggest a consistent theme faced by the Vietnamese leadership that we attempted to highlight in *Sunshine* – the difficult balancing act of acquiring valuable information on citizen preferences and views of the regime, while at the same time maintaining order and stability in an authoritarian parliament.

I begin by discussing the intellectual history of *Sunshine*, highlighting the key puzzles about the "assertiveness" of the VNA that piqued our curiosity. Along the way, I attempt to place *Sunshine* in the context of the reforms that have garnered so much attention among Vietnamese analysts and media. I show how recent debates over the Vietnamese Constitutional reforms and the defense by the regime of one of their most outspoken critics can be understood within the theoretical framework of the article. Finally, I discuss the motivation, organization, and the results of the confidence vote, demonstrating how this unique new mechanism, unprecedented in the annals of authoritarian regimes, further elucidates the tension between transparency, access to information, and stability faced by Vietnam's leadership. It is noteworthy that while the results of the transparency were made public, the actual confidence voting itself was done with a secret ballot. Neither citizens nor elites knew which delegates actually voted for or against a particular minister. As in *Sunshine*, the protection of voting delegates' identity allowed for a more honest assessment of their perceptions about top leaders. In fact, more delegates gave low confidence votes to the State Bank governor and prime minister than they would have actually spoken out in query sessions!

The intellectual history of the article

When we first sat down to design the online experiment described in the article, we had both broad and narrow intellectual goals. For general political science audiences, we intended to test the effects of transparency interventions on performance in authoritarian legislatures (McGee and Gaventa 2010). For the subfield of authoritarian regimes, we wanted to explore a critical mechanism of the co-optation theory, the notion that authoritarian regimes use parliaments to co-opt potential opposition (Wright 2008; Gandhi 2009; Svolik 2012). We were worried that the literature had emphasized the benefits of co-optation without paying enough attention to the threat of punishment, which was necessary to ensure regime stability.

In addition to these broader claims, we also had a narrow goal of pinpointing the role of the VNA in elite Vietnamese politics. Unfortunately, this motivation is somewhat buried in the disciplinary jargon, experimental design, and complex statistics. Yet, this agenda is critical for how we, as Vietnam specialists, view the implications of the experimental results.

It has become conventional in analyses of Vietnamese politics to refer to the VNA as increasingly "assertive." The phrase is so ubiquitous in descriptions of the body, that the words "National Assembly" alone appear almost naked.[1] Moreover, the reference is always meant to connote a recent development, even though some of the usage goes back over a decade. What is unclear is what assertive actually means, and especially what assertive implies when used to describe a political institution in its entirety rather than to refer to individual delegates or leaders. The usage gives the impression that a once tame institution, suddenly and on its own, decided to challenge higher authorities. We are guilty of the turn of phrase ourselves, but our own culpability does not diminish the fact that "assertive" is shorthand that obfuscates more than it explains.

There is no doubt that the role of the body and quality of delegates has changed over time. In our work, we have chronicled the increasing professionalism of the VNA. With each new session, the share of full-time delegates has risen, and our work has charted a steady increase in educational attainment and professional expertise in the body over time (Thayer 2003; Malesky and Schuler 2010). As a result, the level of legislative debate and query sessions has improved. Furthermore, elections, while still far from truly free and fair, have become uniquely competitive for single-party regimes. Candidate-to-seat ratios now range between 1.7 and 2 (depending on electoral district characteristics). This means that voters have some choice among the candidates nominated and vetted by central institutions or local election commissions (Gainsborough 2005). In the past two elections, 2007 and 2012, a large number of centrally nominated candidates (those designated for leadership positions) have lost and an even larger number barely eked out a victory (Malesky and Schuler 2008, 2011). Increasing professionalism and functional expertise has in turn allowed the VNA to take on new responsibilities, including the query sessions, where delegates are able to grill ministers on their performance and policy choices, legislative debates, where delegates debate draft laws, and public hearings, where committees (the Economic Committee being the most active) have solicited testimony from experts on policy debates of national import.

These are important developments to be sure, and they have certainly raised the profile of the parliament as well as that of individual delegates, but do they constitute "assertiveness"? Champions of the assertiveness thesis cite a few well-worn anecdotes: the active query sessions and fierce criticism of ministers (including the sacking of an education minister after a poor showing), rejection of the prime minister's sponsored resolution for a high-speed railway, and the occasional low vote total for a ministerial appointment (i.e. Deputy Prime Minister Hoang Trung Hai received a VNA approval vote of 73% in 2007). For each of these anecdotes, however, there is an equally compelling counternarrative. Query session participation is actually quite low with only 30 percent of delegates asking any questions at all, and only 5 percent asking questions that could be perceived as critical of a minister, ministry, or government action (Malesky and Schuler 2010). The rejection of the high-speed rail was truly remarkable, but as we have argued in another work, it occurred during a unique set of circumstances – when Vietnamese Communist Party (VCP) leaders were not unified in support for the initiative. The 2008 Hanoi merger with Ha Tay province was equally controversial initially, but passed with over a 90 percent of the vote after a Central Committee Resolution signaled unified elite support (Malesky et al. 2011). Finally, the cherry-picking of low votes totals for particular ministers ignores the obscenely high vote total for most other appointments. In 2007, for instance, 21 out of 31 ministers were approved by the VNA with votes over 90 percent.

Moreover, the Hanoi merger reminds us that the VNA is not an autonomous institution. It is embedded within a web of institutions controlled by a single-party regime (Thayer 1995; Gainsborough 2005). Over 90 percent of delegates are VCP members and beholden to the party line, established through elite resolutions. The greatest predictor of leadership in the VNA is not a large vote total in the popular election, but party membership and nomination by a central institution (Malesky and Schuler 2013). The institutional changes that have professionalized the body, and provided it with a prominent, televised forum, were allowed by the VCP, and in many cases were conceived of at the highest levels of the VCP leadership. An "assertive" VNA did not simply burst on the political landscape. Its reforms have been carefully designed and cultivated to achieve regime goals, and its powers have been parameterized to avoid destabilizing single-party control of the country.

In our research agenda, we have highlighted four benefits that the reforms of the VNA accomplish for the regime: information, professionalism, co-optation, and power sharing. *Information*: elections, query sessions, and legislative debates provide valuable information on popular support for the regime, the strength of potential opposition, public perceptions of national policy, and the geographic distribution of policy preferences. *Professionalism*: better educated and professional, full-time delegates means that laws can be designed with more complexity and specialization. *Co-optation*: query sessions and debates provide an outlet for potential critics, who otherwise might seek external outlets for their dissent. These potential critics can be co-opted by the limited ability to influence policy and direct access to high-ranking politicos. *Power-sharing*: the institutionalized rules and evaluations provide a powerful ability for elites to check the power of other political elites. In *Sunshine*, we focused our attention on elucidating the co-optation mechanism.

A fascinating illustration of the value elite regime leaders place on the information and policy ideas revealed during VNA debate and the lengths they will go to protect it occurred in early 2012, when Hoang Huu Phuoc, a VNA delegate from Ho Chi Minh City, criticized fellow delegate Duong Trung Quoc as one of the four "great idiots" in the VNA for his criticism of the government. Duong had been an outspoken in his dismay at the Vinashin bailouts, opposition to a Chinese bauxite investment in the Central Highlands, and had famously called for the resignation of the prime minister. In Phuoc's blog post, which he admitted to writing, he suggested that Quoc "shut his mouth" so that other delegates could speak (Truong Son 2013). However, Phuoc's ploy quickly backfired. The government chose to take no action against its most famous gadfly (*GiaoDuc Vietnam* 2013). Instead, it was Phuoc who was publically chastised by the VCP leadership and was ultimately forced to apologize publicly for his actions (Schuler 2013: ch. 6).

The benefits that VCP elite receive from its parliament, however, are not risk free. By expanding membership beyond a narrow, loyal circle, opening the scope of debates, and allowing a wider audience to view them, the regime places itself at serious risk. An outspoken critic could use the powerful forum to mobilize an opposition movement. Fierce debate in the VNA might spill over into the public, igniting popular discontent and protests. Limited evidence for both of these threats can be found in the debate over a Chinese bauxite firm's investment in the Central Highlands and in the collapse of *Vinashin*, the state-owned shipping conglomerate.

For a current example of this, witness the 2013 debates about the draft Constitution. Seeking to generate public support and solicit helpful advice, the National Assembly circulated a draft version of the Constitution for public comment. Intellectuals, bloggers, and advocates took advantage of the opening to post their own draft constitution online, which removed Article 4's stipulation of the VCP as the sole political force in the country. The intensity of emotion and the number of participants in the debate surprised the leadership, forcing leaders like Party Secretary Nguyen Phu Trong to take to the media in an attempt to tame the critics by calling their positions "political, ideological and ethical deterioration" (Brummit 2013a). Nguyen Sing Hung, chairman of the National Assembly, put it most directly, "Abusing the garnering of ideas on the revised constitution to propagandize and lobby for the people to oppose the party and the government...must be resolutely prevented" (Brummit 2013b).

The tension between the benefits of an active VNA and the risk to regime stability are felt directly by delegates, who must do their jobs professionally (speaking, researching laws, and caucusing with other delegates) while avoiding actions that might endanger regime stability. In *Sunshine*, we sought to probe this tension directly. By providing citizens information on what their delegates were doing in an easy to use and follow format, we hoped to see how delegates might toe this fine line.

At the same time, we hoped to learn something about the representativeness of delegates to their underlying constituencies. In previous work, we identified a strongly robust pattern between vote shares and delegate activity in the query session. Holding characteristics of the delegate constant, representatives who performed worse in the most recent query session tended to be more active than then delegates who had won by large margins. As Figure 5.1 shows, delegates with safe seats simply did not feel as obligated to challenge ministers. While confident of the correlation, we were always unsure of the specific mechanism driving the results. On the one hand, the relationship could be viewed as evidence for delegates competing for the votes of citizens; on the other, delegates might care more about the provincial leaders who nominate local candidates and structure the electoral districts. Thus, their query performance might be a signal to provincial elites rather than citizens. A third possibility was reverse causality – active delegates were less popular among citizens and/or provincial elites.

By randomizing whether or not citizens learned about the activity of particular delegates, we hoped to determine which of these three

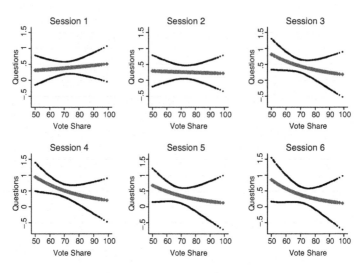

Figure 5.1 Relationship between vote share and participation

Note: This figure provides a bivariate correlation between vote share and participation in query sessions in all six sessions. The statistically significant negative relationship in the final four sessions indicates that delegates are responding either to voters or local leaders who arrange provincial electoral districts. Note that Session 6 (the time of the *Sunshine* intervention) demonstrates the same pattern as previous sessions and the relationship is not altered by proximity to the 11th Party Congress.

mechanisms was most likely doing the work. If it was the popular representation mechanism, then transparency should have led to greater delegate participation in query sessions, as delegates tried to impress voters. We did not observe such behavior.

An agenda for future work

As we discuss in the *Sunshine* article, the experiment sheds light on how transparency affects political processes in a single-party state. Legislative transparency initiatives have often been promoted by international donors as a shortcut to generate accountability of an authoritarian regime without institutional reform. While laudatory, we sought a direct test of these claims. We suspected that while transparency certainly has benefits, there are our occasions when it might not work as expected. Indeed, our research found that legislative transparency did not have the salutary effects on performance that it has in a democratic setting. While the experiment had no direct effect on participation and criticism in the VNA, it actually curtailed activity for those in provinces where there was a high degree of internet penetration. Delegates, who knew their actions in the VNA would be visible, were reluctant to make statements that they deemed might be destabilizing. In other words, delegates internalized the trade-off between information and stability that the regime faces and responded accordingly to the incentives. A few delegates miscalculated, speaking even though their statements were posted online. In these cases, the increased exposure also had an effect on re-election prospects, with delegates undergoing the treatment facing a lower probability of being re-nominated and elected to the VNA.

These findings are sobering for two groups. For advocates of an assertive "VNA," the results expose clearly the constraints that even the most active and critical VNA delegates operate within. They also present important cautionary evidence to those who would promote transparency interventions in authoritarian settings.

That said, it is important to bound our findings as well. Our conclusions do not rule out the possibility that certain types of transparency can also have benefits. We studied only one effect of transparency – the influence on delegate behavior during VNA sessions. There are other areas where transparency might be extremely beneficial. Of particular importance in the case of Vietnam has been the expansion of the number of sessions that appear on television. Televised query sessions were first introduced in 1994, and have since expanded to other debates within the VNA such as the debates over the government's implementation of the socioeconomic plans and debates on constitutional revisions. The effect of television is difficult to ascertain, given that the sessions to be televised are not randomly assigned as in *Sunshine*. Therefore, it is not easy to assess whether or not the tenor of the debates or the types of delegates that speak in these sessions differ from those sessions that are not televised. However, one possible benefit touched upon by Schuler (2013: ch. 2) is the effect of debates on public opinion. Schuler shows that speeches made on the floor of the VNA can have a direct impact on public interest in an issue. For instance, the mention of the bauxite issue on the floor of the VNA increased the number of *Google* searches for information on bauxite in Viet Nam. If the proceedings of the VNA were not made public similar to the debates within the VCP Central Committee, such discussion could not generate public debate.

What this suggests is that when assessing the impact of transparency on performance in an authoritarian legislature, it is important to consider the metric used to measure performance. As *Sunshine* shows, transparency may not improve the performance of individual delegates. In fact, in some cases it may depress their activity. On the other hand, the presence of transparency also enables activity within the VNA to reach the public. Therefore, if a delegate makes an incendiary speech, the presence of television cameras ensures that they will have an audience for their critiques.

Once again, we return to the inherent tension between the benefits and risks of policy changes that enable the VNA. In the next few pages, I look at how events that followed the publication of *Sunshine* shed additional light on this tightrope walk.

The Confidence Vote

The origins of the no confidence vote

The discussion of a "No Confidence" vote first arose during the VNA's debates over the Vinashin bankruptcy in the fall of 2010. Although Prime Minister Nguyen Tan Dung admitted partially responsibility (*VietnamNet* 2010), critics argued that ultimately the buck stopped with him, because state conglomerates officials reported to the PM's office and the PM appoints their leaders according to a 2006 decree (Decree 86/2006/ND-CP). The issue was first raised by Nguyen Minh Thuyet in a bold speech on the VNA floor, but he received support from a handful of other delegates, including Duong Truong Quoc, who would continue the calls for the PM's resignation in subsequent sessions (Hookway 2010). Importantly, although interviews suggest that the prime minister was clearly upset with Nguyen Minh Thuyet's proposal, neither he nor any of the delegates who supported him were removed. Furthermore, not only were the delegates who supported Thuyet not punished, but some of them were actually re-nominated, including Truong Quoc (Schuler 2013: ch. 5).

New momentum for a no confidence vote picked up after the 11th National Congress of the Communist Party of Vietnam, which was rife with internal debates and divisions (Clark 2011). The Congress opened with an apology for corruption and inefficiency, which spurred critics to ask for leadership changes. At the 6th Plenum of the 11th Central Committee (October 2012), internal division re-emerged during a debate about whether to discipline certain members of the Politburo for the underperformance of state corporations and elite-level corruption. Members of the Politburo engaged in self-criticism for their actions, but the Central Committee did not think leadership change was warranted at that time (An Dien 2012). Immediately after the session, critics in and outside the top echelons of the party hierarchy hoped that there would be greater opportunities to hold particular officials accountable in the VNA, which had a more diverse membership than the VCP Central Committee (Thayer 2013a). In the aftermath of the 6th Plenum, General Secretary Nguyen Phu Trong noted his support for continued self-criticism of top officials along with the resolution permitting no confidence voting in the VNA (An Dien 2012).

Critical to the main thesis of our argument is the fact that internal divisions within the elite ranks of the VCP facilitated the move to empower the VNA with this unique new authority, unprecedented in other authoritarian and single-party regimes. The VNA did not seek this power on its own accord; it was invested with it by the VCP to provide a check on elite actors in government.

The structure of the Confidence Vote

On November 21, 2012, the internal critics succeeded in passing Resolution No. *35/2012/QH13* in the VNA, which called for a no confidence vote, but was thin on details. Resolution *561/2013/UBTVQH13* (February 2012) provided the framework for how the VNA would be administered. According to the two resolutions, the VNA laid out a two-tier process: a preferential ranking of confidence ranking, followed by a no confidence vote.

During the preferential ranking stage, delegates of the VNA would be asked to fill out a form with names of the individuals, who had been elected to position subject to the approval of the VNA. This list included all members of the National Assembly Standing Committee (NASC), and VNA committee chairs, the president, prime minister, chief justice, and head of the procuracy, an official charged with the observance of the law by all government officials. On each form, delegates were asked to tick the cell for "highly confident about," "confident about," and "low confident about," depending on their evaluation of the official's performance. The slight semantic gamesmanship did not go unnoticed by observers of Vietnamese politics – the ballot expressly did not present an option to demonstrate "no confidence."

According to Article 6.4, officials receiving over two-thirds of the VNA expressing low confidence votes, or receiving over 50 percent low confidence votes for two successive years would be provided with the opportunity to resign. In case they did not, the VNA could begin procedures for an actual "No Confidence" vote, where the official simply received an up or down vote. The second stage would take place in the next VNA session following the disappointing preferential ranking. The mechanism for discharge of an official receiving low confidence votes is not direct (Article 8), but can be requested by the Standing Committee of the

VNA in accordance with the Law on Oversight of the National Assembly (2003: Article 13). Ultimately, the Standing Committee will ask the institution that nominated the official who failed the confidence vote to dismiss him or her.

Following the vote, Article 6.1 mandated that the vote totals be publically posted. While this was a tentative move to transparency, delegates were provided with a secret ballot (using paper instead of the usual electronic voting) to ensure their anonymity from citizens and elites. This partial transparency, in line with our argument in *Sunshine*, protected delegates, so that they could vote more honestly without fear of retribution or endangering regime stability. Thus, VCP leaders could receive far more accurate information on the perceptions of delegates, which we document below.

Results of the preferential confidence ranking

The preferential confidence ranking was held on June 11, 2013. On the face of it, the vote in the VNA was a failure for critics hoping that particular officials would be held accountable. Focusing on the "low confidence" vote that triggers further proceedings, not a single official received a share over the 50 percent threshold to be monitored over two years or the two-thirds criteria necessary for immediate action. All top officials kept their jobs and stability was preserved among the elite VCP leadership.

On the other hand, the vote provided an incredible amount of information to the Vietnamese leadership and outside observers about perceptions of the performance of individual officials and satisfaction with governance. For instance, it was notable that the officials most associated publically (fairly or not) with the economic importance of the country received the highest share of "low confidence" votes (State Bank Governor Nguyen Van Binh [42%], Prime Minister Nguyen Tan Dung [32%], Minister of Industry and Trade Vu Huy Hoang [25%]). As the Vietnamese economy has struggled to regain its dynamism, a share of delegates appear to be willing to identify the leaders they deem to be most responsible.

The health (29% low confidence) and education ministers (36%) rounded out the top five lowest performers. These scores also provide valuable information, because these ministries are of critical importance to Vietnamese citizens. In the annual Provincial Administration Performance Index (PAPI) survey conducted by UNDP every year, the strongest correlates of citizens' satisfaction with government (measured on a 100-point feeling thermometer) are perceptions of health and education services. This is the reason that PAPI weighs the public services index so highly (about 44% of the total index), above measures of participation, transparency, and corruption control. Further disaggregating the different public services that are measured, it is clear that education and health stand alone. Their relationship with citizens' satisfaction is twice the level of assessments of "infrastructure" and "law & order" (UNDP 2012).

Scrutiny and performance

Digging further into the vote totals, it becomes clear that level of scrutiny applied to particular officials had a large impact on their confidence ranking. On average, National Assembly Standing Committee (NASC) and committee heads performed much better than ministers. The average share of "low confidence" votes for members of the NASC was 3.4 percent, ranging from 1 percent to 12.6 percent. For members of government, the mean share of "low confidence" was 15.1 percent, ranging from 2.6 percent to 42 percent. This is a statistically significant difference. There are three possible reasons for the differences in scores. First, this may be professional, as delegates may be reluctant to vote against their bosses and colleagues. Second, it may be that delegates truly value the government NASC leadership over government for meritocratic or political reasons. But a third aspect may have to do with process and opportunity. Heads of the NASC did not have to participate in query sessions, and therefore were less subject to intense scrutiny.

To see how the level of scrutiny affects the confidence votes, I next analyze the data on ministers and whether they were subject to the query session. Ministers who never appeared before query sessions (i.e. defense, foreign affairs, justice) had the best scores. They received a "low confidence" average of 5.4 percent, compared to 19.5 percent for ministers who were queried. This difference is also statistically significant. Another way to see this is to rank order the scores with the individual receiving the lowest number of "low confidence" votes as number one. Not a single minister, who was subject to a query session, ranks in the top 25 delegates who received a confidence vote.

Moreover, there is a strong correlation between the number of times a particularly ministry (not necessarily the individual) was queried and the share of low confidence votes (bivariate correlation = .71). More precisely, Figure 5.2 shows that every time a ministry was subject to a query session between 2007 and today, they received 3.5 percent more "low confidence" votes.

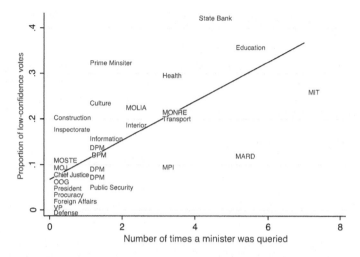

Figure 5.2   Relationship between query appearances and confidence voting

Note: This figure provides a bivariate correlation between number of total query appearances by a government official and the share of low confidence votes. The line represents the fitted values, with observed values labeled by the official's position. DPM is Deputy Prime Minister.

It is hard to prove statistically, but if you compare the no confidence vote to general impressions about how a minister performed in the query sessions (Did they give respectable answers? Were they well informed? Did they appear to understand how problems in their Ministry would be addressed? A number of follow-up questions?), ministers who performed adequately (judging by the analysis on blogs and media), received reasonable votes of confidence (Ministry of Planning and Investment = 9.2% low confidence; Ministry of Agriculture and Rural Development = 11.6% low confidence). Ministers who were thought to perform poorly received very low scores as you note. The best examples of this are health and education, where the query sessions were quite vigorous and the delegates were panned in the media for having underperformed.

Information on elite-level politics

The VNA vote also provided a great deal of information on internal rifts. Figure 5.3 creates a measure of polarization for all government offices, which is essentially a standardized difference between high and low vote totals. A high polarization means that delegates were strongly divided in their position of candidates. One figure stands out as extremely polarized, PM Nguyen Tan Dung. This was expected, given that it was the

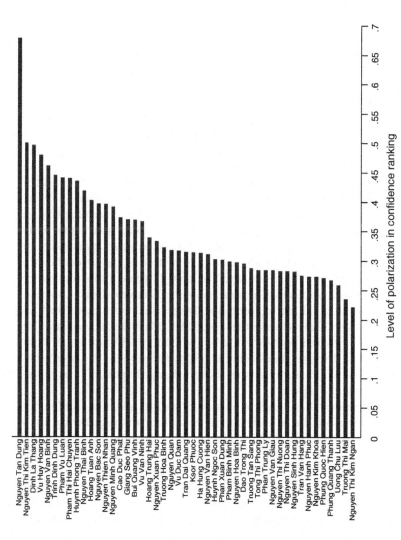

Figure 5.3 Polarization of confidence ranking of government officials

Note: Polarization is the scaled difference between the number of "high confidence" and "low confidence" votes received by a delegate. It is calculated using the formula: $polarized = \left(1 - \sqrt{(high\% - low\%)^2}\right) * (1 - medium\%)$

debate over his performance in the 6th Plenum, which stimulated the confidence proceeding in the first place (Thayer 2013). Two other officials, the ministers of transport (D. L. Thang) and health (N. T. K Tien) also stand out with close to 0.5 scores on polarization. Notably, the state bank governor (N. V. Binh), while unpopular, was not extremely polarized, as delegates converged in their negative views about his performance. Also notable were the extremely low polarization scores of other Politburo members, which congregate at the bottom of the chart.

Conclusion

Overall, the results of the confidence vote point in the same direction as conclusions in *Sunshine*. Both the query sessions and the confidence votes provide critical benefits to regime leaders. Valuable information is being revealed and delegates have an opportunity to probe issues that are of importance to Vietnamese citizens, as measured by independent public opinion surveys. And when ministers do not perform adequately, a portion of delegates are willing to use the no confidence vote to let them know. It would be even more useful if all officials were subject to the intense scrutiny of the query session. The strong variation in which ministries are subject to query sessions is very hard to explain.

How much the confidence vote really matters for promoting change in Vietnamese politics is hard to predict. I noted above that only 30 percent of delegates can be characterized as *active participants* in the query sessions. This again appears to be true in the no confidence vote. The very worst performance had only 42 percent low confidence votes. Because of this large number of fairly inactive delegates, there is very little danger that a top official will ever be removed by the institution. Schuler (2013) refers to this as the "Yes, Man" insurance plan. The Vietnamese government is best served when it gains information from a few active delegates, but stacks the body with enough "Yes, Men" that there is no risk of a surprise vote, sudden change in policy, or mobilization against the regime.

Thus, rather than playing a transformative role, the confidence vote appears to be a mechanism for information gathering in a semi-transparent setting. Top officials in Vietnam can learn about which issues are of important to Vietnamese citizens and can adjust policy and personnel to make improvements, if they choose. Similarly, individuals who received relatively low confidence votes can adjust their own performance, if they choose. The system is designed to be highly stable, providing opportunities for policy voice and information acquisition without putting top leaders or delegates at risk through full transparency.

For outsiders attempting to derive normative lessons from VNA reforms in Vietnam, the results of the confidence votes and *Sunshine* pose a conundrum. It is impossible to understand the institutional reforms in the country as simply black or white. On the one hand, it is clear that nominally democratic reforms, such as opening electoral completion and increasing the power and professionalism of VNA delegates, strengthen Vietnam's current leadership as Vasavakul explains in her chapter. Far from being a vehicle for democratic reform as hoped by the dissidents profiled by Kerkvliet in his chapter, they actually postpone it. On the other hand, these reforms have increased the responsiveness of VNA delegates to civil society (as Wells-Dang explains) and local economy (as Jandl demonstrates), enhanced the quality of policy and public services, and ultimately improved the lives and welfare of Vietnam's citizens today.

Note

1. A *Google* search of the words "assertive" and "Vietnamese National Assembly" together yields 15,100 citations including country reports, journalistic accounts, academic articles, and even the *Transparency International* webpage. Early examples include Abuza 2001: 99; Thayer 2003: 28; Dalpino and Steinberg 2005: 84; Vo X. Han 2008: 34.

6

Government Repression and Toleration of Dissidents in Contemporary Vietnam

Benedict J. Tria Kerkvliet[1]

Introduction

All governments, including democratic ones, use repression against their own citizens. What varies is the intensity, form, and scope of repression. Governments in authoritarian political systems, according to conventional thinking, are far more repressive than those in democratic systems. Among the most repressive, by many accounts, are single-party communist governments such as those that ruled in the Soviet Union and much of Eastern Europe after World War II until the early 1990s, and that still rule in China, Cuba, Laos, North Korea, and Vietnam.

Foreign critics often describe Vietnam's Communist Party-run government as a totalitarian or authoritarian system that countenances little or no criticism. "The government," says an Associated Press report in 2001 from Hanoi, "does not tolerate any challenge to its one-party rule" Freedom House's 2010 report refers to the Communist Party government "silencing critics" through numerous means (*The Nation* 2011; Freedom House 2010). The only book-length examination of how Vietnamese authorities deal with dissent concludes that the government "tolerates no dissent or opposition" (Abuza 2001: 238). Expressing similar views have been several members of the US Congress. Recent annual reports about Vietnam from Human Rights Watch and the US State Department, while avoid glossing the Vietnamese government as totally repressive, depict it as extremely intolerant of political dissent of any kind.[2]

These portrayals of Vietnam are troublesome to me as I research state–society relations in the country today. Public dissent and criticism of state officials, their actions, and policies have grown considerably in

Vietnam during the last dozen or so years (see Wells-Dang's chapter in this book). The criticisms are wide ranging – from lambasting corrupt local authorities to opposing the political system, from alleging repression against religious organizations to demanding a multiparty political system, from protesting working conditions in factories to questioning the state's foreign policies. The critics are also diverse: rural villagers, urban workers, religious leaders, intellectuals, students, environmental activists, professional association leaders, and former government and Communist Party officials. Groups advocating major changes in how Vietnam is governed have formed organizations, even political parties, and they regularly produce internet newspapers and other literature about their activities and goals. The extent, diversity, and vibrancy of public political criticism in contemporary Vietnam do not correspond to reports such as those just mentioned. Even if one focuses on the people most critical of the government – those calling for an end to a one-party political system and the rise of a multiparty system and other democratic institutions – the characterization that Vietnamese authorities tolerate no dissent or opposition is erroneous.

Better than depicting a regime as being repressive is to examine how, when, and to what extent its leaders resort to repression and study the mix between repression and other actions toward protests and other forms of public political criticism. As Jonathan London suggests in this book's opening chapter, understanding authoritarian systems requires nuanced analysis. Rarely does an authoritarian regime rely only or even primarily on repression to deal with critics and dissenters. Toleration, accommodation, dialogue, and concession also figure in the mix. Scholars studying contemporary China, whose political system is most similar to Vietnam's, have begun to do this kind of analysis, contributing a more nuanced understanding of how the Communist Party regime there deals with burgeoning Chinese unrest and dissent in recent years (Yongshun Cai 2008: 38; Xi Chen 2009; Baogang He and Thørgersen 2010; Hongyi Lai 2010; Mackinnon 2011; Ogden 2002; Tong 2002; Tsang 2009; Wright 2002). For contemporary Vietnam, only a few academic studies have been done on protests, dissent, and other forms of public criticism and how the Vietnamese Communist Party regime responds (Zinoman 1994; Thayer 2006; Angie Ngọc Tran 2007, 2008; Koh 2008b; Thayer 2009a; Thayer 2010b; Hayton 2010: 113–34; Kerkvliet 2010a, 2010b). Material in this small body of work suggests that Vietnamese authorities also mix repression with toleration, dialogue, and accommodation.

The literature on China and Vietnam suggests some patterns of how authorities react to public political criticism. Authorities are generally more tolerant of criticism about particular government policies or programs or of particular nonsenior officials than they are of criticism about top national leaders, the form of government, or the entire political system. Within this pattern, individual critics are more tolerated than are large groups that publicly rebuke a policy or program. Yet even large congregations of protesters against, say, a local official or a project that would deprive an entire village of its farmland frequently occur without hostile reactions by police or other authorities. Another pattern is that authorities are more tolerant of protests by peasants and workers than they are of demonstrations by middle class, rather well-educated urbanites even though they too are criticizing specific policies, programs, or practices. For example, in recent years throngs of Vietnamese farmers regularly travel to Hanoi and Ho Chi Minh City to demonstrate in front of government offices against corruption, environmental degradation, land confiscations, and other issues adversely affecting their rural communities. Usually such protests occur with little or no intervention by police or security forces. Demonstrations in those cities that police and security forces have tended to suppress quickly are the ones staged by writers, scholars, musicians, office workers, small business owners, and the like who oppose China's encroachment into Vietnamese territory and the Vietnamese government's seemingly tepid responses.

What about authorities' actions toward individuals and groups that publically criticize the form of government and openly favor major reforms of the political system? For this question too little research has been done on China or Vietnam to identify several patterns. The only clear generalization emerging from the scholarly literature is that authorities in neither country are uniformly repressive even against these regime dissidents. Some of these dissidents suffer little or no adversity; others go for years without much government interference but then suddenly are arrested and imprisoned. Still others get arrested immediately. The authorities' actions toward regime dissidents seem to vary considerably.

The purpose of this chapter is to analyze Vietnamese authorities' actions toward regime dissidents and try to find some patterns and explanations for the variety of those actions. Such an examination has not been done previously for contemporary Vietnam nor, as best as I can tell, for post-Mao China. The chapter first synthesizes Vietnamese dissidents' main criticisms and objectives and then analyzes state authorities' actions toward them. The analysis reveals a degree of toleration by authorities and a lack of uniformity in their repression.

Regime dissidents, their aims, and approaches

Regime dissidents

Regime dissidents in my definition are citizens in Vietnam who publicly criticize and often oppose their country's system of government, the Communist Party's domination of the state, and that party's efforts to control society. Because they seek fundamental political changes, not just changes in particular policies or projects, their criticisms are among the most sweeping in the broad range of public criticism heard and seen in Vietnam today. Consequently, regime dissidents are presumably the most troublesome and threatening critics in the eyes of Vietnamese authorities.

Among the regime dissidents are a few peasants and workers, but mostly they are writers, scholars, lawyers, priests, monks, and former government officials. They express their dissent primarily through their writings, although several, especially since about 2006, have formed or joined organizations aimed at channeling criticism and changing the political system. The number of regime dissidents is unclear. One indicator might be that about 2,000 people in Vietnam signed a "Declaration on Freedom and Democracy for Vietnam," which began to circulate in April 2006.[3] A better indicator might be the number of people who, through their writings, their prominence in organizations that defy authorities, and/or their pronouncements, publicly rebuke the regime or its primary institutions and advocate reforms that would remake the political system. That figure would be in the hundreds.

Most of this chapter's material concerns 62 individuals who have publicly criticized Vietnam's political system during the last ten to fifteen years and for whom I have been able to find, as of May 2011, rather complete and, as best as I can determine, reliable information regarding their residence, occupation, political activities, and other factors, especially whether or not authorities have detained them, arrested them, brought them to trial, and/or sentenced them to prison. The information comes from material on the internet and in publications that dissidents themselves, their sympathizers, interviewers, and other people, including Vietnamese authorities, have provided. There being no way yet to determine how representative these 62 people are, my analysis applies to them, not necessarily to the whole "universe" of which they are a part.

The ages of the 62 people as of 2011 range from early thirties to late eighties; their average age is about 55. Three elderly ones passed away in the early 2000s. Roughly half of these dissidents were born after 1955; a quarter were born prior to 1941. A large proportion of those born prior to 1956 had careers in the government, military, and/or Communist Party, whereas only two of those born after 1955 had worked for the government. Occupations of those born after 1955 are scattered among several categories – telecommunications, journalism and writing, teaching, manual labor, and engineering; the two most numerous are business people and lawyers (eight each). All but nine of these 62 regime dissidents are men. The homes for about one-third of these dissidents are in Hà Nội, another third in Hồ Chí Minh City, and one-third are from other parts of the country, such as Hải Phòng and Thái Bình in the north, Huế in the center, and Đà Lạt and Đồng Nai in the south.

What all these individuals have in common are writings, extended interviews, and/or leadership positions in unauthorized organizations and publications that are highly critical of the regime.[4] Sometimes these public critics refer to themselves as *người phản kháng* [resister], *nhà hoạt động dân chủ nhân quyền* [democracy and human rights activist], and *nhà đấu tranh dân chủ* [one who struggles for democracy]. Their most frequent terms, however, are *nhà bất đồng chính kiến* and *người bất đồng chính kiến*, which literally mean a person with different political views but can be more loosely translated as political dissident or political dissenter. I often refer to them as "regime dissidents" so as to indicate more precisely the political content of their criticisms.

Criticisms and objectives

Regime dissidents criticize many aspects of Vietnam's existing governmental system and discuss numerous aspects of a different one to replace it. In this array of commentary, three themes stand out: corruption, democracy, and national pride.

For many dissidents, the extent and scale of corruption in Vietnam is what ignited their disgust with the political system. One of the earliest groups to openly criticize the government was the Association of Vietnamese People Against Corruption [Hội Nhân Dân Việt Nam Chống Tham Nhũng], formed in September 2001 by Phạm Quế Dương, Trần Khuê, Nguyễn Thị Thanh Xuân, Nguyễn Vũ Bình, and Lê Chí Quang, people from Hà Nội and Hồ Chí Minh City. Soon a dozen or so others joined them. Some members were retired military officers and former Communist Party members. Their stated main objective was not to oppose the party; instead, they wanted to help it root out corruption. Indeed, when they announced the association's formation, they wanted officials to recognize it.[5] National authorities, however, spurned the group and soon harassed and eventually arrested and imprisoned some of its members for "misusing democratic freedom."[6]

The corruption that angers dissidents is not the petty favors and bribes that local police and government officials solicit. What upsets them is the corruption they say is pervasive at higher levels. One writer in Hồ Chí Minh City likened the Communist Party to a "gluttonous monster" [*quái vật*], sucking the life out of the people and the country (Nguyễn Hải Sơn 2004: 22). Corrupt officials, critics claim, include thousands of high-ranking authorities who get millions, even billions, of US dollars (Trần Độ 2004, no. 31: 2; Phạm Quế Dương 2007).[7] According to a brief account based on information in 2005 from an un-named high-ranking official in the Ministry of Security [Bộ Công An], senior leaders who are inordinately wealthy thanks to kickbacks, embezzlement, and other corruption include former secretary generals of the Communist Party Đỗ Mười ($2 billion) and Lê Khả Phiêu ($500 million); the then secretary general of the party Nông Đức Mạnh ($1.3 billion); former national president Lê Đức Anh ($2 billion); the then president Trần Đức Lương ($2 billion); the then prime minister Phan Văn Khải ($2 billion plus); and the then National Assembly president Nguyễn Văn An ($1 billion plus) (*Điện Thư* 2005: 1).

Often, contend regime dissidents, relatives of top officials reap inordinate benefits through their connections to and protection from senior authorities. For instance, Secretary General Nông Đức Mạnh, claim some dissidents, has pulled strings to get his son higher positions in the government and party (Đỗ Mậu 2006: 22).[8] A son-in-law of former Secretary General Đỗ Mười is said to be a billionaire largely because of his father-in-law's name and connections (Lê Chí Quang 2004: 3; Hai Cù Lần 2005: 10–11).[9] A son of former Prime Minister Phan Văn Khải is rumored to have made millions from kickbacks and other illicit activities in the construction industry (Lê Chí Quang 2004: 4; Hai Cù Lần 2005: 9–10). A son and a son-in-law of former national president Trần Đức Lương, critics claim, have also become wealthy through business deals facilitated by their connections (Nguyễn Thiện Tâm 2005: 32).[10] A son of Nguyễn Chí Thanh, one of Vietnam's famous generals, reportedly has ridden extensively on his family's connections to rise up party and government hierarchies, obtain several houses, and become extremely wealthy through illegal deals.[11]

I am not concerned here with exploring the veracity of these and other claims about high-level corruption. The point is that many regime dissidents believe them to be true. Moreover, they think corruption is so entrenched that it can only be rooted out through fundamental changes in the political system. This and their naming senior national officials whom they think are corrupt distinguishes their condemnations from those in Vietnamese daily newspapers, arguments by people advocating modest reforms, and speeches by state authorities. Those accounts rarely implicate top officials, and they imply or argue that corruption can be dealt with by measures within the existing system. Most regime dissidents, by contrast, insist that the system itself must change.

Indicative of their thinking are the words scrawled on a banner hung from a large bridge in Hanoi in October 2008. After listing "corruption that sucks blood from the people" and two other huge problems in the county, the banner called on the Communist Party to immediately "democratize the nation" and bring about "pluralism and multipartyism."[12] The line of argument by many regime critics is that corruption flourishes because power is concentrated in one political party, a situation that precludes democracy. The root cause of corruption, argue Nguyễn Xuân Nghĩa and many other regime dissidents, is "dictatorship" [*chế độ độc tài*] and the "mother" [*mẹ*] of that system, as one critic put it, is the Communist Party's domination of the country.[13] To fight corruption, critics often argue, the Communist Party's power must be reduced so that other actors can play significant roles in the political system. For instance, to root out corruption, Vietnam needs an independent judicial system, an independent press, and opposition political parties (Tống Văn Công 2009).[14]

The absence of democracy is a second prominent theme in regime dissidents' statements and activities. Democracy, to most dissidents, requires the protection and fostering of basic human rights and pluralist political institutions. Initially, these critics often note, the independent republic that the Vietnamese people established in 1945 advocated and promised democracy.[15] Rather quickly, however, the freedoms and institutions essential for democracy were sidelined then squashed. The primary culprit, many dissidents contend, is the Communist Party, which usurped power and changed the Constitution to make itself the country's supreme leader.

Dissidents often cite the United Nation's Universal Declaration of Human Rights as the standard which Vietnam should follow. Among those rights, critics typically stress freedom of press, of speech, of association, of religion, and of trade union formation.[16] (Rarely do they mention what might be called the "economic rights" listed in that Declaration – rights to social security, adequate standard of living, and education, for example.) The essential democratic political institutions that dissidents frequently demand are rule by law; separation of executive, legislative, and judicial functions of government; fair and impartial trials; and regular elections with candidates from various political parties.[17] The last of these is what many regime critics stress most, frequently sounding as though a multiparty system would be a panacea for Vietnam.[18]

A third prominent theme in regime dissidents' writings and other activities is "national pride," a term I use to include three, often entwined, issues – Vietnam's low level of development, its poor standing compared to other Asian countries, and its relations with China.

To regime dissidents, development includes economic conditions, but it is much more than that. Besides a strong economy, a developed country has a high-quality educational system, opportunities for people to use their ingenuity to better themselves and their community, a robust civil society, and a democratic political system (Phạm Hồng Sơn and Thu Lê 2002; Trần Độ 2004, no. 29: 3; Trần Độ 2004, no. 31: 5–6; Nguyễn Khắc Toàn 2006).[19] To dissidents, Vietnam falls far short of these standards. Despite rapid economic growth since the mid-1990s, many argue, Vietnam remains poor with a large percentage of citizens living essentially hand to mouth. Several dissidents are appalled at the widening gap between the "haves" and "have nots." Many blame this on Vietnam's wholesale move into a capitalistic economy in which foreign investors are welcomed to establish factories that pay miserable wages to teems of people desperate for work (Vi Đức Hồi 2008).[20] Others say the opposite: Vietnamese authorities have not embraced capitalism fully enough and should rid the country of all state enterprises and other vestiges of a socialist economy (Lê Hồng Hà 2004: section 2; Radio Free Asia 2007b).[21] Dissidents also often bemoan the low quality of education and backward pedagogy in Vietnam's schools and universities (Trần Khải Thanh Thủy 2006).[22] Authoritarian conditions in the country stifle educational reform as well as innovation and independent thinking. The same authoritarian conditions impede civil society ("Tiến sĩ Phan Đình Diệu" 2005; Đỗ Nam Hải 2008).[23] All these shortcomings, dissidents often argue, are contrary to what Vietnam could be and are an affront to Vietnam's majestic history.

Adding to this affront for dissidents is that Vietnam lags far behind most Asian neighbors. Look, they frequently say, at the enormous economic improvement during the last 50 or 60 years in South Korea, Japan, Singapore, Malaysia, Thailand, and Indonesia. Even in terms of democracy, several dissidents argue, these countries are now further developed than Vietnam: they have multiparty political systems, vibrant civil societies, and considerable freedom of press. That Vietnam had a long war is not a sufficient explanation for its laggard position; South Korea and Japan, too, critics stress, had major wars; yet, they have prospered economically and have democratically elected governments.

Vietnam's unfavorable comparison to numerous Asian countries, dissidents declare, insults the Vietnamese nation and people (Hoàng Tiến 2005: 8; Nguyễn Khắc Toàn 2007; Phạm Quế Dương 2007; Bạch Ngọc Dương 2007; Trần Lâm 2009b).[24]

Vietnam's relationship with China in recent years is a huge aggravation to numerous regime dissidents, who take pride in their nation's long history of defending the country against Chinese encroachment and meddling. China, many contend, is Vietnam's gravest external threat. Yet, instead of standing up to China and protecting the nation and its people's interests, Vietnamese authorities have made concessions to China's claims to Spratly and Parcels islands in the South China Sea, ceded territory along the China–Vietnam border, opened roadways to accommodate Chinese traders and companies, and let a countless number of Chinese people live and work in Vietnam, many of whom do not even have visas. To some dissidents the gravest concession is allowing Chinese to exploit natural resources, especially bauxite, in the Central Highlands. This, numerous critics contend, will irreparably damage Vietnam's economy and environment and greatly compromise Vietnam's national security (Nguyễn Chính Kết 2009; Trần Khuê 2001; Nguyễn Thanh Giang 2004: 3–6; Trần Lâm 2009b; Phạm Đình Trọng 2009: 6–7).[25]

Two things, according to some regime dissidents, explain Vietnamese officials' apparent timidness toward China. One is that the Communist Party leaders are bending over backwards to keep China as Vietnam's closest ally. The regime desperately needs China's support because it can turn to no other power to stand with Vietnam against China and because Vietnamese authorities cannot even rely on the support of the Vietnamese people. A second explanation is that by collaborating with China, many Vietnamese authorities become extraordinarily rich.[26]

Forms of struggle

All the regime dissidents for whom I have credible information advocate peaceful, nonviolent political change ("Tuyên Ngôn Tự do Dân chủ cho Việt Nam" 2006; Nguyễn Chính Kết 2006a: 24–5; Phạm Quế Dương 2007: 15; Phạm Hồng Sơn 2009b: 5). Most also favor being open, not secretive, about their criticisms of the existing system and their desires to revamp it.[27] Nonviolent change, dissidents suggest, can come in a couple of ways: state authorities' leaders may see the handwriting on the wall of their inevitable demise and simply concede, or a peaceful mass uprising will cause the regime to collapse.[28] For examples of both, dissidents point to political transformation processes in Eastern Europe and the former Soviet Union during the late 1980s and Indonesia during the late 1990s.

Debated among regime dissidents is how to bring about such scenarios. All advocate struggle [*đấu tranh*] but they emphasize two different forms. One form stresses participation and engagement with authorities and state institutions. Such participatory struggle, say dissidents with this orientation, has already figured prominently in Vietnam's mutation and conversion toward a more open society since the mid-1980s and gradually will bring about full democracy. The other form advocates direct confrontation and opposition to the regime's authorities and institutions. Dissidents with this orientation attribute little importance to alterations in recent years and instead see the regime as stubbornly opposed to significant change and highly prone to repression. Hence, the only way for Vietnam's political system to improve is to replace the Communist Party regime with democracy.

The basic course of participatory struggle is to engage particular state officials, actions, policies, and institutions on matters that directly affect people's lives. Where people – be they workers, peasants, students, intellectuals, entrepreneurs, businessmen/women, or anyone else – see that authorities and policies make life better for them and their communities, they should show support. But where people deem authorities' actions, programs, and policies are wrong or need modification, they should struggle to stop or correct them. Such efforts, say these dissidents, further Vietnam's economic and social development. Even though they are not directly attacking or confronting the political system, they gradually and cumulatively contribute to political change and democracy. Indeed, it is better "not to politicize struggles about people's livelihood and welfare" [*không nên chính trị hóa các đấu tranh dân sinh*]; otherwise, authorities are apt to be repressive rather than responsive (Hà Sĩ Phu 2007a; Lữ Phương 2007). The struggle, to paraphrase one critic, is not about overthrowing or bringing down the government. It is about stopping policies that hurt people and the nation.[29]

Evidence shows, these critics say, that struggles for better living conditions and other specific issues influence the Communist Party government and help the country to develop. They point to the remarkable rise of family farming, which the Communist Party ultimately had to endorse on account of persistent opposition among rural people to collective farming. Other evidence is the demise of centrally planned economy and the revival of private enterprise and a market economy. These were major concessions that authorities had to make during the 1980s–90s in the face of people's poverty and seething discontent. These and other changes also mean "communism" and "socialism" no longer have much importance or meaning among most Vietnamese, another reality to which the Communist Party has had to adjust. Thus, on the economic and ideological fronts, people's struggles for better living conditions have defeated some objectives of the Communist Party government (Lê Hồng Hà 2007b; Trần Lâm 2009a: 6–7).[30]

Associated with participatory struggle are some specific stances, although not all dissidents in this school endorse every one. A widely shared stance is to recognize the achievements of the Communist Party regime. These include the party's leadership in overthrowing colonial rule and reuniting the nation and the party and government leaders' ability to bend to pressures from the people. Regime dissidents favoring participatory struggle are wary of overseas individuals and organizations who want to play significant roles in Vietnam's democratization movement (Hà Sĩ Phu 2007b; Trần Bảo Lộc 2007).[31] Among their reasons is that such people include Vietnamese refugees who may be trying to restore the Saigon regime or something similar. Also foreigners, they contend, inadequately understand the dynamics and conditions in today's Vietnam.

Dissidents with a participatory struggle orientation also tend to be dubious about trying to organize big demonstrations or even petition campaigns demanding democratic institutions (Lê Hồng Hà 2006). Instead, they favor dialogue and interaction with government and Communist Party authorities at all levels (Trần Bảo Lộc 2007; Hà Sĩ Phu 2008). That can include working within existing institutions, such as helping democratic leaning journalists and lawyers to do their jobs well, which in turn will strengthen and expand civil society (Hà Sĩ Phu 2009b). It can include changing how National Assembly [Quốc Hội] delegates are elected. Right now, 90 percent or more of the Assembly's delegates are Communist Party members. Through persuasive argumentation, that situation could change to allow a wide range of people to be candidates for seats in that legislative body (Lê Hồng Hà 2007a). The Communist Party itself might be reformed such that its internal procedures become more democratic and that it recognizes the value of a free press and a multiparty political system (Phan Đình Diệu 2004: 22; Trần Lâm 2006). If the Communist Party proves incapable of reforming itself, some dissidents think, participatory struggle can, over time, contribute to the regime's self-destruction [*tự vỡ*] under the weight of vast corruption, major conflicts and debates within the party, and widespread animosity (Lê Hồng Hà 2007b; Hà Sĩ Phu 2007a).

Regime dissidents favoring confrontational struggle stress direct opposition to the Communist Party and its government. They say little about changes that have occurred from the bottom-up. Even if authorities in the past have made adjustments in the face of indirect and widespread pressures, these dissidents see no evidence that such engagement can force the Communist Party regime to change fundamentally the political system. That change, democracy in particular, is what Vietnam needs now, not years from now. Violent revolution is not a viable way to bring that about; the only way is through straightforward and open advocacy for a multiparty, pluralistic political system that protects free speech and other human rights. The present system, in the words of the "Declaration on Freedom and Democracy," should be "completely replaced" [*phải bị thay thế triệt để*]; it is "incapable of being renovated or modified" [*không phải được đổi mới hay điều chỉnh*].[32]

That declaration is a prominent example of direct confrontation. It openly demanded democracy, freedom of press and association, and an end to Communist Party rule. Other actions advocated by dissidents taking this confrontational approach include boycotting elections for the National Assembly unless opposition parties are allowed to run candidates, demanding an internationally supervised national referendum on whether the present government should continue or not, and encouraging nation-wide mass demonstrations against the regime.[33] The type of confrontation about which there is the most agreement is establishing organizations that publicly oppose the Communist Party government and insist on democracy. Besides confronting the regime, say these dissidents, such organizations will give the democratization movement continuity and sustainability even though the regime suppresses, arrests, and imprisons individual activists.

During recent years, several opposition organizations have emerged. One is Khối 8406 [Bloc 8406], which the declaration spawned and takes part of its name from the date on which that statement was issued. The organization claims to represent those who signed the declaration. Regime dissidents have also formed political parties that champion democracy and human rights. They have such names as Đảng Dân Chủ Nhân Dân [People's Democratic Party, secretly formed in mid-2003; publicly announced in June 2005], Đảng Dân Chủ [Democratic Party, formed in June 2006; its full name is Đảng Dân Chủ thế kỷ XXI, the Twenty-first century Democratic Party], and Đảng Thăng Tiến Việt Nam [Vietnam Progressive Party, launched in September 2006]. They have not registered with proper government agencies – although some have tried – and hence have no legal standing.

Whether to have many organizations or to consolidate them into one or two is a question these dissidents are discussing.[34] Another issue is the role of Vietnamese living abroad and of other foreigners. To some dissidents with a confrontational orientation, overseas supporters are

vital. One dissident even says that leaders of the democratization movement should be outside Vietnam until it becomes strong inside the
country (Phạm Quế Dương 2007).[35] Others say that material and moral
support from abroad is helpful but the movement must rely on domestic
resources and leadership.

Underlying the two forms of struggle are divergent arguments about the
relationship between development and democracy. Dissidents favoring
participatory struggle tend to emphasize development, especially improved
living conditions, welfare, and happiness for citizens across the country.
Implicitly (explicitly for some) democracy is an aspect of development.
The two are linked, but development is, as Lê Hồng Hà says, overarching
and comprehensive – democratization is an important aspect of development, not independent from it. Hence, fighting for democracy by itself
does not make sense. The struggle is for the development and democratization of Vietnam [*đấu tranh vì sự phát triển và dân chủ hóa đất nước
Việt Nam*] (Lê Hồng Hà 2007b: par. "Với vấn đề thứ nhất … "). Thinking
along similar lines, Lũ Phương says democratization in Vietnam need not
start with a multiparty political system. Indeed, he says, a multiple party
system is likely to come in the late stages of the whole democratization
process (Lũ Phương 2007: par. "Dân chủ hóa … ").

For those favoring confrontational struggle, however, democratization
is primary. Development cannot happen until Vietnam has democratic
institutions, especially multiple political parties competing for government positions in free elections. Without such institutions, they argue,
corruption will continue, creative thinking and innovation will remain
stifled, and human rights will be suppressed.[36] Without such political
institutions, Vietnam cannot catch up with other Asian countries.[37]

Authorities' views and actions

In the second half of the 1950s, faced with public criticism involving
some of the issues posed by dissidents today, the then newly established Communist Party government in northern Vietnam initially
reacted with a "vacillating admixture of official repression and tolerance" (Zinoman 2011: 77).[38] But by late 1959–early 1960, authorities
decisively suppressed their critics.

Authorities in contemporary Vietnam have been unable, or maybe
unwilling, to suppress regime dissidents so resolutely. Similar to how
authorities initially reacted some 50 years ago, authorities today respond
with a mixture of tolerance and repression. A striking difference now,
however, is that this mixed approach has persisted not just for three

or four years but for well over a decade. During that time, since the mid-1990s, the critics include not just people opposed to particular policies and programs but critics of the regime. These regime dissidents seek significantly more than the moderate reforms in the Communist Party system that critics in the 1950s advocated. The number of dissidents today has also grown and their activities have become more diversified than those of critics years ago.

Consequently, authorities today face a greater challenge from public political criticism and dissent than they did 60 years ago. Tuong Vu's chapter in this volume shows that Vietnam's Communist Party has had to deal with many challenges since it began to govern in the mid-1940s. Whether its leaders today can adapt to this new challenge while preserving the political system is unpredictable. What we can do is examine authorities' actions now.

Perceptions

At one level, state authorities and regime dissidents today have a lot in common. Development, democracy, and nationalism – themes championed by the dissidents – are also ideals that the Communist Party and its government celebrate and subscribe to. The words "Independence – Freedom – Happiness" [*Độc lập – Tự do – Hạnh phúc*] form the header on official documents. Vietnam's Constitution provides for freedom of press, speech, association, religion, and numerous other human rights ("Constitution of the Socialist Republic of Vietnam" 1992/2001).[39] Government leaders regularly talk about democracy and how it should be strengthened in Vietnam. Authorities also frequently condemn corruption and wage campaigns against it that often result in arrests and imprisonment of offenders, usually sub-national officials but occasionally national ones.

Major differences between dissidents and national authorities are the meanings of democracy, development, and freedom and how to counter corruption. So large are these differences that party and government authorities frequently regard dissidents as significant threats to the party, the government, and the stability of Vietnamese society. Such threats, according to authorities, are violations of the Constitution and numerous laws. Among the dissidents' objectives that officials commonly see as especially dangerous are a multiparty political system, which is at odds with the Constitution and laws stipulating that the Communist Party is the "leading force of society and the state" [*lực lượng lãnh đạo Nhà nước và xã hội*], and independent organizations and media outlets, which contravene the state's claimed authority over all such entities.

Engagement

How to deal with dissidents has been a major issue in long-running debates among Communist Party and government authorities over "the scope and pace of political reform" (Thayer 2010b: 201). Although few details of the debates are public, some authorities have urged engagement and dialogue, a position somewhat symbiotic with those dissidents who advocate participatory struggle.

Võ Văn Kiệt, Vietnam's prime minister from 1991 to 1997 and a senior advisor to the government for years afterward, favored "expanding dialogue" [*mở rộng đối thoại*] between authorities and activists in the "democracy movement" [*phong trào dân chủ*]. Authorities, he elaborated in an interview, should foster an open exchange of views with people in the movement. That, he added, is a better approach than being heavy handed. Moreover, he said, officials should treat people in the movement with civility rather than imposing degrading labels on them. He also supported revamping National Assembly elections so as to significantly increase the number of delegates who are not members of the Communist Party (BBC 2007). Although Võ Văn Kiệt died in 2008, I suspect other prominent officials express similar views during their closed deliberations about responses to regime dissidents.

Another indication of some willingness among officials to dialogue with regime dissidents is a lengthy conversation in 2008 between a colonel in the security police [*công an*] and Nguyễn Khắc Toàn, a dissident whose activism had earlier landed him in prison for four years (2002–06). The colonel, who had often questioned Nguyễn Khắc Toàn in police headquarters about the latter's whereabouts and activities, invited him for tea at a shop near Toàn's home in Hà Nội. For hours the two men had a rather frank exchange of views about Vietnam's political system, corruption, laws, legal system, and other topics. Whether either man's positions changed as a result is unknown. Nguyễn Khắc Toàn noticed, however, that the colonel referred to him and others like him as *nhà hoạt động chính trị* [political activists], which Nguyễn Khắc Toàn regarded as more respectful than the terms often used in official news sources: *kẻ cơ hội chính trị* [political opportunists], *kẻ bất mãn chế độ* [regime malcontents], and *đối tượng vi phạm luật pháp hình sự* [transgressors of criminal law; criminals] (Nguyễn Khắc Toàn 2008).[40]

Intimidation

State authorities in the various agencies discussed in Carlyle A. Thayer's chapter of this volume use numerous methods and instruments to intimidate and repress regime dissidents. Detention, arrest, and imprisonment are the most severe, but, as Thayer's chapter shows, there are many other less onerous measures.

One is to publicly critique, denounce, and, in the eyes of many dissidents and observers, slander those who dissent. Previously, officials and the authorized mass media rarely commented in public about individual dissidents. In recent years, however, newspapers and television stations, all under the purview of government and Communist Party authorities, have produced numerous accounts alleging nefarious activities of individual dissidents. One frequent allegation is that the named individuals are in league with outsiders, often overseas Vietnamese, who viscerally oppose the Communist Party's government. Another theme is that dissidents, by verbally berating the government and Communist Party, are unpatriotic and dismissive of the huge sacrifices their forebears made in order to overthrow colonial rule, defeat aggressors, and secure the nation's independence.[41] A third theme is that dissidents use their activist persona to make a living from the contributions they receive from relatives, friends, and supporters, especially those living abroad.[42] Accounts also allege that particular dissidents have illicit sexual affairs and relationships, swindle fellow citizens of money and property, misrepresent themselves, and malign authorities.

Authorities also harass regime dissidents and their families. Authorities tap and cut phone lines to dissidents' residences, block or disrupt their mobile phone numbers, hack into their email correspondence, track their internet usage, and confiscate files, books, letters, and computers from their homes. Over 30 percent of the 62 dissidents under study have endured these adversities.[43] Authorities often interfere with and sometimes manage to shut down dissident organizations and newspapers' websites and other internet locations that regularly post dissidents' writings and interviews. Security police typically shadow dissidents wherever they go, keeping a record of whom they meet, when, where, and sometimes what was said. Dissidents who have served prison sentences often remain on parole and are closely monitored for years afterward. Spies among dissident groups are also a distinct possibility, say some activists (Nguyễn Vũ Bình 2008). Some dissidents also report that speeding motorcycles and cars try to hit them or family members ("Nhóm phóng viên Phong trào tranh đấu vì Dân chủ, Hà Nội" 2008).

An example of someone who has endured harassment is Lê Trần Luật, a lawyer who has represented several regime dissidents and who himself condemns the regime for systematically violating human rights. In early 2009, he said, officials prevented him from meeting his clients. Harassment then intensified. For instance, police raided his office and seized his computers, files, and other possessions. Ultimately, a provincial association for lawyers expelled him on the grounds that he had violated an article in the profession's code against using legal skills to endanger national security. The expulsion effectively prevents him from practicing his profession.[44] Intense intimidation to the point of people losing their livelihoods has also happened to several other dissidents.

Sometimes harassment turns violent. Numerous signers of the "Declaration on Freedom and Democracy" reported being beaten up by men thought to be plain-clothed police or tough guys hired by local authorities (Vũ Hoàng Hải 2006; Radio Free Asia 2006a, 2006b). Security police and their hired men have waylaid and mugged dissidents while traveling. One such victim was 35-year-old Nguyễn Phương Anh. His parents – a retired university teacher and retired government employee – complained to authorities in detail about the beating he suffered along a provincial highway.[45] Sometimes dissidents are attacked near their homes, which Trần Khải Thanh Thủy says happened to her and her husband in October 2009, after which the security police made the event look like she and her husband had attacked them (Đỗ Bá Tân 2009). Dương Thị Xuân claims, with photos as supporting evidence, that security police in late 2008 destroyed her entire house and the makeshift quarters her family erected afterward. Authorities say that the structures are illegal because the area, on the outskirts of Hà Nội, is zoned for agriculture. Neighbors report, however, that no other homes in the vicinity were touched ("Công An CS Hà Nội tiếp tục đàn áp dã man, khốc liệt gia đình nữ nhà báo tranh đấu Dương Thị Xuân" 2009; Vietnam Sydney Radio 2009). Apparently Dương Thị Xuân's family home was targeted because she is the secretary for the unauthorized publication *Tập San Tự Do Dân Chủ* [Freedom and Democracy Magazine]. She is also a cousin of another regime dissident, Nguyễn Khắc Toàn.

Confinement

The most severe forms of repression are various types of confinement: detention and interrogation, arrest, and imprisonment. Curiously, confinement does not happen to all dissidents, and the extent of their confinements varies. The other remarkable thing is that confinement rarely stops people from continuing their dissent. Using these two variables – extent of confinement and persistence of dissent – I see six clusters in the 62 regime dissidents under study (see Tables 6.1 and 6.2).[46]

Table 6.2 Summary table of 62 regime dissidents in Vietnam*

Cluster	Freq	Birth year (%)			Avg age (yrs)	Residence (%)			DRV (%)**	CP memb (%)	Mil vet (%)**	Public Dissent Activities (%)***			
		>1941	1941–55	>55		HN	HCMC	Other				Solitary	Poli party	Newspaper, etc	Advocacy organ.
	62	26	16	58	55.2	34	31	35	39	51	53	24	19	29	39
1	4	100			81.5	50	25	25	100	100	100	50	9	50	
2	11	36	9	55	56.5	36	27	36	50	57	71	27	19	36	27
3	21	33	10	57	55.9	52	33	14	40	50	60	29	33	29	33
4	6	17	50	33	61.8	33	17	50	33	33	40		18	50	83
5	17		24	76	47.5	12	41	47	21	36	43		18	18	47
6	3			100	41.7			100	0	0	0	29	67		33

Notes:

Cluster code:

1. No detention or arrest despite frequent public political dissent.
2. Arrest and/or detention, often frequently, but no conviction and imprisonment even though public political dissent continues.
3. Convicted and imprisoned once but not imprisoned again even though public political dissent continues.
4. Convicted, imprisoned, released; resumed public political dissent; convicted and imprisoned again. (Three of the six are currently in prison. Of the other three, one died in 2008, one is very ill, and one has resumed public political dissent.)
5. Currently in prison after being convicted for the first time.
6. Stopped public political dissent after being detained, tried, and convicted.

Notations:

* Details are reported in Table 6.1 Sixty-two regime dissidents in Vietnam clustered according to their confinement by authorities and persistence of their dissent (as of May 2011) [http://ips.cap.anu.edu.au/sites/default/files/IPS/PSC/Table_1_for_Government_Repression_and_Toleration_of_Dissidents_in_Contemporary_Vietnam.pdf].
** Percentage of people for whom the information is available.
*** Some rows for Activities total more than 100 percent because a few regime dissidents are involved in more than one type.

HN = Hà Nội; HCMC = Hồ Chí Minh City; Othere = elsewhere in Vietnam
DRV = active supporter of or participant in the Democratic Republic of Vietnam government (1945–75)
CP memb = Communist Party member
Mil vet = military veteran
Solitary = not publicly a member of a dissident political party (Poli party), publication (Newspaper, etc), or formal organization (Advoc organ.)

In the first cluster are four dissidents who, as best as I can determine, suffered no confinement – police have neither detained nor arrested nor imprisoned them. The four are Đặng Văn Việt, Lữ Phương, Trần Đại Sơn, and Trần Lâm. Partial explanations for this exceptional treatment may be that all were advanced in age when they began to openly criticize the regime, had served in the government and or military during Vietnam's wars against France and the United States, and had been Communist Party members.

Trần Đại Sơn (1931?–2006), a Communist Party member for over 50 years and an army veteran of several wars, began in 2003 to publicly chastise the security police and other government institutions.[47] Đặng Văn Việt (1920–), an army veteran who later was a high-ranking official in a government bureau for irrigation, signed the "Declaration on Freedom and Democracy" and was a founding editorial board member of the internet-based dissident newspaper *Tổ Quốc* [Homeland] in 2006.[48] Trần Lâm (1924–) had a long career in the Vietnamese government, including being a member of Vietnam's supreme court [Tòa Án Nhân Dân Tối Cao]. Since about 2005, he has sharply criticized authorities and has been the trial lawyer for several dissidents; he was also on *Tổ Quốc*'s editorial board when it started and remains an advisor to the publication.[49] Lữ Phương (1938–) served in the underground movement fighting the government in southern Vietnam and the United States. He has publicly criticized the current regime since the early 1990s.

The most common confinement is detainment and interrogation at police stations. Euphemistically described by authorities as requiring a person to "work" [*làm việc*] with the police, the sessions can last for hours and sometimes days. Police may allow the person being questioned to go home between sessions but occasionally they hold the individual for several days. According to dissidents' accounts, the police want details about their political views, involvement in unauthorized organizations and newspapers, and relations with other critics. Besides getting information, police also use the interrogations to frighten dissidents and threaten harsher measures if they continue to criticize the government and Communist Party.[50] Sometimes the police become physical, slapping, punching, and beating the people being questioned.[51]

Among the 58 dissidents who have been detained and/or arrested, often several times, eleven have always been released without being tried and imprisoned, and all eleven resumed their public political criticisms. They compose Cluster 2 of the dissidents under study.

One person in this cluster is Trần Độ (1923–2002), whom most public dissidents today greatly admire. He was a general in Vietnam's military and held several prominent positions in the government before his retirement. But starting in the late 1990s, he openly criticize the party and the political system he had served for decades.[52] He was detained once, in mid-2001. Perhaps his advanced age and long-term service to the regime protected him against harsher treatment.

In four cases it is easy to explain why, despite continuing to be outspoken, the dissidents were not arrested and imprisoned: they fled the country. Bạch Ngọc Dương went to Cambodia in May 2007 after being hounded by police.[53] Bùi Kim Thành, the only dissident, so far as I know, whom authorities confined in a mental hospital (not just once but twice), was reportedly released on the condition that she leaves Vietnam. She is now active in anti-Vietnam government organizations in the United States ("Internet writer Bui Kim Thanh released" 2008; "Bóc trần dã tâm của bọn khủng bố" 2009). Nguyễn Chính Kết, who left in December 2006, is the foreign representative of Khối 8406 [Block 8406], which claims to represent those who signed the Declaration on Freedom and Democracy (Khối 8406 2007). He apparently resides in the United States. Lê Trí Tuệ is one of the founders in October 2006 of the Công Đoàn Độc Lập Việt Nam [Independent Trade Union of Vietnam] and reportedly fled to Cambodia in 2007 to escape constant harassment, more interrogations, and possible arrest.[54]

Why six people in this second cluster who remain politically active in Vietnam have not been brought to trial and imprisoned is unclear. Only in the case of Bùi Minh Quốc might an explanation be that he has acted on his own. The other five have been active participants in organized dissent – four in unauthorized internet newspapers critical of the government and one in an organization representing signatories of the 2006 Declaration on Freedom and Democracy. Advanced age may be a factor in cases of Bùi Minh Quốc (b. 1940), Hoàng Tiến (b. about 1932), and Vũ Cao Quận (b. 1932). The three also have been Communist Party members or served the government. Of the remaining three – Dương Thị Xuân, Đỗ Nam Hải, and Nguyễn Phương Anh – two have parents who served the Democratic Republic of Vietnam, which fought in 1945–75 for independence from France, against the United States, and for the country's unity.[55] (Hereafter, I label such connections "DRV credentials.")

Such family connections to the regime and resulting ties to relatives and friends still in the government and Communist Party may provide these individuals and other dissidents like them with some protection against extreme repression. Much in Vietnamese politics, argues political scientist Martin Gainsborough, involves personal relationships and networks, which can provide advantages and safeguards. The viability and reliability of such linkages, however, are typically in flux and unpredictable (Gainsborough 2010: 177–90). Linkages that dissidents might have to individual authorities are no guarantee against more severe confinement. Indeed, as indicated by dissidents or their parents' DRV credentials and Communist Party membership, a significant proportion of those who end up being arrested and imprisoned have personal connections to authorities in the regime (see the summaries for Clusters 3–6 in Table 6.2).

Cluster 3 has 21 dissidents who served their prison terms and afterwards resumed their public political criticisms yet have not been rearrested. Why authorities have not imprisoned them again is a puzzle. My initial speculation was that these critics are acting individually, rather than being prominent members of dissident organizations, and possibly subscribe to the participatory struggle orientation discussed earlier rather than the confrontational one. This pattern, however, fits only five people: Dương Thu Hương, a famous novelist, has been an outspoken political critic since the early 1990s; Hà Sĩ Phu, a biologist in a government research institute who was forced to take early retirement because he refused to join the Communist Party, has written essays critical of the party and its government since the late 1980s; Lê Hồng Hà, who held numerous government positions before retiring in the 1993, has openly criticized various aspects of the regime since about 1995; Nguyễn Vũ Bình, who initially ran afoul of the Communist Party when he asked permission in 2000 to establish an opposition political party, appears not to be prominent in any organized opposition since resuming his public political criticism; and Trần Dũng Tiến, a former body guard for Hồ Chí Minh, has signed petitions and written letters since the early 2000s that criticize political leaders and institutions.

Another similarity among these five is their DRV credentials. Dương Thu Hương, Lê Hồng Hà, and Trần Dũng Tiến were Communist Party members and fought under the party and Hà Nội government's leadership for Vietnam's independence and unification. So did Hà Sĩ Phu, although he never joined the party. Nguyễn Vũ Bình, too young to have participated in the DRV, is the son of revolutionaries. Also, he himself was a party member and on the staff of the party's foremost journal, *Tạp Chí Cộng Sản* [Communist Review] before being forced to resign.

Three others in this cluster – Phạm Quế Dương, Nguyễn Thanh Giang, and Trần Khuê – also have DRV credentials, and Phạm Quế Dương was a Communist Party member. That background and their age (all are in their seventies) may help to explain why they have not been rearrested despite their leadership positions in dissident newspapers. Advanced age may also be giving Chân Tín some protection for further arrest and imprisonment, although he has no DRV credentials. Lê Chí Quang, Nguyễn Khắc Toàn, and Phạm Hồng Sơn have neither age nor, as best as I can tell, DRV credentials for possible protection. Yet they have not been imprisoned again even though the first two are prominent in dissident newspapers (*Tổ Quốc* and *Tự Do Ngôn Luận*, respectively) and the third is a leader in an advocacy group for prisoners of conscience (Hội Ái Hữu Tù Nhân Chính Trị và Tôn Giáo).

Five in this cluster – Hồ Thị Bích Khương, Nguyễn Ngọc Quang, Vũ Hoàng Hải, Huỳnh Việt Lang, and Lê Thị Công Nhân – have been out of prison for less than three years as of May 2011. The last two are leaders in opposition political parties, which may make them vulnerable to rearrest. Hồ Thị Bích Khương and Nguyễn Ngọc Quang, not leaders in opposition political parties, may be less liable for rearrest, although, like nearly every other regime dissident, they are harassed. Extensive harassment and the trauma it caused his family reportedly prompted Vũ Hoàng Hải to seek help from the United States consul general in Hồ Chí Minh City and leave Vietnam with his wife and child (DVR radio 2010). Another three individuals in this cluster – Lê Nguyên Sang, Nguyễn Kim Nhàn, and Nguyễn Văn Đài – have been out of prison for less than a year.

Only six previously convicted and imprisoned dissidents who resumed their political dissent have been convicted and imprisoned again. They form Cluster 4. It is unclear why people in this cluster have multiple imprisonments while people in Cluster 3 have had but one despite resuming their political dissent. One difference is Cluster 4 has no "solitary" dissidents – that is, people not active in dissident organizations (see Table 6.2). That, however, probably explains nothing because most of the *initial* imprisonments of those in Cluster 4 were for offenses done as individuals, not as members of organizations. In most respects the differences between the two clusters are slight. Cluster 4 people tend to be somewhat older, are less likely to live in Hà Nội or Hồ Chí Minh City, and somewhat less likely to have been Communist Party members.

One significant difference is that four of the dissidents in Cluster 4 are among the earliest and most determined regime dissidents. Three of these four have been imprisoned three times each, and their first imprisonment came prior to 1990.

Two of the four at one time served the Communist Party government. Hoàng Minh Chính, a former head of a national philosophy institute, was purged from the party and imprisoned during 1967–72 for criticizing, not publicly but within party circles, top leaders' positions regarding China and the Soviet Union. In 1981, soon after he had accused top party leaders of violating several provisions of Vietnam's Constitution, authorities imprisoned him for another seven years. In November 1995, at the age of 73, he was imprisoned another year after he distributed writings critical of the party's hold on power and advocated reinstatement of Communist party members who were purged in the 1960s (Đài Việt Nam California Radio 1996; Hoàng Minh Chính 1993). After being released from prison in 1996, he was not arrested and imprisoned again, however, even though his public dissent intensified. In 2006 he was a founding member and leader of a new opposition political party, Đảng Dân Chủ [Democratic Party]. By then he was 84 and sickly, conditions that may have stayed authorities' repressive hand until his death in 2008. Trần Anh Kim is a former officer in Vietnam's military. He was first imprisoned in 1995–97 for, he says, exposing the corruption by authorities in his home province of Thái Bình. In 2009, his political opposition resulted in being sentenced to five and a half years imprisonment on charges of trying to overthrow the government ("Cựu trung tá Trần Anh Kim, nhà tranh đấu và bất đồng chính kiến, bị công an bắt giữ 3 giờ đồng tại Hà Nội" 2006; Radio Free Asia 2009).

The other two long-time dissidents in Cluster 4 never served the Communist Party government. Nguyễn Đan Quế, a physician in Hồ Chí Minh City, began in 1976 to criticize the government's health care and human rights policies and created a short-lived dissident newspaper. In 1978 he was arrested for rebellion and for organizing a reactionary organization. He was imprisoned for ten years. In 1991, authorities sentenced him to twenty years imprisonment for attempting to overthrow the government. After seven years in jail a government amnesty freed him. His third jail term was July 2004 to September 2005 for abusing his democratic rights and jeopardizing the state and society ("Vụ án Nguyễn Đan Quế" 2004; "High Cost of Lifelong Commitment to Human Rights" 2004; Voice of America 2006). Disturbing the peace was Nguyễn Văn Lý's offense when this Roman Catholic priest in Huế was imprisoned the first time, 1983–92. Parole violations and sabotaging national unity were the charges against him when imprisoned again in 2001. After he served more than four years of a fifteen-year sentence, authorities released him. In early 2007, a court convicted him of spreading propaganda against the state and sentenced him to eight years imprisonment. After he suffered several strokes, authorities freed him, perhaps temporarily, in March 2010 (Công An tỉnh Thừa Thiên Huế 2007; Reuter News 2010).

Trần Khải Thanh Thủy and Nguyễn Tấn Hoành are considerably younger than the others in Cluster 4. A writer whose parents have DRV credentials, Trần Khải Thanh Thủy (b. 1960) has been on the editorial board of the dissident newspaper *Tổ Quốc* since October 2006 and in that same month was a founding board member of the Công Đoàn Độc Lập Việt Nam [Independent Trade Union], which the government deems illegal. In early 2007 a court convicted her of disturbing the peace. After nine months, authorities released her from jail because, they said, she had tuberculosis and she promised not to violate the law again. Nevertheless, she resumed making sharp criticisms of the regime. In 2010, authorities put her and her husband on trial for assaulting police officers and sentenced her to three and a half years imprisonment (BBC Vietnamese 2008; *VietCatholicNews* 2010). Nguyễn Tấn Hoành (b. 1976), a southern factory worker and a founding member of another nongovernment labor union, Hiệp Hội Đoàn Kết Công-Nông Việt Nam [United Workers-Farmers Association of Vietnam], was arrested in 2007 on charges of spreading propaganda against the state and collaborating with foreigners to oppose the regime. He was imprisoned for eighteen months. In February 2010, he was arrested again, apparently after being heavily involved in several strikes in Trà Vinh province south of Hồ Chí Minh City. A court convicted him of disturbing the peace and abusing his democratic rights; it sentenced him to seven-year imprisonment (Nguyễn Văn Huy 2009; Thân Văn Trường 2010; Committee to Protect Vietnamese Workers 2010).

In Cluster 5 are 17 people convicted for the first time. Because they are still serving prison sentences, we do not yet know whether they will resume their dissident activities after being released. Cluster 5 has the largest proportion of people born after 1955, the lowest proportion with DRV credentials, and next to the largest proportion of dissidents not from Hà Nội or Hồ Chí Minh City. All but four of the people have been members of outlawed opposition political parties, dissident internet publications, or other anti-regime groups and organizations.

Cluster 6 has three people who, as best as I can determine, stopped their public political dissent after being confined. I am guessing that the confinement experience contributed to dissuading them from being openly critical. (Possibly their dissent continues but not publicly.) Trần Thị Lệ Hồng, convicted in 2007 for her involvement in the United Workers-Farmers Association, was released from prison two years later. Hoàng Thị Anh Đào and Lê Thị Lệ Hằng received suspended prison terms in 2007, a condition that may also be influencing their lie-low behavior.

That Cluster 6 has only three people indicates that detaining, arresting, and imprisoning critics are only marginally effective repressive measures. Forty-four other dissidents, fourteen times the number in

Cluster 6, continued their open opposition to the regime despite having been confined, frequently more than once and sometimes even imprisoned.[56] This suggests considerable determination and commitment on their part. It also suggests more tolerance on the part of authorities and/ or considerable less ability to stifle dissidents than might be expected of an authoritarian regime.

Sentences

Dissidents sentenced to imprisonment are guilty, according to the government, of violating Vietnam's criminal laws. Hence, authorities claim, no one incarcerated is a political prisoner. According to government officials, people are in prison because they violated Vietnam's Constitution and laws.[57]

Before 2000, nearly half the thirteen charges leading to convictions and imprisonments were rather heavy-duty: espionage, revealing state secrets, inciting rebellion, and joining reactionary organizations (see Table 6.3, top half). Since 2000, such charges constitute less than one-fifth of the 50 offenses for which dissidents have been sentenced to prison. The rest of the offenses have been of a lighter nature: abusing one's freedom or democratic rights, disturbing the peace, assaulting police officers, and spreading propaganda against the state. The last of these, which does not appear prior to 2000, has constituted over half of all offenses for which dissidents have been incarcerated in the last eleven years.

Prison terms, too, have tended to be lighter in recent years (see Table 6.3, bottom half). All four prison terms prior to 1990 were five years or longer; two were ten years. In 1990–99, only one prison term was more than four years; most were less than two years. From 2000 onward, over half the imprisonments have been less than four years, and that includes dissidents still serving sentences that could end up being shortened. In the 26 instances for which there are data for both sentences and prison terms (see Table 6.1, Clusters 3, 4, and 6), only eight served the full sentence. The remaining eighteen, nearly 70 percent, were released before, sometimes years before, completing the original sentences. In several cases, sentences were reduced by appellant courts. Other people were released early due to their good behavior as inmates, their poor health, or intervention from influential relatives.

The relationship between offense and prison term is elusive. People convicted of rebellion, trying to overthrow the government, or inciting others to rebel tend to have longer prison terms than those convicted of abusing their freedom and democratic rights (Table 6.4). But for other

Table 6.3 Offenses and imprisonments for 47 regime dissidents*

Offense code

Offense code	\<1990	1990–94	1995–99	2000–04	2005–09	2010–11	Total
1				1	25	2	28
2		1	1	3	1		6
3			1	4		1	6
4		1			7		8
5					1		1
6	1				1		2
7	1						1
8			1				1
9	3	1	2	1	1	2	10
Total	5	3	5	9	36	5	63

Time period when convicted

Years in prison**	\<1990	1990–94	1995–99	2000–04	2005–09	2010–11	Total
\<1		1	1	1	3		6
1\<2			3	2	2		7
2\<3			1	2	4		7
3\<4		1		1	7	1	10
4\<5				3	4		7
5\<6	1				6		7
6\<7					4		4
7\<8	1	1				2	4
8 or more	2				1	1	4
Total	4	3	5	9	31	4	56

Notes: Offense codes: 1 spreading propaganda against the state; 2 espionage; 3 abusing freedoms and/or democratic rights; 4 trying to overthrow the government and/or inciting others to oppose the government; 5 working with foreign elements against the state; 6 joining reactionary organizations; 7 rebellion; 8 revealing state secrets; 9 other or unknown.
* The number of offenses and imprisonments exceeds 47 each because some dissidents were convicted of more than one offense and imprisoned more than once.
** For the dissidents convicted during 2000–11 and still in jail, this tabulation uses sentences. In the past, over half of those convicted were in prison fewer years than their original sentences stipulated.

Source: Data comes from Table 6.1 Sixty-two regime dissidents in Vietnam clustered according to their confinement by authorities and persistence of their dissent (as of May 2011) [http://ips.cap.anu.edu.au/sites/default/files/IPS/PSC/Table_1_for_Government_Repression_and_Toleration_of_Dissidents_in_Contemporary_Vietnam.pdf].

Table 6.4 Offense with prison terms for 47 regime dissidents

Imprisonment (yrs)*	Offense code												
	1	2	3	4	8	9	1&2	1&4	1&5	1&6	3&9	6&7	Total
<1	2	2				2							6
1<2	1	2	1		1	1			1				7
2<3	4		3										7
3<4	6		1			2		1					10
4<5	2	1	1			1	1	1					7
5<6	2			3		1				1			7
6<7	3												3
7<8	1			2		1					1		5
8 or more	1			1		1						1	4
Total	22	5	6	6	1	9	1	2	1	1	1	1	56 **

Notes: Offense codes: 1 spreading propaganda against the state; 2 espionage; 3 abusing freedoms and/or democratic rights; 4 trying to overthrow the government and/or inciting others to oppose the government; 5 working with foreign elements against the state; 6 joining reactionary organizations; 7 rebellion; 8 revealing state secrets; 9 other or unknown.

* For dissidents convicted during 2000–11 and remaining in jail this tabulation uses sentences rather than years in prison. In the past, over half of those convicted were in prison fewer years than their original sentences stipulated.

** The number of offenses and imprisonments exceeds 47 each because some dissidents were convicted of more than once and some convictions were for more than one offense.

Source: Data comes from Table 6.1 Sixty-two regime dissidents in Vietnam clustered according to their confinement by authorities and persistence of their dissent (as of May 2011) [http://ips.cap.anu.edu.au/sites/default/files/IPS/PSC/Table_1_for_Government_Repression_and_Toleration_of_Dissidents_in_Contemporary_Vietnam.pdf].

offenses, prison terms have varied considerably. Stated differently, in many instances, people convicted of the same offense are in prison for significantly different lengths of time. Incarceration for espionage convictions and the closely related offenses of working with foreign elements against the state and revealing state secrets have ranged between less than one year and five years; prison terms for spreading propaganda against the state vary between less than one and more than seven years. Even people charged with the same offense and tried at the same time frequently are sentenced to different prison terms.

Lawyers have told me the main reason for this variation is authorities deem some accused's actions to be more onerous than others even though the charges are the same. The criminal code allows authorities to make such assessments and impose different sentences accordingly. Often trial judges themselves are not the ones making these determinations; instead higher authorities decide.[58] Observers have speculated that sentences can vary because of the accused's demeanor, connections, and other personal circumstances.[59] A defendant who acts contrite is likely to get a shorter sentence than another one who, in the eyes of interrogators, prosecutors, and other government officials, is beligerant. An accused who has relatives in influential positions within the government, military, police, or Communist Party may also be treated less harshly than others. Being known internationally, especially among vocal human rights organizations and United Nations agencies, might also help to explain lighter sentences.

Prison conditions, according to the few accounts I have seen thus far, are dismal. Prisoners live in cramped cells, often with poor sanitation and ventilation. Imprisoned regime dissidents typically are not separated from other inmates; they live with people serving sentences for a wide range of crimes. Meals are spare and sometimes so awful that inmates refuse to eat and demand better food. Prisoners work most of the day: gardening, raising pigs and other livestock, doing handicrafts, cleaning and repairing prison facilities, and doing other chores. Apparently much of the food fed to them comes from what they produce themselves. Recreation time and resources are sparse. Usually prisoners are allowed to read newspapers and magazines provided by authorities, watch some television programs, and listen to selected radio broadcasts. Visits from relatives and friends are restricted and closely monitored. Occasionally, authorities permit foreign diplomats and representatives from international organizations to visit imprisoned regime dissidents (Hoàng Minh Chính 2004; Voice of America 2010b).

Infrequent forms of repression

Worth mentioning are forms of repression Vietnamese authorities apparently have rarely used against regime dissidents. Unlike in China, and before it the Soviet Union, authorities in Vietnam have not made a habit of depicting and treating dissidents as mentally deranged.[60] As noted earlier, only one of the 62 regime dissidents discussed in this chapter was put in a mental institution. Sometimes authorities beat imprisoned dissidents, place them in stocks, or put them in solitary confinement for weeks. But reports of such violence or other physical abuse against imprisoned regime dissidents are rare. I have no evidence of imprisoned regime dissident being brutalized further, confined in "tiger cages," or held in other extreme conditions.[61]

Conclusion

Being a regime dissident is risky. Even though the 62 dissidents considered in this chapter do not use or threaten violence and are not involved in armed struggle, authorities often are heavy handed in their reactions. Officials can and do mess up critics' lives – take away their jobs, intimidate their relatives and friends, interfere with their daily lives, interrogate them, sometimes beat them, and frequently detain or imprison them.

Nevertheless, data used for this chapter do not support a conclusion that Vietnam's Communist Party government tolerates no dissent or opposition. Instead, data show that the government is somewhat tolerant of dissidents who advocate major political reforms and oppose the present political system. The degree of toleration of political dissent would be even greater and the extent of repression much less, I suspect, were the data expanded to include how authorities react to public political criticism that does not call for overhauling the political system.

Another significant finding in this chapter is that the repression against regime dissidents is not uniform. A few regime dissidents have not been detained despite years of public criticisms of the political system. Many more who were detained have never been imprisoned even though they have persistently and openly criticized the political system. Others have been imprisoned, but after getting out of jail and resuming their political dissent, they were not rearrested. Only a few have been rearrested and served additional prison terms.

Analysis of the data provides no clear explanation for such varying degrees of repression against dissidents. The most that can be determined from the information collected thus far is that being elderly and having a history of service to the government and/or Communist Party appears to reduce the likelihood of a dissident being arrested and imprisoned and, if imprisoned, the risk of being arrested again after being released and resuming public dissent. Not being a prominent member of a dissident organization may also help to reduce one's risk of confinement beyond occasional detainment and interrogation. That there are numerous exceptions to these generalizations means that other factors are at work but not detectable with the material in hand.

Notes

1. I am most grateful to Phạm Thu Thủy of the Department of Political and Social Change, The Australian National University, for collecting and organizing many of the materials used for this chapter. My gratitude as well to the Australian Research Council for its financial support to our materials collection process. I thank Jonathan London for organizing the "Authoritarianism in East Asia" conference at City University of Hong Kong in June 2010 to which the initial version of this chapter was presented. I greatly appreciate, too, helpful comments and suggestions from Jonathan London, Đặng Đình Trung, Philip Taylor, David Marr, Nguyễn Hồng Hải, Drew Smith, and people attending my talks based on this chapter at George Washington University and The Australian National University.
2. Human Rights Watch (2013: Vietnam chapter); United States Department of State (2011). A more measured report from the Department of State is a subsequent one: United States Department of State (2012).
3. "Tuyên Ngôn Tự do Dân chủ cho Việt Nam" April 8, 2006, initially signed by about 300 Vietnamese; at year's end, about 2,000 people had signed, including several Vietnamese living abroad. The "Declaration" is on numerous websites, for example, Mạng Ý Kiến [Opinion net], <http://www.ykien.net/>, accessed May 12, 2006. For an English version, see Lẽ Phải [Justice] website <http://lephai.com/uni/n2006/dt20060720h.htm>, accessed July 28, 2006. The declaration calls for replacing the current Communist Party-dominated political system with one featuring multiply political parties, protected human rights, and other democratic institutions. Note, this statement came more than a year and a half earlier than a similar one in China, called Charter 08, issued by Chinese political dissidents in December 2008.
4. Not included are other political critics who voice their objections and disapproval primarily through demonstrations and/or signing petitions.
5. The organization's full name was Hội Nhân Dân Việt Nam Ủng hộ Đảng và Nhà Nước Chống Tham Nhũng [Association of Vietnamese People to Support the Party and State to Fight Corruption]. Its open letter, dated September 2, 2001 was sent to national authorities (Hội Nhân Dân Việt Nam Ủng hộ Đảng và Nhà Nước Chống Tham Nhũng 2001). For accounts of the association's founding, see Phạm Quế Dương (2002), and Phạm Quế Dương and Trần Khuê (2004), an article about its first anniversary in September 2, 2002.

Phạm Quế Dương is a former military officer and Communist Party member. *Điện Thư* [Electronic letter], which appears in several of my citations, was an online publication of the Câu Lạc Bộ Dân Chủ Việt Nam [Club for Vietnamese democracy] inside the country, started in April 2003 and, as best as I can tell, stopped in July 2007. The page numbers for *Điện Thư* that I cite are my printouts of the issue on A4 paper.

6. The offense was "*lợi dụng các quyền tự do dân chủ,*" quoted in an editorial of *Thông Luận* (2004: 2). The publication is also online (http://www.ethongluan.org).

7. Trần Độ, who died in 2006, had been a military officer and Communist Party member.

8. Đỗ Mậu held high positions in the Communist Party and Vietnamese army.

9. Lê Chí Quang is a lawyer in Hà Nội.

10. The author, writing in Hồ Chí Minh City, says he is a former professor and revolutionary fighter.

11. Nguyễn Thanh Giang (2004: 6–7), quoting at length an unidentified source; news item in *Điện Thư* 2004: 1; and Võ Đồng Đội 2005. Nguyễn Thanh Giang is a scientist and military veteran in Hà Nội.

12. The banner said (capitalization in the original):

    THAM NHŨNG LÀ HÚT MÁU DÂN!
    LẠM PHÁT, GIÁ CẢ TĂNG CAO LÀ GIẾT DÂN!
    MẤT ĐẤT BIỂN ĐẢO LÀ CÓ TỘI VỚI TỔ TIÊN!
    Yêu cầu đảng cộng sản thực hiện ngay:
    DÂN CHỦ HOÁ ĐẤT NƯỚC!
    ĐA NGUYÊN – ĐA ĐẢNG!

    Arrested for hanging it was Vũ Văn Hùng, a school teacher in Hà Tây province, adjacent to Hà Nội. For a photo of the banner and account of Vũ Văn Hùng's arrest, see Nguyễn Phương Anh (2008).

13. Radio Free Asia (2005). Nguyễn Xuân Nghĩa is a journalist and writer in the city of Hải Phòng. Also see Đặng Văn Việt (2006a: 5), Radio Free Asia (2004), and previously cited items by Phạm Quế Dương, Lê Chí Quang, and Trần Độ. Đặng Văn Việt, a veteran of the revolutions against France and the United States and a long-time Communist Party member, lives in Hà Nội. *Tổ Quốc*, a source for several citations in this chapter, is a web-based dissident publication (www.to-quoc.net) from Vietnam that started in September 2006.

14. Tống Văn Công, a Communist Party member for over 50 years, is a former editor of the newspaper *Lao Động* [Labor] and other government authorized publications.

15. Several regime dissidents say that Vietnam's 1946 Constitution was essentially a democratic one and should be reinstated today. See, for instance, Trần Dũng Tiến (2001), Đỗ Nam Hải (2004c: 38), and Nguyễn Thanh Giang (2006: 46). Trần Dũng Tiến, a revolutionary and one of Hồ Chí Minh's guards, lived in Hà Nội and died in April 2006. Đỗ Nam Hải lives in Hồ Chí Minh City; his parents were Communist Party members who fought in Vietnam's wars for independence.

16. For example, see the "Declaration on Freedom and Democracy for Vietnam," ("Tuyên Ngôn Tự do Dân chủ cho Việt Nam" 2006), Trần Lâm (2005b), Đỗ Nam Hải (2008), Phạm Hồng Sơn (2009a: 8–10). Trần Lâm lives in Hải Phòng,

is a lawyer, and is a former judge in Vietnam's supreme court. Phạm Hồng Sơn is an information technology specialist in Hà Nội.

17. For example, see Nguyễn Thanh Giang (2006: 22–3); Nguyễn Vũ Bình, interview with BBC radio, June 15, 2002, from Mạng Ý Kiến http://www.ykien.net/ mykbdv45.html, accessed February 4, 2004; and "Lời Kêu Gọi cho quyền thành lập và hoạt động đảng phái tại Việt Nam" [Calling for the right to establish and run political parties in Vietnam, signed by 116 advocates for democracy] April 6, 2006, from Lê Phai website, http://lephai.com/uni/n2006/dt20060406a.htm, accessed April 7, 2006. Nguyễn Vũ Bình lives in Hà Nội; he was an editor for a Communist Party journal but was fired after he requested permission to establish an opposition party in 2000.

18. An exception is Đỗ Nam Hải's remark that a multi-party system, although much needed, will not solve all of Vietnam's problems (Đỗ Nam Hải 2004a: 2–3).

19. Nguyễn Khắc Toàn has owned and operated an electronics shop and real estate office in Hà Nội. /D\PhamHongSon\The nao la dan chu Jan 2002, par Vai dong, 1; Nguyen Khac Toan\Khat Vong tu do 25 Apr 2006, p'out 13 m/

20. The relevant passages are on pages 19 and 21 (printing on 8 ½ by 11 inch paper) in this lengthy account about how and why Vì Đức Hồi, a provincial official, and Communist Party member, joined the pro-democracy movement in recent years.

21. Lê Hồng Hà is a former Communist Party member, government official, and revolutionary living in Hà Nội. /D\Le Hong Ha\ TrachNhiem TriThuc 2004, sec 2, first several # items; Le Hong Ha\Nhung Van de ...1 Feb 2007, "Nha tu ban/.

22. Trần Khải Thanh Thủy, a writer in Hà Nội from a family that joined the revolution for independence, was imprisoned in 2007 and again in 2010.

23. Phan Đình Diệu is a retired professor of mathematics in Hà Nội.

24. Hoàng Tiến, a writer in Hà Nội, participated in the revolution for independence; Bạch Ngọc Dương is an engineer living in Hải Phòng.

25. See also numerous materials on the Bauxite Vietnam website, available at <http://boxitvn.wordpress.com>. Besides regime dissidents, many other Vietnamese, including war hero General Võ Nguyên Giáp, have publicly opposed government plans to allow Chinese to mine bauxite and other minerals in the Central Highlands. Nguyễn Chính Kết was a religion teacher living in Hồ Chí Minh City until he left Vietnam in 2006 to become the overseas representative of Khối 8406 [Block 8406], an opposition organization; Trần Khuê is a military veteran and academic living in Hồ Chí Minh City; and Phạm Đình Trọng, a writer in Hồ Chí Minh City, recently quit the Communist Party because of his disgust with the regime's policies about China and several other matters.

26. Tống Văn Công 2009; Hà Sĩ Phu 2009a, 2009b. Hà Sĩ Phu, a scientist forced to take early retirement because of his political views, is a writer in Đà Lạt.

27. For a forceful argument of this position, see Nguyễn Chính Kết (2006b: 23–5).

28. Đỗ Nam Hải, open letter to national authorities and other people (Đỗ Nam Hải 2004b), Đỗ Nam Hải (2005: 4), and Hoàng Bách Việt, member of the Đảng Dân Chủ Nhân Dân [People's Democratic Party] (Hoàng Bách Việt 2005: 1–2).

29. "Đây là một cuộc đấu tranh nhằm chấm dứt những chính sách sai lầm của Đảng Cộng sản cầm quyền, những chính sách phản dân hại nước nhưng không phải là một cuộc đấu tranh để lật đổ chính quyền hiện nay." (Lê Hồng Hà 2007b). Lê Hồng Hà, a former government official, lives in Hanoi.

30. Related, although taking issue with aspects of Lê Hồng Hà's discussion, is Tống Văn Công, a dissident who says Communist Party leaders' initiatives, too, explain the country's economic renovation policies. The party in Vietnam, he contends, has never been strongly wedded to communism and has long had a give-and-take approach to governing (Tống Văn Công 2009).

31. Trần Bảo Lộc, like Hà Sĩ Phu, resides in Đà Lạt, central Vietnam.

32. "Declaration on freedom and democracy" ("Tuyên Ngôn Tự do Dân chủ cho Việt Nam" 2006: part III, and par. "Mục tiêu cao nhất ... ").

33. Essay by Chân Tín and three other Roman Catholic priests calling for election boycott (Chân Tín, Nguyễn Hữu Giải, Nguyễn Văn Lý, and Phan Văn Lợi 2006); see also Nguyễn Văn Lý (2007); Minh Chính, secretary of the Đảng Dân Chủ Nhân Dân [People's Democratic Party] in Ho Chi Minh City, public letter to Nguyễn Minh Triết, secretary of the Communist Party in Ho Chi Minh City (Minh Chính 2006); Trung Hiếu 2006. Chân Tín, Minh Chính, and Trung Hiếu were writing in Hồ Chí Minh City. Nguyễn Văn Lý, a priest from Huế, was arrested and imprisoned in February 2007.

34. Huỳnh Việt Lang, member of the Đảng Dân Chủ Nhân Dân [People's Democratic Party] (Huỳnh Việt Lang 2006: 39–40), Lê Quang Liêm, member of Phật Giáo Hòa Hảo Thuần Túy [Hoa Hao Buddhist religion] (Lê Quang Liêm 2006: 17); Nguyễn Vũ Bình (2008: part 3, point 3). Huỳnh Việt Lang, a resident of Ho Chi Minh City, was arrested in August 2006 and then imprisoned; Lê Quang Liêm is in Vietnam but I do not know where.

35. The writer lives in Hanoi.

36. See, for instance, Đảng Dân Chủ Nhân Dân (2005), especially 1, 5–6, and Đảng Thăng Tiến Việt Nam 2006, parts I and II.

37. See, for instance, Đặng Văn Việt (2006b: 15) and Trần Anh Kim (2006: par Đảng man lại ...). Đặng Văn Việt is in Hanoi; Trần Anh Kim is in Thái Bình City, Thái Bình province.

38. This article thoughtfully analyzes the movement and the government's various reactions. Its footnotes also guide interested readers to other studies of the movement.

39. See especially Articles 69 and 70.

40. The session may have cost Nguyễn Khắc Toàn some credibility among fellow regime dissidents. See the account by "NH" in Hà Nội (2010).

41. An example is the article, in a security police publication, "Nguyễn Khắc Toàn, kẻ vụ lợi bằng việc làm phản dân hại nước" (2009).

42. For instance, see "Sự thật về 'tờ báo lậu' Tổ Quốc" (2008).

43. The percentage would likely be much higher if I had complete information on this factor. As Table 6.1 reflects, information for "other hardships," which includes harassment, is missing for nearly half of the 62 dissidents emphasized here.

44. Among the relevant accounts about Lê Trần Luật are "Tước giấy phép hoạt động văn phòng luật sư pháp quyền" (2009); "Khi nhà nước đè bẹp công lý"

(2009); Phạm Văn Hải (2009); "Lê Trần Luật bị xóa tên trong danh sách Luật Sư Đoàn" (2009).

45. See Ủy ban Nhân Quyền Việt Nam (2007), and complaint letter from Nguyễn Văn May and Lê Thị Thúy Minh (May 2007), parents of Nguyễn Phương Anh.

46. Table 6.1, being extremely large, with columns of details about each of the 62 dissidents, could not be printed here. But it can be viewed and downloaded at http:// ips.cap.anu.edu.au/sites/default/files/IPS/PSC/Table_1_for_Government_ Repression_and_Toleration_of_Dissidents_in_Contemporary_Vietnam.pdf. It is summarized in Table 6.2, which is printed in this chapter.

47. One of his early public criticisms was the article Trần Đại Sơn (2003: 8–9).

48. His name disappears from the editorial board list by the *Tổ Quốc*'s third issue, October 15, 2006. I have found very little indication of his public political criticism since then. Perhaps his age (he is in his nineties) has forced him to stop.

49. For an early public statement of Trần Lâm's views, see Trần Lâm (2005a).

50. Vi Đức Hồi describes numerous such interrogation sessions he endured in early 2007(Vi Đức Hồi 2008: 23–37, 53–64, pagination when printed on 8 x 11 ½ inch paper). For another example, see the account of Nguyễn Khắc Toàn's lengthy detention in Hà Đông security police offices during May 2009 (Nguyễn Khắc Toàn 2009).

51. Examples of reports about physical abuse are an open letter by Vũ Hoàng Hải (2006), an interview of Bạch Ngọc Dương (Radio Free Asia 2007a), and Vũ Hùng's letter to the United Nations (Vũ Hùng 2008). Vũ Hùng is also known as Vũ Văn Hùng.

52. One of his early public critiques was made on January 8, 1999 and published as "Phát biểu của tương Trần Độ" (1999). A few days earlier, the Communist Party's leadership had expelled him from the party, which he had joined in 1940, after he refused to rein in his public criticisms.

53. A self-proclaimed sympathizer with the pro-democracy movement warns that Bạch Ngọc Dương may now be working with the security police (Hoàng Hải 2007).

54. In Cambodia, some allege, Vietnamese security police had Lê Trí Tuệ murdered (Lê Minh 2009). An article in the security police force's magazine, *An Ninh Thế Giới*, claims Lê Trí Tuệ is a charlatan labor leader ("Lê Trí Tuệ đã lừa đảo người lao động như thế nào?" 2007).

55. Explaining why he has not been arrested, Đỗ Nam Hải speculated that authorities weigh the advantages and disadvantages to the regime before arresting dissidents. Thus far, he speculated, officials probably think arresting him would not be worth the trouble. He did not elaborate why. (*Tập San Tự Do Dân Chủ* 2010: 31–2).

56. The 44 are the 11 in Cluster 2, the 21 in Cluster 3, the 6 in Cluster 4, and the 6 in Cluster 5 for whom I have the necessary information (see Table 6.1, Column V, "R'smd PC.")

57. Examples of such official justifications are reported in BBC Vietnamese (2009), VietnamNet (2009a). Inside the prisons, according to some regime dissidents, authorities typically do refer to them as "political prisoners" [*tù nhân chính trị*]. See Dân Luận (2009).

58. Discussions with attorneys in Hanoi, September 2012.
59. Phone interview with a Vietnamese political activist, June 2012. See also Gillespie (2012: 13), *Tập San Tự do Dân chủ* (2010: 30–1), Voice of America Online (2010a).
60. For a recent study of this practice in China, see Munro (2006).
61. "Tiger cages" are prison cells so tiny that a person cannot stand or lay down. Authorities of the Republic of Vietnam (the pre-1975 government based in Sài Gòn) frequently incarcerated prisoners, especially dissidents, in such cells.

7
The Apparatus of Authoritarian Rule in Vietnam

Carlyle A. Thayer

Introduction

This chapter examines the repressive role of four key state organs in buttressing Vietnam's one-party state: Ministry of Public Security (MPS), People's Armed Security Force (PASF), General Directorate II (military intelligence), and the Ministry of Culture and Information (MCI). The analysis that follows explores how authoritarian rule is implemented by examining the methods and tactics used to repress pro-democracy activists, bloggers, journalists, and religious leaders in Vietnam. This examination reveals that Vietnam's one-party state is a divided entity and its organs of repression are manipulated by leaders engaged in factional in-fighting. This finding parallels similar conclusions on the role of China's state security apparatus that historically has exerted influence on Vietnam.[1]

Vietnamese security authorities invariably charge political activists under the vaguely worded Article 88 of the Penal Code on "Conducting propaganda against the Socialist Republic of Vietnam." Article 88 states:

1. Those who commit one of the following acts against the Socialist Republic of Vietnam shall be sentenced to between three and twelve years of imprisonment:
   a. Propagating against, distorting, and/or defaming the people's administration;
   b. Propagating psychological warfare and spreading fabricated news in order to foment confusion among people;
   c. Making, storing, and/or circulating documents and/or cultural products with contents against the Socialist Republic of Vietnam (Socialist Republic of Vietnam 1999: 22).

Repression in Vietnam consists of three overlapping components: monitoring and surveillance, harassment and intimidation, and arrest detention, trial, and sentencing. Each of these components is used to coerce politically active citizens whose views and actions are deemed unacceptable by party and state officials.

Political repression in Vietnam has largely been neglected in the scholarly literature by political scientists who focus on relations between society and the state. One notable exception is Ben Kerkvliet's chapter in this volume that argues there is considerable toleration of dissent and criticism in Vietnam where the regime relies on a mix of accommodation, dialogue, concession, and repression. Kerkvliet's analysis therefore focuses on uncovering explanations for this mix of patterns. This chapter, in contract, focuses on patterns of state repression.

The number of political dissidents, pro-democracy activists, and religious freedom advocates in Vietnam is quite small; yet, the state devotes enormous resources to monitor and repress this tiny group. One reason may be that Vietnam's one-party state's claim to legitimacy on rational-legal and ideological grounds is weak (Thayer 2009a, 2010a). This heightens the state's sense of vulnerability and the vigor of its response to dissenting views. Thus the state relies on repression to silence individuals and groups constituting "political civil society" to shore up its authority and prevent the undermining of the authoritarian basis of its rule (Thayer 2009b).

The apparatus of repression

Ministry of public security

The MPS (*Bo Cong An*, formerly the Ministry of Interior) is the lead organization responsible for national security. The MPS forms a bloc on the Central Committee of the Communist Party of Vietnam (CPV) representing 4.4 percent of its 160 members elected at the tenth congress in 2006. The Minister of Public Security is also a member of the party's Politburo. From 2006 until July 2011 this position was held by General Le Hong Anh. Anh was listed first in protocol rankings after the party Secretary General based on voting results at the 2006 national party congress. He was replaced after the eleventh national party congress in 2011 by General Tran Dai Quang. The MPS bloc comprised eight members of the new 175-member Central Committee or 4.6 percent. The Minister of Public Security is assisted by six deputy ministers, all of whom are members of the party Central Committee.

The MPS currently comprises six General Departments: Police, Security, Strategic Intelligence, Education and Personnel, Logistics, and Science and Technology. The General Department of Police is primarily a law enforcement agency and is estimated to have 1.2 million officers nationwide (Thayer 2008: 303). The General Department of Security has responsibility for collecting information related to national security and advising on policy, protecting political and economic security, protecting cultural and ideological security, immigration control, and international terrorism.

The General Department of Security has a specialist unit, A42, that monitors telephones, emails, and the internet (Hayton 2010: 122).[2] In 2002, Vietnam acquired the Verint mobile phone monitoring system. In 2005, the MPS acquired additional sophisticated mobile/cell phone monitoring equipment known as the Silver Bullet system that included two P-GSM portable mobile phone monitoring devices.[3]

The General Department of Strategic Intelligence focuses on Vietnam's "enemies both foreign and domestic" and has responsibility for collecting and processing information to identify external threats to national security, including international terrorism.[4]

People's armed security force

The PASF (*Cong An Vu Trang Nhan Dan*), established in 1959, operates primarily in rural areas at district and, in some cases, village level. It is charged with responsibility for dealing with ordinary crime, illegal political activity, and insurgency.

According to one authoritative account, in the 1980s the PASF largely bypassed or coordinated only laterally with the Ministry of Interior (now Public Security), its nominal superior, and reported directly to the party Secretariat (Library of Congress 1987). In this sense, the PASF may be viewed as an extension of party control at the local level where it comes under the direction of the People's Committee. In recent years the MPS has assumed greater vertical control over the PSAF.

General directorate ii

The Ministry of National Defence (MND, *Bo Quoc Phong*) has primary responsibility for the external defense of Vietnam's sovereignty and territorial integrity. Units under its control coordinate closely with the MPS and other agencies on internal security matters.

The MND comprises an Office of the Minister and six major divisions: General Staff Department, General Political Department, General Logistics Department, General Technical Department, General

Department of National Defence Industry, General Department II
(GD II), "and other directly subordinate agencies" (Socialist Republic
of Vietnam 2004: 42). The General Political Directorate contains an
internal military security component (*To Chuc va An Ninh*). GD II is the
military intelligence service of the MND.

GD II was reportedly established in the early 1980s when General Le
Duc Anh was Minister of National Defence. Under the terms of Decree
96/ND-CP (September 1997) Vietnam's military intelligence is charged
with collecting news and documents related to national security with
special attention to foreign countries, organizations, and individuals,
at home or abroad, "who plot or engage in activities aimed at threatening or opposing the Communist Party of Viet Nam or the Socialist
Republic of Viet Nam" (quoted in Nguyen Nam Khanh 2004). According
to Chapter 1, Article 1 of the Ordinance on Intelligence (1996), GD II is
empowered to be "active in the fields of politics, defence, security, foreign
relations, economics, science and technology, industry and the environment, science and culture" (quoted in Nguyen Nam Khanh 2004). GD II
was reportedly upgraded in the 1990s with Chinese technical assistance
to enable it to better monitor internal threats to national security.[5]

Very little was known about the operations of GD II until March–April
2001 when it attracted public attention for its role in tapping the telephones of senior party officials. Party Secretary General Le Kha Phieu
reportedly used the dossiers complied by a specialized wire tap unit
known as A10 within GD II to influence factional in-fighting on the eve
of the ninth national party congress.[6]

According to the then Prime Minister Vo Van Kiet:

> [t]here was a general reminder to the Politburo that they should not
> use this instrument [military intelligence wire tapping] for personal
> purposes after some allegations made by people and the public.
> Normally in the tradition of the communist party here, the general
> secretary has the right to use party and state organisations to monitor
> the domestic and foreign situation. The important thing is to use that
> apparatus to cope with the internal situation. It is unacceptable for
> anyone, and I mean anyone at all, to use this instrument for personal
> purposes. It's something that should be roundly criticized because it
> is forbidden.[7]

Le Kha Phieu failed to gain re-election as CPV Secretary General at
the ninth party congress in April 2001 in part due to the wire tapping
scandal. The Chief of the General Staff and the Head of the General

Political Department were both reprimanded but their careers were not affected otherwise (Thayer 2003).

In 2004, two of Vietnam's most respected retired military generals raised the issue of GD II's interference in internal party affairs in private letters to the senior leadership.[8] No less a figure than General Vo Nguyen Giap demanded an investigation into the "extra-legal" activities of GD II. Giap noted that the party Central Committee, Politburo, Secretariat, and Central Control Committee had all considered the matter without taking any corrective action. Giap charged that for many years GD II had tried to manipulate factionalism within the CPV to its advantage and had smeared the political reputations of many leading figures including himself (Vo Nguyen Giap 2004).

General Giap's allegations were supported by retired Major General Nguyen Nam Khanh in a letter to the senior party leadership on the eve of a plenary meeting of the Central Committee. Khanh accused the GD II of "slandering, intimidation, torture, political assassination," and manipulation of internal party factionalism for its own partisan purposes. Khanh provided excerpts from the GD II's classified *News Bulletin* (*Ban tin*) to back up his accusations (Nguyen Nam Khanh 2004).

Ministry of culture and information

The MCI traditionally has played a major role in controlling information available to society at large. The Ministry has oversight of the publishing industry, including books, periodicals, and newspapers, and uses its powers to censor views and ban publications that were perceived to be at odds with party policy. The rise of the Internet has posed major challenges to the traditional role of the MCI. The MCI has become one of the most proactive institutions in promulgating regulations to counter the use of the Internet by so-called cyber dissidents, politically active individuals and groups, and bloggers.

Since 2001, the MCI has issued a stream of directives in an attempt to keep up with advances in the spread of Internet technology in Vietnam. For example, Decree 55/2001 ND-CP on Internet Management and Use (August 23, 2001) made the owners of cyber café legally responsible for monitoring their clients and reporting breaches of the law. Another MCI regulation, issued in August 2005, prohibited the use of Internet resources to oppose the state; destabilize security, the economy or social order; infringe the rights of organizations and individuals; and interfere with the state's Domain Name System servers.[9] A third MCI Decision (October 10, 2007) required that all businesses obtain a license before setting up a new website and that they could only post information for which they had been licensed. The Decision also made it illegal to post information that incited people against the government or caused hostility between different ethnic groups. A fourth MCI Circular, No. 7 (December 2008), mandated that bloggers must restrict their postings to personal matters and that blogs commenting on politics, matters considered state secrets, subversive or a threat to social order and national security were proscribed.[10]

In 2007, the MCI conducted a national audit of Internet access sites in all provinces and major cities in order to determine whether the Ministry's directives were being complied with. This survey identified nearly 2,000 subversive Internet sites, including *Thong Luan, Han Nam Quan, Con Ong, Con Vit, Vietbaoonline,* and *Ky Con.*

The MCI took immediate steps to reinforce firewalls to block material deemed subversive and harmful to national security. The Ministry directed Vietnam Data Communications Co., Vietnam's only Internet gateway, to block websites based on a list drawn up and regularly updated by the MPS. This was an onerous requirement because the Vietnam Data Corporation could only manually filter these sites.

The MCI also issued further regulations requiring Internet café owners to obtain special licenses requiring checks into their family, professional, and financial backgrounds. The Ministry also announced that Internet Service Providers would be held responsible for blocking anti-government websites. They were required to obtain photo IDs and monitor and store information on the activities of online users.

In 2008, Chinese bauxite mining activities in Vietnam's Central Highlands attracted widespread criticism by a diverse network of citizens who used social websites, such as *Facebook*, to express their views. This novel use of social media on the Internet to criticize government policy led public security officials late that year to aggressively interfere with if not shut down *Facebook* and other sites where anti-bauxite blogs had been set up.[11] In this respect Vietnamese security authorities were mimicking China where authorities blocked *Facebook* in July 2008 and subsequently imposed restrictions on *Twitter* and *YouTube.* When Vietnamese Catholic activists set up websites to publicize their land disputes with government authorities, public security officials also blocked these sites.[12]

In another manifestations of the state's attempt to gain control over an ever-changing Internet, the Hanoi People's Committee issued Decision No. 15/2010/QD-UBND (April 26, 2010) requiring the installation of Internet Service Retailers Management Software (or Green Dam) in all computers used by Internet cafés, hotels, restaurants, airports, bus stations, and other locations providing access to the Web by the end of the year.[13] This software will allow the government to track user activities and block access to websites.

Under Decision 15, Internet users in Hanoi are prohibited from doing anything online to

> oppose the government of the Socialist Republic of Viet Nam; endanger national security, stability, public safety; disrupt the unity and harmony of the people; propagate war; create hatred, conflicts between minority groups, religious groups; provoke violence, pornography, crimes, social unrest, stereotypes; impair cultural values; or call for illegal demonstrations, boycotts, unlawful gatherings for grievances and complaints.[14]

Groups targeted for repression

This section reviews state repression directed against four distinct groups: pro-democracy activists, Catholic land rights activists, Zen Buddhists, and the Christian Degar ethnic minority group.

Pro-democracy activists

During the late 1980s and 1990s political dissent in Vietnam was mainly the province of individuals or small groups (Thayer 2006). In 2006, Vietnam's network of pro-democracy activists and groups coalesced into an identifiable political movement. On April 6, 2006, 116 persons issued an Appeal for Freedom of Political Association that they distributed throughout Vietnam via the Internet. On 8th April, 118 persons issued a Manifesto on Freedom and Democracy for Vietnam. These pro-democracy advocates became known as Bloc 8406 after the date of their founding manifesto.

Bloc 8406 issued a number of statements that called upon the Vietnamese state to respect basic human rights and religious freedom and to permit citizens to freely associate and form their own political parties (Thayer 2009b).[15] They argued that these freedoms were rights guaranteed by the 1992 state constitution and by international agreements and covenants the Vietnamese government had signed. Bloc 8406 was the most prominent political network but other political groups and networks were also active at this time.

In August 2006, Bloc 8406 publicly announced a four-phase proposal for democratization including the restoration of civil liberties, establishment of political parties, drafting of a new constitution, and democratic elections for a representative National Assembly. On October 12, 2006, members of Bloc 8406 issued an open letter to the leaders of the Asia Pacific Economic Cooperation (APEC) Leadership Summit, who were scheduled to meet in Hanoi in November, asking for their help in promoting democracy in Vietnam. Four days later, Bloc 8406 attempted to transform itself into a political movement by uniting with the outlawed Unified Buddhist Church of Vietnam (UBCV) to form the Vietnam Alliance for Democracy and Human Rights.

Vietnamese security authorities held off taking action against Bloc 8406 until the eve of the APEC Summit. Once the summit concluded, security authorities rounded up key leaders of the network. They were summarily tried in court and sentenced to imprisonment. In 2009, Vietnam renewed its crackdown on political dissent by arresting up to thirty political activists.

In some respects the crackdown in 2009 represented a mopping-up operation of Bloc 8406. But in other important respects it reflected a new development in domestic politics. In the past, political activists focused their protests on issues relating to freedom of expression, association, and belief. In 2009, political dissidents expanded their reform agenda to include environmental issues raised by bauxite mining, relations with China, corruption by senior officials, and other issues.

Since 2009 political activists have increasingly taken to the Internet to voice their criticisms of Vietnam's one-party state. The use of the Internet by individual bloggers with a popular following emerged as another new development. Bloggers quickly picked up on topical issues and posted their views on the Internet and invited readers to provide feedback. No issues had more salience than the South China Sea, where Chinese assertiveness raised the hackles of Vietnamese nationalists, and abuse of power by party officials. In 2012, at least 25 pro-democracy activists, including bloggers and songwriters, were sentenced to lengthy prison terms. During the first half of 2013, 46 pro-democracy activists and bloggers were arrested (Thayer 2013b).

The expanded reform agenda represented a new challenge to the legitimacy of Vietnam's one-party state. In addition to the challenges to rational-legal and performance legitimacy, the state now found its claim to legitimacy based on nationalism under challenge. This represented a serious threat to the authority of the party-state as the growing anti-China backlash spread from the political fringe to the political elite who questioned the state's perceived inadequate response to Chinese heavy-handiness in the South China Sea (Thayer 2009a).

Catholic Church land protests

Vietnam's Catholic community numbers approximately six million. Church authorities estimate that Vietnam's communist regime confiscated 2,250 church properties since 1954. In recent years friction has arisen between church and state over ownership of confiscated land and property. In late 2007 and continuing throughout 2008, for example, the Catholic Church in Hanoi and local government authorities became embroiled in disputes over land claimed by Thai Hoa parish and property of the former Vatican representative in Hanoi. Local officials rejected these claims and this sparked nonviolent mass protests in the form of prayer vigils and other public religious ceremonies.

In 2009, the Catholic Church became embroiled in another major land dispute this time with local authorities in Dong Hoi town, Quang Binh province. At issue was ownership of land that surrounded Tam Toa Cathedral. The cathedral was bombed by the United States during the Vietnam War. Local authorities took possession in 1996 and the following year designated the Tam Toa ruins an American War Crimes Memorial Site.

The issue of land ownership over Tam Toa continued to fester over the next twelve years. In 2009, Catholic Church officials became more assertive in their claims by holding open air masses on the grounds of the cathedral and calling for the return of church land. This prompted the official state Commission on Religion to declare that the government "has no intention of returning any property or goods to the Catholic Church or any other religious organization" that was confiscated by the state.[16]

Throughout the remainder of 2009 matters escalated. In July, when 150 local Catholic parishioners erected a tent chapel on the contested land they were promptly evicted by police who arrested eleven Catholic activists. These arrests sparked a series of massive public protests by Catholics in the provinces of Quang Binh and neighboring Nghe An and Ha Tinh in late July. Catholics marched behind flags bearing the Vatican's colors.

By early August Catholic media reported that the entire diocese of Vinh, numbering up to half a million persons from 178 parishes, rallied to protest police violence.[17] In mid-August, on the Feast of the Assumption, the Catholic Church held another show of force by staging a rally of 200,000 in front of the Bishopric of Vinh in Nghe An province.[18] Banners and placards protested police brutality and persecution and called for justice. The rally was addressed by leading church dignitaries and was probably the largest religious protest in Vietnam's history.

Zen Buddhists

Thich Nhat Hanh, a Zen Buddhist and religious activist, was one of the founders of the UBCV in South Vietnam during the Vietnam War. He opposed the war and went to France to live in exile; there he founded Plum village, a Zen Buddhist monastery. After reunification in 1975 the UBCV refused to give up its autonomy and merge with the state-sponsored Buddhist Church of Vietnam. The UBCV was declared illegal and its leaders subject to house arrest. They have nevertheless posed a continued thorn in the side of the Vietnamese state.

In 2005, Vietnam permitted Thich Nhat Hanh to return to Vietnam. He was welcomed by government officials who may have hoped to use his message of reconciliation to undermine the leadership of the UBCV. Thich Nhat Hanh's followers were invited by the Abbot of Bat Nha monastery in Bao Loc, Lam Dong province, to take up residence and worship. Soon crowds as large as 800 from surrounding provinces and further afield gathered for monthly services.

In 2007, Thich Nhat Hanh returned to Vietnam on a second visit and incensed government officials by presenting a ten-point proposal calling for greater religious freedom to the state president. Thich Nhat Hanh's proposal stated:

> Please separate religion from politics and politics from religious affairs. Please stop all surveillance by the government on religious activities, disband the Government Department for Religious Affairs but first of all disband the Religious Police. All religious associations should be able to operate freely in accordance with laws and regulations, just like any cultural, commercial, industrial and social associations.[19]

Thich Nhat Hanh further angered government authorities by his public support for the Dalai Lama and condemnation of Chinese persecution of the Dalai Lama's followers in Tibet. Thich Nhat Hanh's comments resulted in unwelcomed Chinese diplomatic intervention with the Vietnamese government. In these circumstances, the government's attitude toward Thich Nhat Hanh and his followers turned vindictive and they were violently expelled from Bat Nha monastery.

Degar ethnic minority

Vietnam is a multiethnic state. Ethnic minorities comprise about fifteen percent of the total population. During the Vietnam War several ethnic minority groups (also known as Montagnards) developed a collective sense of identity in response to the migration of lowland Vietnamese into the Central Highland. Collectively they adopted the name Degar. In the mid-1960s the Degar ethnic minority formed a political movement known as Front Uni de Lutte des Races Opprimées or FULRO to advance their cause. After unification some elements of FULRO resisted the imposition of communist rule; however, by the mid-1990s they were a spent force.

In February–March 2001 a major outbreak of unrest involving several thousand Degar took place in three provinces in the Central Highlands. National security authorities were quick to blame "outside hostile forces" whom they identified as the Montagnard Foundation in the United States and FULRO remnants.

The regular Vietnam People's Army (VPA) has been very circumspect about becoming involved in internal security that involves a direct confrontation with the public. The VPA prefers that the PASF assume primary responsibility for internal security. Nevertheless, at least thirteen army regiments were posted to the Central Highlands to provide area security by manning checkpoints and securing the border with Cambodia to prevent the flight of ethnic minorities (Thayer 2011). Soldiers were billeted with local families and political cadres directed a campaign of public education designed to calm the situation and prevent illegal departures. Further waves of unrest broke out in the Central Highlands in August 2001 and April 2004.[20]

In 2009, one hundred Degar, who had been arrested and imprisoned following disturbances in 2001 and 2004, were released. International human rights groups claim that several hundred ethnic minority demonstrators associated with the 2004 Central Highlands protests still remain incarcerated. These same sources claim that the Degar, who converted to Christianity, are subject to religious persecution and continued political repression (Human Rights Watch 2011).

The three components of repression

This section analyzes the main components of state repression: monitoring and surveillance; harassment and intimidation of individuals of concern, family members, and employers; and arrest, detention, trial, imprisonment, and house arrest after release.

Monitoring and surveillance

Vietnamese security forces employ both a widespread territorial surveillance network and sophisticated electronic monitoring technology to identify and surveil individuals and groups that are considered politically subversive. Once sufficient information has been gathered to confirm that an individual or group has engaged in activities in violation of Article 88 (or other articles) of the Penal Code, the individual or group is then subjected to harassment and intimidation.

The MPS's General Department of Public Security is organized territorially with offices in all of Vietnam's 59 provinces and five municipalities (Hanoi, Ho Chi Minh City, Can Tho, Da Nang, and Hai Phong). Public Security officers are also assigned at district and city ward levels where they conduct surveillance and report on the activities of pro-democracy and religious freedom advocates. Territorial surveillance includes the extensive use of local informants.

The case of Bloc 8406 is illustrative of how public security conducts monitoring and surveillance. Prior to and during the 2006 APEC summit in Hanoi, for example, the security police cordoned off the streets where members of Bloc 8406 lived, disconnected their phones, and restricted their movements. Notices were posted barring foreigners from entry and uniformed police were conspicuously posted to enforce these measures.

When the Internet was first introduced in Vietnam government authorities set up firewalls to prevent access to sites they considered politically subversive. These included sites maintained by overseas Vietnamese anti-communist groups, international human rights organizations, and international news outlets such as the Vietnamese language services of Radio Free Asia and the Voice of America. The restrictions on Voice of America were relaxed in 2009 but remain in place for Radio Free Asia. In late December 2009, these firewalls were extended momentarily to the Vietnamese service of the BBC and intermittently to *Facebook*.

The MPS and General Directorate II regularly monitor telephones, facsimile transmissions, post, email, Internet, and mobile phones. Members of Bloc 8406 have attempted to evade detection by utilizing digital telephone and encryption technology on websites provided by Voice Over Internet Protocol (IP) providers such as *PalTalk*, *Skype* and *Yahoo! Messenger* to organize chat room discussions within Vietnam as well as overseas.

In 2008–09, Vietnamese officials faced a growing challenge to their authority by bloggers who posted political commentary on the Internet and who had no discernable connections to pro-democracy activists (Hoang et al. 2009). For example, in early 2009 a group of seven hundred individuals signed up to a *Facebook* site to promote their opposition to bauxite mining.[21] Other environmental activists founded an extremely popular website devoted to the bauxite mining controversy. A number of independent bloggers also became active and attracted popular interest in their blogs.

CPV leaders were placed in the uncomfortable position of having to defend their handling of Vietnam's relations with China from criticism by nationalist-minded patriotic citizens including members of the political elite. The regime responded by cracking down on its critics and moved to curtail blogging on the Internet. In May 2010, Lt. Gen Vu Hai Trieu, Deputy Director of General Directorate II, announced to a press conference that his department had "destroyed 300 bad internet web pages and individual blogs."[22]

Government critics charged that GD II had come under Beijing's political influence and was using its sophisticated electronic equipment to identify anti-China activists.[23] In 2010, a series of Denial of Service Attacks on *Thong Luan*, a political commentary website, and *Dong Chua Cuu The Viet Nam*, a Catholic website, were traced to IP addresses belonging to Viettel, a company owned by the MND.[24]

It is likely that specialists units within the MPS were also involved in the unprecedented cyber attacks directed against independent blog sites that began in September 2009 and intensified in April–May 2010. During this period cyber attacks were launched against more than two dozen websites and blogs maintained by Catholic land activists, political discussion forums, opposition political groups, and environmentalists concerned with bauxite mining.

Hackers penetrated the *Osin* blog site in January 2010 and posted fabricated messages stating that the owner, journalist Huy Duc, was retiring because he "ran out of new ideas."[25] A fabricated note also appeared on *DCVOnline*, a news and discussion site, announcing the site's closure due to internal conflict. Hackers accessed the discussion forum *x-cafevn.org's* database and posted the login names, email, location, and IP addresses of over 19,000 users on the web. Fabricated profiles of administrators and activists associated with *x-cafevn.org* were posted on www.x-cafenv.db.info. In sum, "[t]he objective was to make the web community believe that Hanoi's intelligence agents working with hackers could obtain dossiers on virtually any Vietnamese activist or internet user."[26]

Independent investigations by Google and McAfee, a reputable major Internet security company, determined that the majority of command and control servers involved in the cyber attacks were executed through IP addresses inside Vietnam. McAfee's chief technical officer, George Kurtz, concluded, "we believe that the perpetrators may have political motivations and may have some allegiance to the government of the

Socialist Republic of Viet Nam ... This is likely the latest example of *hacktivism and politically motivated cyber attacks.*"[27]

Investigations conducted by Google and McAfee determined that the cyber attacks used botnet malware (W32/Vulvanbot) disguised as Vietnamese language software VPSKeys to penetrate blog sites, gather information on users, and then direct massive Denial of Service attacks against offending websites and overseas Vietnamese computer users who accessed these sites. Neel Mehta, a member of Google's security team, concluded that the cyber attacks were directed "against blogs containing messages of political dissent. Specifically, these attacks have tried to *squelch opposition to bauxite mining efforts* in Viet Nam."[28] In December 2009–January 2010 Distributed Denial of Service attacks caused the website *bauxiteViet Nam.info* to crash.

Harassment, intimidation, and violence

The use of harassment and intimidation as tactics of repression is not a phenomenon unique to Vietnam; they are employed worldwide by authoritarian regimes. In the case of Vietnam, intimidation and repression have a legacy as old as the communist state itself. These tactics remain in place and are employed by security authorities with no apparent accountability despite a general loosening of state controls over society in the years following the formal adoption of *doi moi*.

Vietnamese state security agencies regularly employ an array of techniques designed to harass and intimidate politically active citizens with the aim of dissuading them from continuing their criticism of government policy. Such techniques include, but are not limited to, cutting telephone service, confiscation of passports and refusal to grant permission to travel overseas, visits by security officials to the homes of individuals of concern, pressure on family members, visits to employers, public denunciation, media vilification, raids on homes and confiscation of electronic devices, long working sessions to interrogate activists, and the use of violence by gangs of plain-clothed police, army veterans, revolutionary youth, and others. The U.S. State Department reported in 2009 "[c]redible reports suggested that local police forces used 'contract thugs' and 'citizen brigades' to harass and beat political activists and others, including religious worshippers, perceived as 'undesirable' or a 'threat' to public security" (United States Department of State 2010).

Prior to and during the 2006 APEC summit in Hanoi, as noted above, the police harassed several of the more prominent signatories of the April 8, 2006 manifesto by sealing off their homes, restricting their movements and disconnecting their phones. Other Bloc 8406 members were picked up for interrogation and detained for varying periods. Employers who were pressured to terminate the employment of Bloc 8408 members complied. For example, in July 2008, as a result of pressure from state security officials, Bloc 8406 activist Vu Van Hung was dismissed from his teaching job.

The experiences of two prominent members of Bloc 8406 illustrate the use of harassment and intimidation by the MPS's A42 unit.

A Hanoi-based journalist reported with respect to lawyer Nguyen Van Dai:

> In September 2006 Nguyen Van Dai was called by his father and told that if he continued to act as a lawyer for dissidents, the two of them wouldn't be allowed to meet. One of the staff in Dai's office, a young woman, described how the police had met her friends and told them that she was working for a bad person and they should try to make her stop. (Hayton 2010: 124)

The same source provided these details on Le Thi Cong Nhan, a lawyer, supporter of Bloc 8406, and founding member of the Vietnam Progression Party:

> Almost immediately after she joined the Progression Party, Cong Nhan was visited at home by officers from A42. She was taken to the police station, told that she was guilty of plotting to bring down the state and questioned for three days, in the course of which she says she was told that, "many bad things could happen to me". When she refused to attend any more questioning sessions the police bombarded her with calls and text messages threatening her with arrest. One officer reminded her that the police were listening to all her phone calls. But then suddenly, the tactics changed. "They sent me flowers, invitations to dinner and the cinema, even a new mobile phone". The emails now called her brave and kind and asked her to explain her motivations and dreams for the country. At the same time, though, A42 were leaning on her family and friends to press her to stop her activities. (Hayton 2010: 124)

The tactic of public denunciation involves the mobilization of neighbors to shout abuse – and occasionally use physical force – to intimidate an individual targeted by public security officials. The examples of Hoang Minh Chinh, Tran Khai Thanh Thuy and Nguyen Van Dai are illustrative.

In 2005, Hoang Minh Chinh, the organizer of the revived Vietnam Democratic Party (XXI), went to the United States for medical treatment. While in the U.S. Chinh testified before the Committee on International Relations of the House of Representatives. This resulted in an orchestrated campaign of denunciation in the Vietnamese state media during the second half of October.

In December 2005, when Chinh returned to his home in Hanoi, he was confronted by a crowd of several dozen demonstrators who denounced him for his action. Members of the crowd threw tomatoes and others struck Chinh with plastic water bottles. The entire incident was filmed by six cameramen. The crowd pursued Chinh into his courtyard and demanded entry into his house. When family members called for police assistance they received evasive replies. Eventually three members of emergency police Unit 113 showed up but declined to take action. According to Chinh's account:

> the crazy crowd ordered us "to open the door in five minutes or it will be destroyed." My children continued to stand fast as some members of the mob successfully broke the window panes, jumped in and tried to force the door down while others used sticks to hit other windows and threw bottles of stinking shrimp paste inside my house. It was a scary horrible moment.

> Then, as suddenly as it began, the crowd dispersed as if on cue. Eyewitnesses reported that a group of ten policemen stood in the alley outside but took no action. Chinh later concluded, "it was the police who organized the disturbances".[29]

The second example concerns Tran Khai Thanh Thuy, a noted novelist and political essayist. In 2006 she founded an association for victims whose land had been confiscated (*Hoi Dan Oan Viet Nam*) and the Independent Workers' Union of Vietnam. She was also an active blogger and member of the editorial board of an underground pro-democracy bulletin, *To Quoc* (Fatherland). In 2006, Thuy was forced to participate in a so-called people's court at which police mobilized 300 people in a public stadium to shout insults at her. She was arrested in April 2007, released in January 2008. Since then she has been subjected to

> relentless harassment from police, local officials, and orchestrated neighborhood gangs.

> During 2009, for example, thugs attacked her house at least 14 times, throwing excrement and dead rodents at her gate. They also inserted

metal into her front door lock on two occasions, locking her out of her own home. When she went to the police to file a complaint, they refused to take any action, even through neighbors reported that police were watching some of the attacks on her home.[30]

On February 8, 2007, lawyer Nguyen Van Dai was brought before a meeting of 200 elderly residents of Bach Khoa Ward in Hanoi and subject to two and a half hours of abuse and accusations. The denunciation session ended after approving a motion finding him guilty of violating Articles 88 and 258 of the Penal Code and calling for the revocation of his law license, disbarment, the closure of his law office, and criminal prosecution (Hayton 2010: 124).

Over the seven-month period from November 2009 to May 2010, Vietnam detained four independent bloggers and subjected them to extended interrogations. In 2009, journalist Huy Duc blogged under the pseudonym *Osin* and wrote commentaries about human rights in the Soviet Union. He was fired from his job with *Saigon Thiep Thi* (Saigon Marketing) newspaper as a result of pressure from security officials.

Bui Thanh Hieu, who blogged under the name *Nguoi Buon Gio* (Wind Trader or Wind Merchant), posted commentary critical of Vietnam's handling of relations with China, Catholic land disputes, and bauxite mining. Hieu was repeatedly interrogated by police in 2008–09 for his role in instigating anti-China protests and arrested in August.[31]

Nguyen Ngoc Nhu Quynh, who blogged under the name *Me Nam* (Mother Mushroom), also posted blogs that discussed relations with China, bauxite mining, and territorial disputes in the South China Sea. She was questioned by police for her involvement in printing t-shirts with the slogan "No Bauxite, No China; Spratlys and Paracels belong to Viet Nam."[32]

Finally, blogger Pham Doan Trang was detained under provisions of Vietnam's national security law for her postings on the South China Sea, the 1954 partitioning of Vietnam, and China's role as a hegemonic power.[33] She was later released when police concluded that she was not linked to any political dissident network. For her part, Trang stated she would only discuss personal matters on the Internet and vowed to steer clear of political topics.

In 2007–08 a land dispute erupted between the Catholic Church and the state over property claimed by Thai Hoa parish and the property of the former Vatican representative in Hanoi. On two occasions crowds were organized to ransack the chapel at the Hanoi Redemptorist monastery. The first attack took place on September 21, 2008 and involved a group of 200 youths wearing blue Communist Youth League shirts.³⁴ The second attack took place under cover of night on November 15, 2008. Local church officials had no doubt that the gangs were organized by local security officers. During the second incident hundreds of police armed with stun guns stood by and took no action.³⁵

During the Catholic Church land protests in Tam Toa parish in central Vietnam in 2009, local authorities resorted to similar heavy-handed tactics. On July 20, after Catholics erected a tent chapel on the cathedral grounds, they were evicted by police who used tear gas and electric stun guns. Local church officials accused the police of brutality and demanded the release of eleven parishioners who had been taken into custody.³⁶

On July 21, 2009, government authorities launched a media blitz in virtually every state outlet characterizing the Catholics who had been arrested as "stubborn, organized criminals" who had disturbed public order and directly challenged the national security and integrity of the state.³⁷ For example, state media reported that the police charged those arrested with "counter-revolutionary crimes, violating state policies on American War Crimes Memorial Sites, disturbing public order, and attacking officials on duty."³⁸ When local authorities summoned Church officials, they refused to comply and demanded the release of those detained, the return of Church property, compensation, and a halt to vilification by the state media.

During July and August 2009, Catholic media reported repeated attacks on parishioners and priests by plain-clothed police and gangs of thugs. On July 26, Father Paul Nguyen Dinh Phu and Father Peter The Binh were beaten by a gang reportedly acting on police instructions when the priests attempted to intervene in a physical confrontation between police and three Catholic women demonstrators in Vinh. Both priests were admitted to hospital in Dong Hoi. The gang of thugs forced their way into the hospital and allegedly threw Father Phu out the second floor window. Witnesses claimed that thirty police stood by and took no action.³⁹

The state further responded to Catholic land protests with an unprecedented campaign of vilification in the state media and by blocking Catholic websites.⁴⁰ The state media also carried government assertions denying any responsibility or involvement in any act of violence. The Catholic land protests in Hanoi and Tam Toa were both ended when local authorities dispatched bulldozers to level the land in order to convert the disputed sites into public parks.⁴¹

Thich Nhat Hanh's Zen Buddhist followers faced similar tactics of intimidation and violence. When the Abbot of Bat Nha rescinded his invitation to Hanh's followers to stay at Ba Nha monastery they refused to leave. The Abbot ordered his monks to cut off power, water, and telephone connections. When these tactics failed, local authorities set a deadline of September 2 for them to leave. This deadline passed. On September 17, the District People's Committee in Lam Dong province issued a confidential memo alleging that Hanh's followers were engaged in illegal activities and "abusing the religious regulations of the Communist Party and the Government, to sabotage the Government and oppose the Viet Nam Buddhist Church."[42] Government officials were instructed to force Hanh's followers to leave Bat Nha and disperse them to Buddhist pagodas that were under the control of the Vietnam Buddhist Church or to return to their home villages.

On September 27, a mob estimated at between 100 and 150, including plain-clothed police, armed with knives, sledge hammers, and sticks, invaded the monastery and forcibly evicted 150 monks and then ransacked the place. Uniformed police sealed off the area but took no action. Hanh's followers were bundled into buses, trucks, and cars and driven some distance away and left by the side of the road. Others were forced to flee on foot. On the following day, the mob returned and set upon 200 mainly youthful nuns and female novices forcing them to flee to nearby Phuc Hue temple where they were placed under police guard. Three leaders were held incommunicado in detention. Uniformed police set up checkpoints to prevent Hanh's followers and local supporters from returning to Bat Nha.[43]

Although the general security situation in the Central Highlands has been brought under control since 2004, there have been continual reports of violent incidents between local security forces and the Degar ethnic minority (Montagnard Foundation 2008). During this period security forces continued to raid the homes of Degar Christians when religious services were being held, and arrest and detain those considered leaders. In 2009, for example, the U.S. State Department reported police harassment of Protestant house churches in Dak Lak and Gia Lai provinces. In other instances, security forces reportedly summoned Degar villages to public meetings and pressured them into renouncing their religion. In April 2010, three Degar Christians were arrested and interrogated for using their homes for worship and refusing to join the official government-approved Protestant Church.[44]

Degar taken into custody report a range of pressures from intimidation to physical abuse to force them to sign a document renouncing their faith and/or declaring their membership in the state-approved Evangelical Church of Vietnam. There are also numerous but unverified reports of regular public protests by Degar outside commune and district offices. On occasion police use chemical sprays and electric stun guns to disperse crowds.

Arrest, detention, trial, and imprisonment

The third major component of state repression involves arrest, seizure of property, interrogation, plea-bargained confession, perfunctory trial, sentencing, imprisonment, rejection of appeal, physical abuse in prison, and house arrest after release. In 2008, government security officials involuntarily committed political activists to mental hospitals as a tactic of repression.

After the 2006 APEC summit, Vietnam brought to trial the leaders of Bloc 8406. Seven members of Bloc 8406 who had been arrested were put on trial during a six-week period commencing in May 2007. On May 11, 2007, Le Thi Cong Nhan and Nguyen Van Dai were given a trial lasting four hours and sentenced, respectively, to four and five years in prison for "spreading anti-state propaganda." Their sentences were slightly reduced later in the year.

Three other political dissidents (Vu Van Hung, Pham Van Troi, and Tran Duc Thach) were given separate trials in Hanoi. Hung was arrested on September 14, 2008 for hanging a pro-democracy banner from an overpass in Hanoi. He was reportedly beaten by police while in custody. He went on a hunger strike and in protest during which his health deteriorated badly. While in custody the police visited his family and pressured them to sign an affidavit indicating he was in poor mental health. They refused. Hung was sentenced on October 6 to three years in prison and three years' probation for violating Article 88. Pham Van Troi and Tran Duc Thach were also tried and convicted under Article 88; they were sentenced, respectively, to four years in prison and four years' probation, and three years in prison and three years' probation.

In May–July 2009, Vietnamese public security officials rounded up seven political activists associated with an informal pro-democracy network. Tran Huynh Duy Thuc, Le Thanh Long, Le Cong Dinh, Nguyen Tien Trung, and Tran Anh Kim were charged under Article 88 of the Penal Code for conducting propaganda against the state or "colluding with domestic and foreign reactionaries to sabotage the state." This offense carried a maximum penalty of twenty years' imprisonment. Le Thi Thu Thu and Tran Thi Thu were not charged but detained pending further investigation.

In December 2009, lawyers representing the five arrested dissidents reported that state authorities had amended the charges to include violation of Article 79 of the Penal Code that carried a maximum death penalty for "carrying out activities aimed at overthrowing the people's administration".[45]

On May 26, 2009, Tran Huynh Duy Thuc was the first to be arrested. He was charged under Article 88 with distorting "the policies, laws, and directions of the Vietnamese government." Information gleaned from Duy Thuc's interrogation led to the arrests of Le Thanh Long and Le Cong Dinh in June. Dinh's arrest was executed by what public security sources called an "expedited procedure."[46] Dinh served as the defense lawyer for Bloc 8406 activists and was a member of the Vietnam Democratic Party.

The state's handling of Le Cong Dinh's case represented an unprecedented use of "information warfare" by security officials (Thayer 2010b). Dinh's arrest was announced at simultaneous press conferences in Hanoi and Ho Chi Minh City by senior officials from the MPS.[47] An orchestrated propaganda campaign was conducted in the state-controlled press, radio, and television. Dinh's affidavit was released publicly and characterized as a confession. The Vietnam Lawyers' Association struck him from its books, effectively barring him from practicing law.[48] In sum, Dinh was virtually tried and convicted before appearing in court. Dinh was later subjected to perfunctory legal proceedings before being sentenced to jail.

In March 2008, after returning to Vietnam, Nguyen Tien Trung was drafted into the army. He refused to swear the oath of allegiance, and in mid-2009 immediately after he was discharged he was arrested for refusing to obey his superiors. The state media reported that Trung played a role in organizing anti-China student demonstrations in late 2007 and protests against China's Olympic torch relay when it passed through Vietnam in 2008. Tran Anh Kim was a retired military officer who became politically active in the pro-democracy movement. Trung and Kim were both arrested in July.[49]

On August 19, 2009, the five above-mentioned defendants appeared on state television with their heads bowed and publicly admitted to "undermining and overthrowing the Vietnamese state." The following day the state media triumphantly reported that the dissidents had "plead guilty and begged for leniency."[50]

In October 2009, security officials bundled together the cases of nine other political dissidents and conducted perfunctory trials in Hanoi and Haiphong. All defendants were found guilty, sentenced from two to six years' imprisonment plus an additional two to three years under house arrest.

Six dissidents were tried as a group in court proceedings in Haiphong for their role in hanging banners in public in Haiphong and Hai Duong in August and September 2008, respectively. The banners displayed slogans reading "no democracy, freedom or human rights because of the communist regime."[51] The banners also accused the government of corruption, failure to control inflation, and "losing the islands to China," a reference to the Paracel and Spratly archipelagos in the South China Sea.

The "Haiphong Six" were charged under Article 88 of the Penal Code. The alleged leader of this group, Nguyen Xuan Nghia, was a writer associated with Bloc 8406. He was charged with posting 57 articles on the Internet. Nghia was sentenced to six years' imprisonment. Nguyen Van Tuc, a farmer and land rights activist, was sentenced to four years. Nguyen Van Tinh, an essayist, and Nguyen Man Son, a former party member who published 22 articles on the Internet, were each sentenced to three and a half years. Nguyen Kim Nhan, an electrician, was given a two-year sentence plus two years on probation. Ngo Quynh, a university student who planned a demonstration timed for the arrival of China's Olympic torch in Ho Chi Minh City, was sentenced to three years.[52]

Degar Christians who were held in detention for long periods report regular beatings and torture at the hands of local police. In May 2008, Y Ben Hdok, a Degar from Dak Lak, died while in detention without a satisfactory explanation by authorities. The U.S. Department of State reported that in 2009, unlike previous years, there were no credible reports of deaths in police custody. However, in March 2010, K'pa Lot, a Degar Christian, reportedly died after a long period of abuse and torture after he was released from custody and moved to a hospital. Human right activists report this is a common practice by police to conceal physical abuse in prison.[53]

The Degar advocacy group, Montagnard Foundation, sums up the situation for ethnic minority Christians in this way:

> This tactic of harassing, beating and torturing Degar Christians is part of the Vietnamese communist government policy to repress house church Christians. Numerous incidents have been reported of security forces randomly summoning Degars for questions regarding their religious beliefs and activities. While some sessions involve Degars detained for long periods of time other involve release under house surveillance. Many arrests involve torture, beatings, imprisonment and even killings of Degars.[54]

Conclusion

As noted in the introduction, the purpose of this chapter is to address an aspect of Vietnamese politics that has largely been ignored by political scientists who focus on the interaction between state and society. This chapter has attempted to break new ground by shifting the focus from political activists and their networks and nascent political groups and parties to the apparatus of state repression in contemporary Vietnam.

This chapter presented an overview of the main organizations involved – the MPS, the PASF, General Directorate II, and the MCI. The chapter has also explored three main components of state repression: monitoring and surveillance; harassment and intimidation; and arrest, detention, trial, and imprisonment.

It is clear from this preliminary analysis that Vietnam devotes massive human and technical resources to monitoring and conducting surveillance over its citizens. Great effort is put into monitoring, controlling, and restricting Internet usage. The enormity of resources devoted for these purposes contrasts with the comparatively small number of political activists, religious leaders, and bloggers who have been arrested, tried, and sentenced to prison. The main exception has been the state's repressive treatment of the largely Protestant Degar ethnic minority in the Central Highlands.

This study highlights that public security authorities in Vietnam conduct their business with impunity and without accountability despite constitutional, legal, and international treaty commitments to the rule of law. The MPS operates within a legal framework that curbs freedom of speech, publication, and assembly. The MPS is free to determine which public manifestations of political dissent should be dealt with under the vaguely worded Article 88 of the Penal Code. The MPS also is not constrained by law from leaking information from its files that is then published by the state-controlled media to smear the reputations of political dissidents. In sum, constitutional and legal provisions are routinely observed in the breach. When all else fails "clubs are trumps" as the state stacks the deck with falsified information and manipulation of the media.

Notes

1. See: Carlyle A. Thayer. Book Review: Zuezhi Guo, *"China's Security State: Philosophy, Evolution, and Politics." Nordic Journal of Human Rights* 31, no. 2 (2013): 279–83.
2. A 2006 study of Vietnam's efforts to control Internet usage revealed that the Ministry of Public Security gave priority to blocking access to websites that

contained information related to Vietnam's 1999 land border treaty with China and other political sensitive commentary; OpenNet Initiative. *Internet Filtering in Viet Nam in 2005–2006: A Country Study*, August 2006. http://www. opennet.net/studies/vietnam/. Accessed July 23, 2011.

3. Robert Karniol. "Vietnamese Army Enhances Monitoring." *Janes's Defence Weekly*, October 31, 2005.

4. Vietnam News Agency, July 12, 2001.

5. Shawn W. Crispin. "Chinese Shadow Over Vietnamese Repression." *Asia Times Online*, September 13, 2009, available at <http://www.atimes.com/ atimes/China/KI12Ad04.html> Accessed September 14, 2009.

6. Confidential email from diplomatic source in Hanoi to the author, March 26, 2001.

7. Agence France-Presse, March 25, 2001; a slightly different translation appears in Agence France-Presse, April 23, 2001.

8. General Department II was also criticized by leading dissidents, see: Nguyen Thanh Giang, "Ve vu an chinh tri sieu nghiem trong lien quan den Tong cuc 2" [About the Very Serious Case Involving Tong Cuc 2], August 19, 2004. This was a letter Giang sent to the leaders of the party, state, government, and National Assembly, available at <http://www.lenduong.net> Accessed September 9, 2006.

9. In August 2007, the Ministry of Culture and Information temporarily closed a popular Hanoi website launched by VVT Innovative Solutions Co. Ltd. VVT was charged with permitting the publication of articles with "inaccurate information" that violated the Press Law and Government Decree No. 55. Authorities took particular exception to material on a web forum that criticized the government for reportedly making concessions to China during negotiations on the 1999 border treaty and material that discussed corruption in the CPV, relations with the United States, and demands for political change.

10. Agence France-Presse, "Amid Crackdown, Two Blogs Shuttered in Vietnam," February 12, 2010.

11. Ben Stocking, "Viet Nam Court Convicts Catholics in Land Dispute," Associated Press, December 8, 2009, available at <http://googe.com/hotednews/ap/article> Accessed December 16, 2009.

12. Thuy Huong. "Catholics Shocked by Press Award Announcement." *VietCatholic News*, January 22, 2009, available at <http://www.vietcatholic. net/News/Html/63467.htm> Accessed January 25, 2009 and Emily Nguyen. "Vietnamese Chairman's Visit to Vatican Under Catholics' Watchful Eyes." *VietCatholic News*, July 28, 2009, Email copy available at <vnews-l@anu.edu. au> Accessed July 29, 2009.

13. People's Committee of Hanoi City. "Decision Promulgating Stipulations on the Management, Provision, and Use of Internet Services at Retails Locations in Hanoi City." Viet Tan Party, June 4, 2010, available at <http://www.viettan. org/spip.php?page=print&id_article=9859> Accessed June 8, 2010.

14. Chloe Albanesius. "Google Criticizes Vietnam's 'Net Sniffing App'." *PC Magazine*, June 11, 2010, available at <http://www.pcmag.com/ article2/0,2817,2364950,00.sap> Accessed June 14, 2010.

15. Members of Bloc 8406 produced a fortnightly publication, *Tu Do Ngon Luan* (Free Speech) that first appeared on April 15, 2006. A typical issue comprised thirty pages of text. *Tu Do Ngon Luan* was published in A4 format in both

hardcopy and electronically. The online version was published as a portable document file. *Tu Do Ngon Luan* was edited by three Catholic priests, Nguyen Van Ly, Phan Van Loi, and Chan Tin.

16. Quoted by *VietCatholic News*, May 26, 2009.
17. Thuy Dung and Trung Tin. "Fresh Mass Demonstrations in Vinh and in Other Parts of Viet Nam in Support of Catholics." AsiaNews.it, August 3, 2009, available at <http://www.asianews.it/viewprint.php?l=en&art=15953> Accessed August 4, 2009.
18. On August 12, 2009, the Conference of Catholic Bishops issued a statement expressing concern over rising tensions and calling for a peaceful dialogue. J.B. An. Dang. "Viet Bishops Call for Peaceful Dialogue." *VietCatholic News*, August 13, 2009, available at <http://www.vietcatholic.net/News/ Html/70124.htm> Accessed August 15, 2009. Available at <http://www. vietcatholic.net/News/Html/61022.htm> Accessed November 17, 2009 and Emily Nguyen. "Catholic Sites Blocked in Viet Nam." *VietCatholic News*, August 5, 2009, available at <http://vietcatholic.net/News/Html/69896.htm> Accessed August 7, 2009.
19. Human Rights Watch. "Vietnam: Sharp Backsliding on Religious Freedom." *UNHCR Refworld*, October 18, 2009, available at <http://www.unhcr.org/ refworld/docid/4add69001a.html> Accessed July 22, 2011.
20. In November–December 2004, over 200 Degar persons were arrested and detained.
21. "Bauxite Bashers." *The Economist*, April 23, 2009.
22. Human Rights Watch Asia. "Viet Nam: Stop Cyber Attacks against Online Critics." May 27, 2010.
23. Crispin. "Chinese Shadow Over Vietnamese Repression." op. cit.
24. Human Rights Watch Asia. "Viet Nam: Stop Cyber Attacks against Online Critics." May 27, 2010.
25. Viet Tan Party. "Denial of Service: Cyberattacks by the Vietnamese Government." April 27, 2010, available at <http://www.viettan.org/spip. php?page=print&id_article-9749> Accessed April 29, 2010.
26. Ibid.
27. Human Rights Watch Asia. "Viet Nam: Stop Cyber Attacks Against Online Critics." May 27, 2010, emphasis in original.
28. Ibid.
29. Hoang Minh Chinh, "Urgent Report No. 2 by Citizen Hoang Minh Chinh of Socialist Republic of Viet Nam to: Secretary General Nong Duc Manh, Chief of State Tran Duc Luong, Prime Minister Phan Van Khai, National Assembly Chairman Nguyen Van An, Director of Public Security, Hanoi, People's Court of Hanoi, People's Court of Investigation of Hanoi, Also to: Ms. Louise Arbour, United Nations High Commissioner for Human Rights, International human rights organizations, Democracies' Congress and Government, National and international media, Vietnamese inside and outside Viet Nam, and concerned people," December 2, 2005.http://www.flickr.com/photos/ saigonusanews/71011141/. Accessed July 24, 2011.
30. Human Rights Watch Asia. "Vietnam: Expanding Campaign to Silence Dissent." February 4, 2010. Thuy was permitted to resettle in the United States in July 2011, available at <http://www.hrw.org/en/news/2010/02/04/ vietnam-expanding-campaign-silence-dissent> Accessed July 24, 2011.

31. Stocking, "Viet Nam Court Convicts Catholics in Land Dispute." op. cit.
32. Ibid.
33. Deutsche Presse Agentur, August 31, 2009
34. J.B. An. Dang. "Redemptorists Threatened to Be Killed. Priests and Faithful Humiliated." *VietCatholic News*, September 22, 2008, available at <http://222. vietcatholic.net/News/Html/58958.htm> Accessed September 23, 2008.
35. J.B. An. Dang. "Pro-Government Thugs Attack Hanoi Redemptorist Monastery." *VietCatholic News*, November 15, 2008, available at <http:// www.catholic.net/News/Htmo/61022.htm> Accessed November 17, 2008.
36. Agence France Press July 21, 2009, Associated Press July 21, 2009 and Reuters July 22, 2009.
37. Nguyen. "Vietnamese Chairman's Visit to Vatican Under Catholics' Watchful Eyes." op. cit.
38. J.B. An. Dang. "Half Million Vietnamese Catholics of Vinh Diocese protest against police's brutality." *VietCatholic News*, July 26, 2009, available at <http://www.vietcatholic.net/News?Html/69468.htm> Accessed August 1, 2009.
39. J.B. An. Dang. "Priest Beaten into a Coma by Police. Catholics Protest throughout Vietnam." *AsiaNews.it*, July 28, 2009, available at <http://www. asianews.it/view4print.php?1-en&artk=15896> Accessed July 31, 2009; J.B. An. Dang. "Anti-Catholic Violence Designed to Hide Crisis and Graft in Vietnam's Communist Party." *AsiaNews.it*, August 5, 2009, available at <http://www.asianews.it/view4print.php?l=en&art=15967> Accessed August 7, 2009; and Nguyen. "Vietnamese Chairman's Visit to Vatican Under Catholics' Watchful Eyes." op. cit.
40. Huong. "Catholics Shocked by Press Award Announcement." op. cit. and Nguyen. "Vietnamese Chairman's Visit to Vatican under Catholics' Watchful Eyes." op. cit.
41. Emily Nguyen. "Tam Toa Parishioners Helpless and in Awe as Their Church Land Being Bulldozed by Quang Binh Government." *VietCatholic News*, August 22, 2009, available at <http://www.vietcatholic.new?News/Clients/ ReadArticle.aspx?ID=70415> Accessed August 24, 2009.
42. Martin Barillas. "Vietnam: Sharp Backsliding on Religious Freedom Harsh Crackdown on Followers of Buddhist Peace Activist Thich Nhat Hanh." October 19, 2009, available at <http://www.impactwire.com/a/517/Vietnam-Shart-Blacksliding-on-Religious-Freedom> Accessed November 9, 2009.
43. Human Rights Watch. "Vietnam: Sharp Backsliding on Religious Freedom." op. cit.
44. Montagnard Foundation. "Three Degar Christians Arrested – One Tortured for Refusing to Joint the Government Church – Security Policy Identified." Press Release, May 21, 2010.
45. Deutche Presse Agentur, December 11, 2009.
46. J.B. An. Dang. "Lawyer Arrested in an 'Urgent Procedure'." *VietCatholic News*, June 13, 2009, available at <http://www.vietcatholic.net/News/Html/68187. htm> Accessed June 15, 2009.
47. Dang. "Lawyer Arrested in an 'Urgent Procedure'." op. cit. and Le Nga, Minh Nam and Thai Uyen. "Lawyer Arrested for Subversion, Police Say." *Thanh Nien News*, June 14, 2009, available at <http://www.thanhniennews.com/ print.php?catid=3&newsid=49796> Accessed June 15, 2009.

48. Dam De and Vu Nhu. "Le Cong Dinh ejected by HCM Bar Association." *VietNamNet Bridge*, June 23, 2009, available at <http://vietnamnet.vn/service/printversion.vnn?article_id=1215620> Accessed June 24, 2009.
49. Ha Truong. "Two Men Arrested for Anti-State Activities." *VietNamNet Bridge*, July 7, 2009, available at <http://vietnam.net.vn/service/printversion.vnn?article_id1220927> Accessed July 7, 2009.
50. "Confessions of Crimes." *Nhan Dan On Line*, August 20, 2009.
51. Agence France Presse, October 8, 2009.
52. John Ruwitch. "Nine Convictions in Vietnam Send Signal before Congress." Reuters, October 9, 2009, available at <http://in.reuters.com/article/worldNews/idINIndia-43040520091009>Accessed October 10, 2009.
53. International Christian Concern, April 30, 2010.
54. Montagnard Foundation. "Three Degar Christians Arrested." op. cit.

8
The Political Influence of Civil Society in Vietnam

Andrew Wells-Dang

A contrast between "glass half-full" and "glass (mostly) empty" portrayals of Vietnam can be found in multiple areas of politics and society: compare the pragmatic policy-making processes described by Jandl in this volume with the persistent rent-seeking found by Vu, or the paradox of a repressive state apparatus (Thayer) with varying degrees of tolerance toward dissent in practice (Kerkvliet). The gap between enthusiasm and gloom is perhaps at its starkest in the analyses of civil society. Some Vietnamese and external observers find encouraging signs of associational growth, while others lament (or celebrate) the Communist Party's continuing control. Is "civil society" (*xã hội dân sự*) at base a cooperative force for sustainable development and poverty reduction, or a political movement aiming for system-wide change?

A few of the stylized facts about civil society and social organizations in Vietnam may be summarized as follows. First, Vietnam has a history of local social autonomy based on clan and religious structures in which, proverbially, "the king's edict stops at the village gates" (*Phép vua thua lệ làng*). National and regional political systems, however, have been uniformly autocratic and relatively centralized. There is no organized democratic political tradition: the diversity of social and political organizations that contended before the 1945 revolution and 1975 reunification was replaced by the victorious communists with a corporatist structure of mass organizations representing various sectors and constituencies.[1] For a time at least, the Party kept a "near-total grip on society" (Vu, this volume), but this has weakened during the Đổi mới ("Renewal") process. The emergence (or reemergence) of urban-based development organizations has occurred alongside an expansion of personal and economic freedoms since the late 1980s (Nørlund 2006).

On paper, the space for civil society action in Vietnam still appears highly restrictive. The Communist Party-dominated state keeps firm control of registration of associations and nongovernmental organizations (NGOs) that are typically viewed as core parts of civil society (Sidel 2010). According to legal regulations, NGOs and other social organizations must submit all projects and foreign funding to their supervising agency for approval (Government of Vietnam 2009). A new Law on Associations has been repeatedly delayed by the Party-state, and internet sites critical of the authorities are routinely blocked – some social media too. For these and other reasons, Vietnam receives uniformly low ratings on international indices of political freedoms, corruption, and human rights, such as those published annually by Freedom House and Transparency International.

Yet this negative picture belies the vibrant reality of civil society in Vietnam. The number of registered NGOs has risen from fewer than 200 in the late 1990s to an estimated 1,700 today. Many more unregistered social groups and informal networks are active in public life (Wells-Dang 2012a). Online and social media are booming and attracting a wide audience in spite of (or sometimes because of) halfhearted restrictions by the authorities. When one blog is shut down, a dozen others arise to fill its space. Vietnamese-language print media, similarly, pushes at the limits of what the Party-state allows: state-owned by law, but increasingly commercially oriented and independent-minded in practice (Heng 2004; McKinley 2008). The social ferment accompanying rapid economic growth and poverty reduction is reflected in an increased incidence of social protest and gradually more open debates in the National Assembly and other political institutions.

What does it mean to talk about civil society (*xã hội dân sự*) in Vietnam in the face of these paradoxical viewpoints? And, more importantly, how are civil society actors able to achieve political influence toward a strong, restrictive single-party state? This chapter offers one set of possible answers to these questions through contrasting an associational and a political-oppositional approach to understanding civil society, examining the responses of the Party-state to nongovernmental organizing, and discussing three recent episodes of contention that involve multiple forms of civil society action. Debates concerning bauxite mining in the Central Highlands, the role of media and bloggers, and constitutional reform, it is argued, have all attained a degree of policy influence, either through or outside the political system. The chapter's conclusion then evaluates the current and potential influence of different forms of civil society on the political process, theorizing a realm of informal politics on the margins of the institutional state.

Recent scholarship on civil society in Vietnam has moved away from firm definitions of what type of organization should or should not be included in civil society to a focus on what various actors actually do (Hannah 2007; Wischermann 2010).[2] Empirical studies have examined how social organizations engage with state authorities (Kerkvliet et al. 2008), how local actors implement "community-driven regulation" (O'Rourke 2002), and how informal networks provide channels for creative advocacy (Wells-Dang 2010, 2012a). Consequently, it makes most sense to speak of "civil society actors," rather than the usual "civil society organizations." The resulting approach to civil society is a broad one, consisting of both formal and informal elements. *Formal civil society* comprises a range of legally registered organizations initiated outside the state, with an office, projects, and paid or volunteer staff. Other expressions of *informal civil society*, including individual activism, networks, blogs and social media, community groups, and religious activity, have fewer or none of these organizational elements. Although many actors operate via direct channels where possible, policy advocacy is frequently screened through unofficial structures, personal connections, and created niches between public and private.

Associational approaches to civil society

In practice, most discussions of civil society conducted inside Vietnam emphasize formal associational roles, classifying all organizations not directly part of the state apparatus as belonging to civil society. The basic unit comprising civil society is presumed to be the organization, or "CSO," which is usually understood as limited to legally registered organizations. CSOs are then grouped into a number of categories based on their structure and relationship to the state. This approach is frequently adopted by donors, international NGOs, and aid programs, as well as many of their Vietnamese partners. For instance, Irish Aid's civil society strategy paper (2012) clusters CSOs into four types: mass organizations, professional organizations, Vietnamese NGOs, and community-based organizations, a typology that originates from the 2006 Civil Society Index conducted by the international coalition, CIVICUS, with a local team of analysts. The "Viet Nam Partnership Document" presented by the Ministry of Planning and Investment (2012) to an aid effectiveness forum uses a slightly different four-part classification, distinguishing between "social-political-professional organizations" and other professional organizations, while not mentioning community-based groups at all.

For historical and political reasons, the various types of civic associations have developed in significantly different ways in Hanoi and Ho Chi Minh City (Wischermann 2010; Taylor et al. 2012) with relatively lower levels of activity in other cities and provinces. With the exception of the mass organizations and other state-sponsored associations, most social organizations are small in size and recently formed, with little experience and capacity in policy advocacy (Taylor et al. 2012). The CIVICUS study found that although space for civil society was opening overall, "virtually all organizations in Vietnam are entangled with the state and each other" (Nørlund 2006: 36).

In order to obtain legal status, new organizations must register with one of a range of "umbrella organizations," which are state-initiated entities with multiple functions, one of which is representing, registering, and managing NGOs and associations (Vasavakul 2003). The most relevant umbrella for many domestic NGOs is the Vietnam Union of Science and Technology Associations (*Liên hiệp các Hội Khoa học và Kỹ thuật Việt Nam*, or VUSTA), which represents its members' interests to government and donors and serves as a clearing house for information and ideas. International NGOs come under a separate umbrella, the Vietnam Union of Friendship Organizations (*Liên hiệp các tổ chức hữu nghị Việt Nam*, VUFO), which supervises the People's Aid Coordinating Committee (PACCOM) and the NGO Resource Center in Hanoi.

Regarding mass organizations, analysts note their hybrid character of being Party-controlled at the central level while having some representational functions at local commune and ward levels (Shanks et al. 2004; Kerkvliet et al. 2008). The Women's Union is generally held to have the strongest civil society character, due to its gendered focus, village-level presence, and ability to deliver services. Although studies of civil society in Vietnam recognize the ambiguous position of mass organizations, most end up including them as a category of CSO. Naturally, this affects the results. If the mass organizations are included as part of civil society, then Vietnam is found to have a very high level of associational participation compared to societies around the world (Dalton and Ong 2004). Without the sometimes compulsory or nominal membership in mass organizations, social participation looks much more shallow (London 2009).

In its favor, an associational approach recognizes that there is no firm line separating state and nonstate actors in the Vietnamese context (and, by extension, in many other contexts too). Drawing on anthropological theories of the state, political theorists contend that the boundaries of the state are fuzzy (Mitchell 2006), the state is multilithic and fragmented (Migdal 2001), and civil society action can at times emerge from within the state itself (Hannah 2007; Wischermann 2010). There is, therefore, a category of "straddlers" (Read and Pekkanen 2009): organizations that are part-state, part nonstate.[3] But are straddlers automatically part of civil society, or only under certain circumstances? And are the mass and umbrella organizations actually straddlers, or are they more accurately viewed as components of a multilithic state?

The argument for including mass organizations in civil society depends on a claim of at least partial autonomy at the grassroots level. In funding terms, this is accurate: local units of mass organizations do raise some of their own budgets from member dues and donor-funded projects. Yet a visit to any commune or district People's Committee will show that mass organizations are very definitely included and housed in the Party-state structure, if perhaps as somewhat junior partners. This is particularly true of the "Fatherland" Front, which is legally "a part of the political system of the Socialist Republic of Viet Nam under the leadership of the Communist Party of Viet Nam" (National Assembly 1999). One possibility would be to classify the Front as part of the state, while the other mass organizations are given a dual state–civil society character. This distinction is itself complicated by the fact that the Front has a mandate to supervise all other mass organizations as well as religious groups.

The place of mass and umbrella organizations in civil society is not merely an academic debate. If donor agencies classify these organizations as CSOs, this makes them eligible for funding under civil society and governance programs along with nonstate organizations. Donors and government bodies then present the results of projects carried out by the Women's Union and other mass and umbrella organization partners as not only effective interventions in poverty alleviation, but also actions to support civil society development. If, instead, the state-like character of these organizations crowds out more independent forms of civil society (and in the case of the Women's Union, achieves token gender balance within a male-dominated structure), the potential for unintended consequences is large.

Professional organizations, such as research centers, and Vietnamese NGOs (VNGOs) comprise the next categories of the "CSO" framework.[4] Many of these organizations are registered under VUSTA or its provincial branches; others register with ministries, city and provincial authorities, universities, or mass organizations. They range in size from dozens of staff to a single founder working with volunteers and consultants. Many VNGOs and research institutes have strong capacity in their respective fields, reflected in technical-sounding names with acronyms that are often difficult to distinguish from one another. Unlike mass, umbrella, and other sociopolitical organizations, VNGOs and professional associations receive little or no funding from the state, relying primarily on international donor funds. Some, such as university research centers, may exist within state structures, but are financially independent and were started through a local initiative. Others are strongly project-driven and operate in the style of nonprofit consulting companies.

VNGOs may be usefully grouped into three generations based on qualities of their founders and directors. The first generation began to form in the 1990s, founded by current or retired government officials, academics, and experts with strong connections to the state system. Since 2000, a second generation of NGOs has emerged, led by younger professionals who have international NGO experience or studied overseas. Compared to the first generation, members of this group are more influenced by business and international models and tend to be more independent in their thinking. The third generation, in recent years, includes student volunteer groups, charitable associations, and community-based start-ups such as self-help groups, with a more voluntary and less technical character.

Vietnamese NGOs have assembled into a diversity of networks. These include working groups with international NGOs, multi-stakeholder coalitions including government, media, and/or business representatives; virtual networks and email groups; and informal advocacy networks based on personal ties (Wells-Dang 2012a). Most are unregistered, since Vietnamese regulations have no legal category for networks. Other networks are officially considered projects of a single registered organization or are affiliated with structures such as the VUFO-NGO Resource Center.

The final category included as a form of "CSO," community-based civil society, receives much less attention from government and most development agencies: ethnic and clan-based associations and religious groups, forest and water users' groups, and farmers' collaborative groups (*tổ hợp tác*), among other types. These groups are either not formally organized and registered at all, or if they are, come under separate legal processes at the commune level, or under the Government Committee for Religious Affairs in the case of religious groups. Since such community-based groups are neither formal organizations nor political in nature, they frequently slip away from all versions of the civil society debate. Adam Fforde (2008) wonders why, if informal farmers' groups are so numerous, most donors and INGOs have not chosen to work with them; the question generalizes to other forms of community-based civil society. There was a brief period of intensive advocacy when the Ministry of Agriculture and Rural Development developed a decree on collaborative groups (Government of Vietnam 2007), but even then the focus was on government policy, not cooperation with the groups themselves. The answer is surely that the international agencies prefer to work with registered partners – and in many cases are compelled to do so by their own internal rules, as well as by the terms of their own registration and legal presence in Vietnam.

Working within an associational framework, Jörg Wischermann concludes that Vietnamese civil society (including mass and professional associations) has a weak democratic basis and that many of its members "enhance and support legitimacy and efficiency of the authoritarian regime" (2011: 408). While this may overstate the point, it is correct that the category of Vietnamese associations presented as "CSOs" includes many organizations that would not meet basic international criteria of autonomy, voluntarism, and representation. Whether arising from an intention to be comprehensive or from wishful thinking, the associational approach to civil society opens itself to the criticism of being overly vague and broad.

Political civil society

External analysts with a lower tolerance for ambiguity have drawn very different conclusions about civil society in Vietnam. If one insists on complete separation of civil society from the state (which hardly exists in any developed country, let alone in Southeast Asia), then the logical finding is that Vietnam has no organized civil society at all, or at least none worthy of the name (Salemink 2006; London 2009). Alternately, observers have looked for civil society in unregistered associations involved in political critique or outright opposition to the system, such as the Club of Former Resistance Fighters, Unified Buddhist Church of Vietnam, Việt Tân, or Bloc 8406 (Abuza 2001; Thayer 2009a). In recent years, the growth of unsanctioned blogs on topics such as bauxite mining in the Central Highlands and perceived Chinese interference in the East ("South China") Sea has added a new source of challenge to the Party's legitimacy (Thayer 2009b). Land protests, such as high-profile cases in 2012 in Tiên Lăng and Vân Giang districts in northern Vietnam, arguably form the newest and most intense form of "political civil society."

Not all of these protesters, to be sure, oppose the Communist Party: many focus on improved treatment and services from the system, such as more secure land rights and an end to corruption in business and local government. Regardless, these are at base political demands.

There is essentially no overlap between the "CSOs" in an associational approach to civil society and the dissidents, bloggers, and demonstrators described in a political-oppositional approach. NGOs and associations are conspicuously absent from land disputes and other forms of political activism, preferring cooperation with authorities through defined projects (such as legal education and capacity building). At the local level, some land protesters and members of virtual networks are connected to mass or professional organizations: for instance, several statements in the Đoàn Văn Vươn case were issued in the name of the Tiên Lãng district Fisheries Association (*Hội nuôi trồng thủy hải sản nước lợ*), and members of the Veterans' Association and the Elderly Association (*Hội Người Cao Tuổi*) have taken a role in other disputes. However, this should be understood as local activists appropriating an association on an ad hoc basis, rather than the association itself taking action.

To many journalists and human rights activists, the type of civil society action identified in a political-oppositional approach begins to resemble international patterns of activism along the lines of the so-called Arab Spring or other social movements. A degree of caution is warranted here: ideal-type conceptions of civil society and its supposed democratizing potential do not necessarily apply well in Vietnam (or elsewhere), and there is a risk of exaggerating the importance of a limited number of cases to construct an imagined or desired challenge to the Party-state that actually remains weak and distant.

Theorists of "political civil society" are right to insist that civil society action has political components that can be found outside as well as within established organizations. But this political engagement does not always lead in the direction of opposition or regime change; in fact, it only rarely does so under specific circumstances. In other instances, the political activity of civil society takes the form of grassroots organizing of people with disabilities or LGBT groups, anticorruption campaigns, and advocacy coalitions on the Land Law, hydropower, or climate change, among other issues. Political engagement can happen through "mere" service delivery as well as policy advocacy. The fact that many of the participants in such actions say nothing about opposing the Party, or even expressly endorse its role, should not be taken as weakness or self-censorship, but rather as evidence of different priorities coupled with smart strategic positioning.

The Party-state and "social organizations"

Officially and in public, the Communist Party and Vietnamese state avoid use of the term "civil society." Instead, the types of organizations donors call "CSOs" are all described in Party-state language as "social organizations" (*tổ chức xã hội*), "socio-professional organizations" (*tổ chức xã hội nghề nghiệp*), or "political–social organizations" (*tổ chức chính trị xã hội*), the last category including the mass organizations. Of these, the "Fatherland" Front and other mass organizations are viewed as first in importance. The 1992 Constitution (and the proposed draft 2013 revision) describes "the Vietnamese Fatherland Front and its member organizations" as "the political base of people's power" (National Assembly 2013: Article 9). In other legal documents, reference is made to "other social organizations," but this is frequently omitted, leaving mass organizations as the only legally recognized representatives of Vietnamese society.[5]

From the Party-state's perspective, no organization is independent: all of them "belong" (*thuộc*) somewhere (Borton 2001).[6] Vietnamese NGOs are, legally speaking, subunits of the umbrella organization or other body where they are registered. In practice, many NGOs and other social organizations act independently from the Party-state in finance, personnel, and programming decisions. But the key, from the Party-state's view, is *political* control: if any organization violates "social stability" or "national security," it could be sanctioned or shut down. In fact, this has rarely, if ever, happened to registered organizations (one VNGO, the Institute for Development Studies, voluntarily closed in 2009 rather than submit to a restrictive new set of regulations). The Party-state's relative light hand toward registered organizations may imply either that the registration process is thorough, only allowing carefully vetted groups to register; that organization staff are themselves not interested in challenging the political system, and indeed share many political views with their Party-state counterparts; or, conversely, that the Party-state has less capacity (or interest) than is often assumed to control the activities of social organizations. Even when the Party's interests are directly challenged, it is as likely to respond with conciliation as with repression (Kerkvliet, this volume).

In practice, attitudes of Party-state officials toward civil society are decidedly mixed. The use of the term in private conversation has increased markedly in the past decade. Newspapers and magazines, including the Party's theoretical journal, *Tạp chí Cộng sản*, have featured lengthy debates on the meanings of civil society and its (non-)applicability in the Vietnamese context (for instance, Nguyen Thanh Tuan 2007 and Nguyen Quang A 2009, among many other examples). The "liberal" view is that civil society is apolitical and can contribute positively as part of a strategy of involving all parts of society in national development.[7] Counterposed to this is a position aligned with the police and military, as well as some Party theoreticians, that civil society poses a security risk to the Party's monopoly on power and could lead to the specter of a "color revolution." It is difficult to say which view is more prevalent; many officials and Party members probably hold some combination of both. This internal debate over the nature and purposes of civil society mirrors external arguments as well, with the reformist viewpoint aligning closely with the associational approach of international donors, and the hard-line security view remarkably similar to the political-oppositional approach that emphasizes links between civil society development and political change. Evidence supporting both views has surfaced in a series of recent episodes of contentious politics linking civil society actors and policy makers.

The controversy over bauxite mining

In November 2007, the Vietnamese government approved a plan by the state-owned mining company, Vinacomin, to exploit bauxite ore in the Central Highlands, a decision affirmed by the Politburo in April 2009. The fact that the bauxite plans were made at the highest level of the Party indicates the importance and sensitivity of the issue. Concerns over the scale of the mining and the involvement of the Chinese mining company, Chalco, led to widespread public debate in 2008–09 that included the voices of Vietnamese NGOs, bloggers, overseas activists, and senior political leaders up to, and including, Gen. Võ Nguyên Giáp. As a result, the bauxite controversy has assumed significance far beyond its environmental impacts to become a test case for civil society involvement in political decision-making.[8]

Public involvement in the bauxite debate can be described in terms of not just one but at least three networks that are loosely connected to each other, if at all. The first network is centered on several NGOs, professional organizations, and their state-affiliated partners. The second circle of bauxite activists extends within the Party-state, including current and retired army officers around Gen. Giáp and other retired officials. The legendary general's open letter about the project in January 2009 was a key rallying point for this network.

The third anti-bauxite network is primarily a virtual one, though based like other informal networks on preexisting personal ties (personal communication, Jason Morris-Jung). A group of bloggers and activists in central Vietnam started an online petition opposing the bauxite project in April 2009 and developed a series of websites to post news and opinions. Over 2,700 people have signed the petition, including many scientists and retired officials involved in the previously mentioned networks, as well as overseas Vietnamese. Online activists have rarely met face-to-face but watch each other's activities on the internet. Each of the sites contains a large variety of material on the bauxite case as well as many other aspects of Vietnamese politics, Vietnam–China relations, and related international news. At times, certain websites have been blocked due to perceived anti-regime political content, but most have either avoided blockage or found ways around the censors.

The most comprehensive research and organizing on bauxite has been conducted by the Hanoi-based Institute for Consultancy on Development (CODE), a VNGO registered with VUSTA. CODE has supported numerous environmental and mining policy initiatives, including advocacy on the Mining Law and the international Extractive Industry Transparency Initiative (Hoang Nghia 2011: 17–19). CODE's report on bauxite mining and the Central Highlands, disseminated to all members of the National Assembly and provincial governments, includes 200 pages of scientific description before proceeding with recommendations. CODE's advocacy approach is scientific and technocratic: if leaders know all the facts, they will make informed decisions. Instead of a total halt to bauxite mining, CODE's politically nuanced recommendation was to speed up construction of one mine (Tân Rai, in Lâm Đồng province) as a pilot, but delay all others in order to study impacts over the longterm (CODE 2010: 199).

Among the internal and online bauxite networks, by contrast, the bauxite mining dispute has been presented in terms of protective nationalism, keeping resources out of foreign hands and opposing perceived external influence in the strategic region of the Central Highlands. Opponents have also expressed concerns about the damage to the ecology, forests, and agriculture, and the consequences for electricity and water, which are in short supply. But these concerns are secondary to the political importance of the case. The bauxite networks include both "respected intellectuals" who wish to reform and democratize the Communist Party and others who seek to abolish it. For the latter group of activists, including bloggers inside and outside Vietnam, bauxite mining was primarily important as a wedge against the current Vietnamese leadership, whose supposed weakness against Chinese interference threatens social stability. Anti-Chinese nationalism can thus be interpreted as hidden criticism of the SRV regime. Other online activists abandoned ambiguity and explicitly questioned the legitimacy of the government, placing blame for environmental problems on the political leadership. This has long been a firm taboo in Vietnamese politics: as one sympathetic activist describes, "Officials will listen to anything except political criticism [against the Party]. Then the two sides are firmly against each other."[9]

Once anti-bauxite mining activists linked their arguments to political opposition, security forces responded with their strongest card, protecting national security and social stability. After April 2009, there was no discussion of bauxite in the Vietnamese media for over 18 months. The involvement of external actors viewed as antigovernment posed a conundrum for domestic activists: opposition groups such as the Việt Tân party were articulate and media-savvy (Hoang 2009) but could provoke repressive measures by authorities against all the bauxite networks. An anti-bauxite group on Facebook was widely believed to be the impetus for Ministry of Public Security instructions to block the social networking site (Clark 2011).

Domestic and international anti-bauxite websites arguably had little direct influence on the Vietnamese government's policy decisions, and perhaps some negative influence. But the virtual network had indirect value by adding technical information and a broad, international view of the issue. This informed Vietnamese intellectuals' opinions and enabled them to frame the issue more effectively toward the government. In late 2010, the bauxite issue resurfaced in the Vietnamese blogosphere as news spread of red mud from Hungarian bauxite mining entering the Danube River (Clark 2011). A petition from prominent intellectuals, including National Assembly members, called on the government to cancel or postpone the mines.

CODE's advocacy efforts on extractive industries have also continued, in cooperation with another respected environmental NGO, PanNature. Their joint efforts have targeted National Assembly members as well as the Ministry of Natural Resources and Environment (MONRE) and the Communist Party's Department of Science, Technology and Environment, using both direct contact and private personal connections (Gainsborough et al. 2011: 23–4). CODE and PanNature's work on mining issues has since expanded to a multi-stakeholder coalition including MONRE, the Vietnam Chamber of Commerce and Industry (VCCI), provincial authorities, and mining companies, aiming to promote revenue transparency and good governance of mineral resources, including but not limited to bauxite.[10]

Meanwhile, the virtual network of bauxite activists has suffered from numerous setbacks since 2009. Yet their long-term influence on political space may nevertheless prove to be positive. As Carlyle Thayer (2009b) perceptively notes, the bauxite campaign exposed a rift between Vietnam's bilateral relationship with China and the Communist Party's historical claim to legitimacy based on Vietnamese nationalism. And in part as a result of public criticism, the scale of bauxite mining being undertaken is much smaller than that originally approved in 2007, with construction underway on two smaller mines, rather than the nine-province proposal originally approved to be in place by 2015 (CODE 2010: 158, 196; Hoang Lan 2011). This outcome demonstrates both the promise and the limits of formal and informal civil society involvement in policy.

Civil society in dispute: the 2012 *Nhân Dân* article

The continuing political sensitivity of civil society issues came to light in the publication and reaction to an editorial in the Party daily, *Nhân Dân*, that appeared on August 31 (Duong Van Cu 2012). The author, later identified as a police colonel, conflated organized and informal forms of civil society as "a trick of peaceful evolution" (*diễn biến hòa bình*), in other words a "plot" by anti-Party forces to implement a Western-style democratic system in Vietnam. The article cited Eastern European experience in which "CSOs" were revealed as fronts for opposition groups with assistance from subversive foreign donors, and concluded with a call for the Party-state to expose and resist such plots in the name of national security.

The editorial's rhetoric was not new: concerns about "peaceful evolution" have been a mainstay of Party hard-liners since the early 1990s, when discussion of a multiparty system became taboo following the Trần Xuân Bách affair (Bui 2013: 46). Nor was the broad-brush, inflammatory language unusual, particularly from security forces. Although *Nhân Dân* is the Party's mouthpiece, one should not conclude that the article represents the view of all Party leaders, rather it gave voice to a certain constituency within the system that may or may not be a majority at any given time.

What was unprecedented was the rapid reaction by organized civil society, namely Hanoi-based Vietnamese NGOs. Within a week of the article's publication, the People's Participation Working Group (currently chaired by two VNGOs, iSEE and CODE) organized a meeting at the VUFO-NGO Resource Center to discuss a response.[11] Over 40 participants attended, including representatives from VNGOs and umbrella associations (PPWG 2012). The gathering resulted in a letter sent to the editor of *Nhân Dân* with 51 signatories (iSEE 2012) stating that "civil society organizations such as we" are patriotic Vietnamese who are working openly and legally to reduce poverty, protect the environment, and promote public health and education, among other positive activities. In what way, the letter asked, is this a threat to the authorities? Subsequent articles posted on the web by other authors expanded on these points. "I'm sure there are some NGOs with political purposes," wrote one online commenter, "but in Viet Nam they aren't many...The vast majority of NGOs are operating for positive ends, with a constructive attitude that is more social than political...their contributions to Viet Nam's development achievements are not small, and the government has recognized this many times" (Nguyen Quang Dong 2012).

The original article, as well as these and other responses, went viral on the Vietnamese blogosphere. Prior to the growth of VNGOs and access to the internet, a similar article would have been critiqued in private discussions, but not discussed publicly or in print. Although *Nhân Dân* never printed the NGOs' letter, it nevertheless reached a wide audience and delivered a clear message.

The NGOs' response seemed to confirm an apolitical narrative of Vietnamese civil society. Yet the meaning of the whole episode may not be so clear-cut. The NGOs assumed that the article was aimed at them as representatives of civil society organizations, and they reacted accordingly. But the article could also be read as a salvo in an ongoing factional struggle within the Party-state. Several weeks after the editorial's publication, Prime Minister Nguyễn Tân Dũng ordered the closure of three blogs, two of which (*Dân Làm Báo* and *Quan Làm Báo*, "The Citizen Reporter" and "The Mandarin Reporter") had been outspoken in their personal criticism of Mr. Dũng. In early October, three bloggers from unrelated sites were sentenced to long prison terms (Brummitt 2012). These actions appeared to galvanize the blogging community rather than suppress it: the censored sites remained online, and web traffic to them spiked. Later in October, the PM narrowly escaped discipline and removal from office by the Politburo (Nguyen Phu Trong 2012). In light of this context, the primary target of the *Nhân Dân* article was arguably critical blogs, not a group of innocuous development NGOs.

In retrospect, a second feature of the editorial also takes on greater significance: its prescient warnings of "a bunch of political opportunists with extreme oppositional views who...demand that the 1992 Constitution revert to the 1946 Constitution and hold a popular referendum on

Article 4 as well as the whole Constitution, set up a Constitutional Court, promote civil society and democratic freedoms...and privatize land" (Duong Van Cu 2012). It is precisely these issues, not "peaceful evolution," that came to dominate Vietnamese political discourse in 2013.

Constitutional reform: opening Pandora's box?

In early January 2013, the National Assembly's drafting committee released a draft of a revised Vietnamese Constitution (*Hiến Pháp*) for public comment. The new Constitution will replace the previous version issued in 1992 and will be the fifth in a series of Constitutions promulgated by the Democratic Republic of Vietnam/Socialist Republic of Vietnam since 1946. The reasons for the timing of the new draft are not entirely clear, coming in the midst of upper-level political turmoil between the prime minister and Party leadership as well as vociferous debate over the revised Land Law. The constitutional revisions appear to have occurred due to a desire to bolster the Party's legitimacy combined with accommodation of pressure from intellectuals and the media to reform the 1992 Constitution, which many commentators view as outdated (Nguyen Thi Huong 2012; Bui 2013).

The January 2013 draft makes adjustments in the political system that could hardly be considered extreme. One such innovation is the addition of a Constitutional Council, not quite the independent court that *Nhân Dân*'s editorialist feared; other new features include the formation of a National Election Commission and a State Audit Office.[12] These amendments result in a slight shift on balance toward the National Assembly and away from the prime minister and government. Most importantly, the Party's role as "the leading force in the state and society" in Article 4 remains unchanged, as does the following clause that "all Party organizations operate within the Constitution and the law" (National Assembly 2013). Civil society has no role in the document outside of the Fatherland Front (Article 9).

The public comment period was set for three months to March 31. On January 19, a group of 72 intellectuals posted an entire alternate draft constitution on the web, making radical changes in almost every article. Article 4, for instance, was replaced by a statement that "political parties are free to set up and operate according to the principles of democracy" (Bauxite Vietnam 2013). The alternate draft called for separation of powers, an independent Constitutional Court, and the depoliticization of the army and security forces – exactly what had previously been termed "peaceful evolution." The signers included a former vice-minister of justice, several prominent economists and former advisors to Prime Minister Võ Văn Kiệt, Catholic bishops, and other professors, writers, and artists. The alternate draft was first posted on the Bauxite Vietnam website that arose from the 2009 mining dispute, and the list of signers includes many contributors to the bauxite campaign, as well as signers of a 2011 call to defend the country from Chinese encroachment (Xuan Dien 2011). By May 2013, over 14,400 people inside and outside Vietnam had signed an online petition in support of the alternate draft. Other online constitutional recommendations followed: one organized by US-based mathematics professor Ngô Bảo Châu titled "Writing the Constitution Together" (Cùng viết Hiến Pháp), http://hienphap.net/, and another, http://hienphap.kienghi.net/, posted by a group of current and former law students within Vietnam. These efforts, as well as the Group of 72 petition, received limited coverage in the official print and online media, showing some evidence of increased space for public discussion.

Democracy manifestos are not unknown in modern Vietnamese history, but most such statements have been made by small groups of dissidents who could easily be repressed or ignored. Earlier activists, such as the 112 signers of the Bloc 8406 statement in 2006, were primarily teachers, priests, engineers, and other white-collar workers in the cities of central and southern Vietnam. The 72 signers of the alternate constitution are a completely different group, predominantly Hanoi-based and with much stronger political and economic connections.

Critical intellectuals working within the system had up to 2013 stayed within the red line of Article 4: criticism of policies was possible, anything except direct opposition to the Party. The alternate constitution breached that line, within the framework of allowable public comment on the revised draft. To be sure, similar debates on the constitution had taken place among intellectuals in 2001 and again in 2010, characterized by a pragmatic call for a state governed by the rule of law (*nhà nước pháp quyền*) without directly challenging the Party (Sidel 2009; Nguyen Thi Huong 2012). Perhaps the closest parallel in recent years was the 2005 alternate draft of the Law on Associations released by VUSTA as a counter to the Government's restrictive draft; this more modest ploy led to the canceling of the entire law (Sidel 2010).

A response from the Party-state was inevitable. In a nationally televised speech on February 25, General Secretary Nguyễn Phú Trọng accused unnamed critics of "political, ideological and ethical decadence" (*suy thoái chính trị, tư tưởng, đạo đức*) for suggesting the removal of Article 4, advocating a multiparty system, and proposing the nonpoliticization of the army. A swift rebuttal came from an unexpected source: a journalist for a state-owned newspaper posted a short blog stating that the real decadence was not different political ideas but rather corruption within the Party (Nguyen Dac Kien 2013). The journalist was summarily fired from his job, but became an instant hero in the blogosphere (Ives 2013). Rather than shut down debate, the National Assembly chairman, Nguyễn Sinh Hùng, announced on March 6 that the time frame for receiving comments on the revised draft would be extended through the end of September (Drafting Committee 2013).

Soon after the posting of the alternate draft Constitution, the People's Participation Working Group entered the debate, organizing a series of events in March 2013 to solicit input from civil society organizations and "disadvantaged social groups": ethnic minorities, people with disabilities, LGBT, migrant workers, youth, HIV-positive people, and women. Thirty-five directors and representatives of VNGOs, networks, professional associations, and informal clubs signed the CSO statement, calling for greater civil and political rights, freedom of assembly, streamlined registration of associations, an independent human rights commission, and Constitutional Court (iSEE 2013a). The social groups' statement, based on the consultation of 17 organizations, 980 individuals, and 2,500 online respondents, made over 20 pages of specific wording changes to the draft, including land rights, free education and health care, and gay marriage (iSEE 2013b). Neither statement mentioned Article 4, but both stressed human rights, equality, and the need for the Constitution to be ratified in a popular referendum. These demands might have seemed radical and new in any other circumstance, but compared to the entire alternate draft, they came across as measured and limited. In this way, the action of the online intellectuals opened allowable space for organized civil society to enter the political arena and deflect potential criticism. PPWG representatives submitted their recommendations to the National Assembly's Drafting Committee according to the law; their input was reportedly "well received" (Nam Pham 2013).

The story of the 2013 constitutional debate – still underway as this chapter was written – seems to provide general confirmation of the "political civil society" narrative. The main actors in the debate are individuals and unregistered groups, not formal CSOs, although they have also joined in using the space available to them. The target of civil society action is unambiguously political and, in many cases, overtly oppositional, engaging in "gradual political fence breaking" (Nguyen Thi Huong 2012: 17). Blogs and the internet have been the main means of communication, demonstrating the power of this new medium as an organizing tool. Yet some features of the debate also challenge a political-oppositional approach to civil society. The leading actors are not wholly separate from the state: the majority of signers of the alternate draft Constitution have strong Party-state connections. Indeed, their actions have the implicit support of some individuals and factions within the system, as can be concluded by the fact that they were not immediately arrested as certain less-connected bloggers have been. Some of the signers and advocates, furthermore, have participated in VNGOs and other social organizations at times, such as VUSTA, VCCI, and the now-closed Institute of Development Studies. Others have played roles in informal networks, such as the 2007–09 campaigns to save Hanoi's Reunification Park. Rather than external, independent voices, the actors in the constitutional debate are shape-shifters who "wear many hats," adopting personae both within and outside the state (Wells-Dang 2012a).

Conclusion: the future of civil society influence

Both organized and informal expressions of civil society are increasingly active in Vietnam. Each of the three controversies profiled in this chapter – bauxite mining, the meaning of "civil society," and constitutional revisions – features the involvement of Vietnamese NGOs as well as informal and virtual activism. Together, the spaces opened by such civil society action comprise a sphere of informal politics in which actors take advantage of opportunities for agency and policy entrepreneurship, within or on the edges of the system's limits. All civil society actors network with other groups to achieve policy objectives, whether this takes place through loose working groups like the PPWG, structured multi-stakeholder cooperation such as the mining/extractives coalition, or via the internet and social media. The capacity and voice of formal organizations is greater than in the past, yet the preponderance of new energy has recently been on the informal side. Any observer who neglects either facet of civil society would miss an important part of the overall picture (CIVICUS 2013: 10).

The Party-state's policies both enable and restrict civil society development, in a process similar to what has been observed in China (Ho 2008). Connections with authorities provide avenues for policy engagement, while also placing limits on what formal civil society actors can do. Similarly, policies to involve the whole of society in national development (*xã hội hóa*), and to encourage the use of information technology, create opportunities for informal activism that other parts of the state sometimes seek to rein in. The ambiguity in many legal documents, the gap between theory and practice, and increasing contradictions between policy and implementation combine to form unexpected political space in which various forms of civil society can thrive.

In a germinal article on state-society relations, Benjamin J. Tria Kerkvliet (2003) noted that in spite of greater numbers and variety of organizations and partially improved legal structures, the initiative in future developments still lay with the state's decision to employ repression or incentives toward civil society. A decade later, the Party-state still holds a very strong position, yet the initiative has surprisingly shifted toward actors outside of state structures. The future potential of civil society's political influence will depend on three as yet uncertain elements, only one of which concerns the Party-state's response.

One area in which greater civil society influence could be achieved is through improvements in transparency and cooperation among groups. If formal organizations as well as informal networks develop more democratic internal governance systems, this would not only strengthen their legitimacy and popular representation, but also pose an alternative to the prevailing political and economic culture. Some VNGOs and networks have discussed voluntary self-certification mechanisms that would encourage organizations to reach a higher standard than required in Vietnamese law; others seek to diversify funding sources through social enterprise initiatives or other local income-generating activities. In addition to potential financial independence, organizations would benefit politically from a stronger domestic constituency base and less dependence on foreign donors. Efforts to promote domestic giving, whether by individuals, corporations, or foundations, are still at their early stages, with Ho Chi Minh City somewhat ahead of other regions (Taylor et al. 2012). Nonprofit governance and fundraising are likely to become key issues as Vietnamese civil society matures.

A second major question for future civil society action concerns the extent to which organizational, informal, and community-based networks come together in joint campaigns, or even develop into full-scale social movements. The previously absolute gap between registered and informal civil society has narrowed in the constitutional debate and land disputes. Local community members – women and men farmers, small business owners, and veterans – have increasingly become engaged in advocacy over land and environmental issues that affect their lives. This informal civil society is not necessarily oppositional in nature: political opposition makes up only a small fraction of all civil society activity in Vietnam. Yet overt criticism of the Communist

Party's monopoly on power emerged in 2012–13 in ways not seen since the early years of *Đổi mới*.

A final uncertain factor is the response from the Party-state. On one pole of the spectrum of possibilities, the constitutional debate could lead to a staged political opening, as has occurred in Myanmar (Burma) since 2008. Such a process would likely continue to be led from above and, as Burmese experience shows, poses numerous risks and obstacles along the path of transition from authoritarianism. The role of various forms of civil society would certainly increase in such a trajectory, but not necessarily in a uniform way. Contrary to the claims of both enthusiastic democracy promoters and hard-line democracy opponents, civil society engagement itself will not be sufficient to bring about political liberalization: that depends on elite decisions, visionary leadership, and external opportunities, among other factors stressed in studies of democratization (Schmitter 1997; Alagappa 2004).

An opposite form of Party-state response to civil society would be increased repression by the security apparatus, which is the logical end point of the "circle-the-wagons" view expressed in the 2012 *Nhân Dân* editorial. Although the political and social climate for civil society in Vietnam has widened considerably over the past decades, these gains are not irreversible. Up to now, for instance, the police and military have mostly avoided use of lethal force in responding to demonstrations, bloggers, and other perceived threats (Kerkvliet, this volume), yet such force remains an available option.

Between these two scenarios lies the possibility of increasing splits among the Vietnamese leadership and competition over resources, resulting in an incoherent, dysfunctional policy response in which uncertainty is a primary instrument of rule (see Gainsborough 2010). In this outcome, some components of the Party-state might become more sympathetic to civil society activities, joining in limited-purpose coalitions at times, while other forces seek to block change. The factional conflicts of late 2012 offer a taste of what could arise if internal disputes move further into the open. While the levels of uncertainty and risk in such circumstances would be high, the opportunities for civil society engagement would also increase. Fragmentation and decentralization of authority, together with bureaucratic competition and personal interests, ensure that civil society actors will be able to identify allies within certain official structures. To the extent that officials and National Assembly delegates become more comfortable in working with civil society, greater cooperation will become possible (Oxfam and OPM 2012).

Division among elites also provides fertile ground for corruption and rent-seeking in Vietnam's political economy, which many civil society actors seek to redress. The grey areas for civil society action and private enrichment may be seen as opposite facets of the same process: investors, ambitious officials, and other interest groups are well (or better) placed to take advantage of opportunities resulting from state fragmentation. Increased freedom for civil society actors, and stronger influence on certain issues, may thus not necessarily result in optimal political outcomes for the country at large. At best, Vietnamese society would "muddle through" uncertainty, with the Party-state remaining strong in some aspects, while social conflicts and inequality increase at the same time.

In either the managed change or muddle-through state responses, civil society actors will become increasingly intertwined in informal politics on the boundaries of the Party-state system. Through media and the internet, research and advocacy projects, and personal connections, the actors involved in recent political controversies have forged pathways around the blockages of institutionalized politics. Such innovation reconciles the paradox of a vibrant civil society in a restrictive political system. It also confirms the importance of a rethinking of familiar concepts of civil society, away from categorizing types of organizations toward a dynamic process of cooperation among both formal and informal actors.

Notes

1. The mass organizations are the "Fatherland" (or "Ancestral") Front (*Mặt trận Tổ quốc,* which is non-gender specific in Vietnamese), the Vietnam Women's Union (*Liên hiệp Hội Phụ nữ Việt Nam*), Ho Chi Minh Communist Youth Union (*Đòan Thanh niên Cộng sản Hồ Chí Minh*), Vietnam Farmers' Union (*Hội Nông dân Việt Nam*), Viet Nam General Confederation of Labor (*Tổng Liên đoàn Lao động Việt Nam*), and the Vietnam Veterans' Association (*Hội Cựu chiến binh Việt Nam*).
2. Internationally accepted definitions have likewise shifted: for instance, CIVICUS' original depiction of civil society as an autonomous realm of organizations has changed to encompass a more fluid and activist-centered approach including individuals and other informal groups who act in the public sphere (CIVICUS 2013).
3. As Read and Pekkanen (2009) demonstrate, the "straddler" concept applies throughout East and Southeast Asia. It also exists elsewhere in the world by the names of "parastatals" and "quangos."
4. This and the following two paragraphs draw on Wells-Dang (2012b), which provides further detail and examples of VNGOs and research centers in the sector of climate change response.

5. There are important exceptions to this rule: for instance, the 2010 Law on Disability specifies roles for self-help groups of people with disabilities, and regulations on HIV-AIDS prevention and treatment recognize the involvement of networks and NGOs. These provisions entered the law due to domestic and international lobbying, and demonstrate the flexibility and diversity possible within the bounds of the Party-state system in particular cases.

6. The Party-state does recognize that some organizations are "nongovernmental": the Ministry of Home Affairs even contains a Department of Nongovernmental Organizations (*Vụ Tổ chức Phi Chính phủ*). This does not mean that NGOs are viewed as independent.

7. This strategy is one meaning of the term *xã hội hóa*, misleadingly (if literally) translated as "socialization."

8. The discussion in this section is based on Wells-Dang (2011).

9. Personal interview, September 2011.

10. The mining coalition is funded by multiple international donors including the UK Government – Oxfam Advocacy Coalition Support Program, of which the author currently serves as Team Leader.

11. iSEE is the Institute for Studies of Society, Economy and Environment. Like CODE, iSEE is a policy-oriented NGO with dynamic young leaders, registered with VUSTA. It has become best known for work on ethnic minority and LGBT issues. The VUFO-NGO Resource Center, jointly sponsored by international NGOs and an umbrella organization, hosts 19 working groups, including People's Participation, which include both domestic and foreign NGOs as members (see http://www.ngocentre.org.vn/workinggroups).

12. Perhaps the most important shift in the draft, outside the scope of this chapter, is the removal of a mandated leading role for the state-owned sector in the economy in favor of an economy with "various forms of ownership" (Article 54).

9
Toward a New Politics?

Jonathan D. London

This book has examined institutional foundations of politics in contemporary Vietnam. It has reflected on continuity and change in the character of Vietnamese authoritarianism. It has sought to better situate Vietnam within the sprawling theoretical literature on comparative politics and authoritarian regimes, in particular. And it has shed light on key tensions and contradictions that animate politics in Vietnam today. Through the contributions to this volume, we have peered into the internal dynamics of the Communist Party of Vietnam (CPV) and the complex relations between central and local authorities in the context of market reforms and economic internationalization. We have scrutinized developments in Vietnam's formal representative political institutions and we have probed the limits of political toleration and dissent. And we have surveyed the country's apparatus of repression. Lastly, we have noted the development of an increasingly vibrant and autonomous associational life and indeed an incipient and a relatively unmediated public political discourse. It will now be useful to reflect on the implications of all this for our understandings of politics in contemporary Vietnam.

In contrast to much of the literature on politics in Vietnam, the chapters in this volume have made conscientious efforts to situate the Vietnamese experience within theoretical literature on comparative politics. Yet, in contrast to much of comparative literature on authoritarian regimes, the contributors to this volume have not sought mainly to understand, explain, or imagine how elections, parliaments, and party organizations serve authoritarian ends. On the contrary, they have sought to observe, understand, and explain the evolution and functioning of Vietnam's political institutions. In so doing, however, the authors have differed from one another; both with respect to their general and specific interpretations of political processes unfolding in Vietnam today. Where some see weaknesses and decay in Vietnam's political institutions (Vu: Ch. 2), others see resilience and strength (Thayer: Ch. 7). Where some see increased accountability (Malesky: Ch. 4) and toleration of dissent (Kerkvliet: Ch. 6), others emphasize the harshness of state repression (Thayer: Ch. 7). Virtually all authors depict an authoritarian regime characterized by considerable intrastate competition and one that is increasingly subject to pressures for fundamental reforms, both from within and from outside. The truth, of course, is that all of these elements may be observed in contemporary Vietnam.

Despite their differences, the chapters in this volume do convey one common sentiment – that contemporary Vietnam is experiencing important changes in its political institutions. Indeed, as we enter the middle years of the twenty-first century's second decade, it appears that Vietnam has entered a new if indeterminate phase in its political development.

But just what sort of phase are we talking about? And in what meaningful respects is it really new? To conclude this volume, this chapter will revisit and relate the various contributions to this volume. And it will do so in light of the most recent developments in Vietnam's politics, that is, those that have occurred in 2012 and 2013. Along the way, the chapter will highlight substantive issues and questions that this volume has mentioned but has not explored in depth. Finally, the chapter will peer into the future and pose important, yet not immediately answerable questions about what might lie ahead. Before doing so, let us take stock of the contributions to this volume and the questions they raise for current and future understandings of politics in Vietnam.

Taking stock

Politics in Viet Nam is not reducible to the CPV. But the party remains the most essential institutional component of Viet Nam's politics. Tuong Vu's contribution to this volume posed perennial but essential questions about the party's status. In particular, he questions whether the CPV is in decline and whether and how this might matter. Departing from the tendency to view Vietnamese political order in isolation, Vu situates Viet Nam within the contemporary historical universe of single-party states. In these states, he notes the special importance of elite politics, violence, war, and rents. He unpacks the significance of these themes in the evolution of single-party dictatorships and the CPV in particular. Vu characterized the period running from 1986 to the present as one of "reform and continuing decay," arguing that "incremental adaptability" (to the market, among others) has nonetheless failed to stem the erosion of the party's autonomy (from its social environment) and hence its power. Vu warns, however, that "decay does not mean immediate or eventual breakdown" (Chapter 2).

An additional strength of Vu's chapter is his analysis of the broader party infrastructure. He notes, for example, that Vietnam's party-controlled mass organizations – once a functional cornerstone of Vietnam's totalitarian social order – have, in the context of markets and increased personal autonomy, declined in their relevance. (One might speculate whether the appointment of Politburo member Nguyen Thien Nhan in late 2013 represents an effort to reverse this trend.) Thinking comparatively, one is reminded of assertions by Stephen Haggard that North Korea's communist party (the Workers Party) appears moribund at the grassroots.[1] This is certainly not the case in Vietnam, where the party remains both active and significant. Be that as it may, the CPV, perhaps unlike the Communist Party of China, has publicly raised the alarm about its own development. This was the central if unapologetic message of Resolution 4 (of 2012), which aims to stanche and reverse the Party's degradation through an increased (albeit all-too-familiar) emphasis on criticism and self-criticism.

Among Vu's most provocative claims is that while revolutionary violence helped build the CPV's rural support base, the transition to a market economy is now destroying it, in large part, owing to a widespread perception that higher- and mid-level operatives who manage "development" in Vietnam are mainly interested in the accumulation of personal fortune. Despite emphasis on erosion and decline, Vu finds that Vietnam's new social order – partly a product of the Party itself – presents ample opportunities for the regime to persist. Looking toward the future, Vu notes the availability of nationalism as a fallback source of regime legitimacy. More provocative still is Vu's contention that the Party has become "seemingly totally beholden to interest groups" and that its survival is in grave danger.

Yet do we, in fact, know enough? The rumor mill is ripe with stories of how interest groups and party membership intersect. But while there is (as there should be) immense interest in the phenomenon of "interest group" politics in Vietnam and its prospective contributions to regime maintenance or decline, there has been no attempt, to my knowledge, to systematically map this phenomenon, or probe its presumptive or real effects on the Party's standing. In general, "interest group politics" in Vietnam is construed as some toxic combination of political elitism and market opportunism. Yet looking forward, it is worth questioning whether the rise of interest group politics in Vietnam necessarily reflects a process of political malaise. Certainly, internal division is nothing new to the CPV. To what extent and how do the "interest groups politics" of today resemble or differ from those of the past?

Let us take, for example, the rather spectacular developments at the 6th Plenum of the 11th Party Congress, in October 2012; an event that will be remembered not only for Nguyen Tan Dung survival of threats to his leadership, but for the Central Committee's open reprimand of the Politburo. While Dung surely tested the limits of naked personal interest, the use of political capital to accumulate personal wealth has become a deeply entrenched feature of party politics in Vietnam. Whether corrupt or not, how and to what extent does the ongoing embourgeoisement of the CPV's elite ranks contribute to the development and character of interest group politics? However corrupted by interests it may be, the CPV's particular brand of interest group politics stands in contrast with China's "one-man show" of Xi Jinping. Does the (apparently) comparatively more decentralized power of Vietnam's party state make interest group politics any more harmful to regime survival? With the improving availability of information – perhaps itself a product of interest group competition – conditions in Vietnam today allow for finer-grained studies of politics, even at the elite level.

One area where interest group politics are widely and with some merit presumed to be undermining party rule concerns the efficacy of the Party's economic stewardship. Thomas Jandl's contribution to the volume is the only one that explicitly addresses economic themes. And while his focus is not specifically focused on interest groups, he is concerned centrally with the political dynamics of market-based economic growth in Vietnam. All market economies are, of course, politically instituted. And in his chapter Jandl unpacks the dynamics of central–local relations in the context of market reforms, with particular attention to foreign direct investment (FDI) and to the politics of state finance. His analysis construes central–local relations as patron–client relations and perceptively identifies the complexities of these relations in the context of uneven development. Jandl demonstrates key differences between China and Vietnam. Notably, his analysis reminds us that Vietnam's political economy is significantly more *redistributive* than China's, in the sense that equalizing transfers – from wealthy to poorer provinces through the central government – are proportionally larger in Vietnam as a proportion of GDP. Jandl also points out that in Vietnam, at least in the first decade or more of reform, local "risers" (rather than central state insiders) have played a relatively more important role than in China in introducing and championing reforms. On the other hand, the very success of provincial elites in championing reforms and rising to the upper echelons of national power circles begs the question of whether it is still meaningful to construe central state and provincial authorities as a patron–client relation; particularly when so many central state leaders have been cut from local cloth. With respect to the broader aims of the volume, Jandl's analysis reminds us of the necessity of understanding Vietnam's economic development as a politically mediated process.

There is, of course, no shortage of economic issues that would benefit from explicitly political analysis. As several chapters in this volume have shown, economic issues concerning land and property rights remain as relevant as ever and stand to benefit from further analysis. As indicated at the outset of this volume, there is already a significant body of scholarship devoted to the political determinants of economic institutions. There has been perhaps less attention to the political effects of economic institutions, economic behavior, and its effects. Vietnam's faltering economic performance since 2008 has brought several interesting issues to the fore, including the politics of (bad) public debt, problems in industrial policy, inadequate skilling, and the political economy of "equitization" and privatization, to name a few. And yet relatively few studies have probed the impacts of how these economic realities have affected the selection and conduct of state policies and the nature of politics in Vietnam more generally. As Jandl's analysis reminds us, the process of administrative and political decentralization that has unfolded in Vietnam has greatly increased the power of provinces and provincial elites, especially those who through trade and investment have come to command large-scale economic resources. In contrast to the China literature, however, comparative research on the local politics of economic governance in Vietnam remains underdeveloped.

Since 1945, Vietnam's formally representative deliberative body, the National Assembly (NA), has been haunted by the possibility that it is a farce. Indeed, the NA has been and remains subordinate to the CPV, formally and practically. The body remains overwhelmingly constituted by Party members and "party people." Be that as it may, Eddy Malesky reminds us that the NA plays a unique functional role in Vietnam's political economy, and the character of this role has evolved significantly in recent years. Moreover, Vietnam's "authoritarian parliament" differs fundamentally from patterns observed in other countries. Perhaps most importantly, the NA is a body in which state officials in Vietnam are increasingly (if unevenly) held to account. In his two contributions to this volume, Edmund Malesky has subjected the body's recent evolution to rigorous empirical scrutiny. In his original contribution to this volume, Malesky discusses the NA's development in light of the historic and unprecedented confidence votes, which were taken in the NA in June 2013. Malesky discusses his findings in "The Adverse Effects of Sunshine," in which he and associates investigated the determinants and effects of publicly broadcast query sessions. Both the confidence votes and the query sessions illustrate the difficult assembly members and regime elite face in acquiring information on citizen preferences while maintaining order and stability in an authoritarian parliament.

What, we might ask, does the recent development of the NA mean with respect to politics in Vietnam more generally and the significance of Vietnam with respect to efforts to understand and explain single-party authoritarian polities more generally? Malesky's piece challenges Vietnam observers to move beyond facile statements about the presumptive "assertiveness" of the NA to substantive analysis of what is actually occurring and whether and how it affects the accountability of the government. His asseveration that we have seen improvements in the quality (i.e., education and training and functional expertise) of assembly members is important as it invites us to consider the somewhat important if potentially discomforting possibility that Vietnamese authoritarianism can be more responsive to national challenges that it has ever been. His observation that confidence votes in Vietnam's NA are unprecedented among authoritarian and single-party regimes, which is a reminder that Vietnam's politics are unusual. On the other hand, Malesky reminds us that not a single official in the June 2013 voting received a share over 50 percent and that government ministers received systematically lower confidence votes than did members of the assembly itself. He concludes that the confidence vote appears to be a mechanism for information gathering in a semitransparent setting, rather than a bold strike for accountability.

Perhaps the most striking change in Vietnam's politics at present has been changes in the politics of dissent. And, in particular, in the rapid development of what might be best characterized as an incipient and largely unmediated public discourse about politics and society, which has unfolded on the net and indeed in communities and workplaces across the country. In his characteristically careful analysis of patterns of dissent and repression in Vietnam up until 2010, Ben Kerkvliet has probed a critical question: Why and under what circumstances do state authorities in Vietnam variously repress or tolerate dissident behavior?

Adopting the departure point that all states use repression to control dissent, Kerkvliet's analysis juxtaposes the experiences of some 62 regime dissidents. He finds that whereas some regime critics are subjected to harsh treatment, others are not. He probes a variety of explanations, finding no single one adequate.

His broader conclusion, that Vietnam's state tolerates many forms of dissent, compels us to examine our assumptions both about the meaning of repression and the character of repression in Vietnam. This question has become if anything more important amid the recent development of Vietnam's political discourse, in which the sheer volume of dissenting speech has grown exponentially. Certainly, the questions Kerkvliet raises deserve continued attention. At a broader and perhaps more controversial level, Kerkvliet's analysis invites us to consider the value and limits of relativistic (versus absolutist) perspective that starts with the assumption that all states (from North Korea to Norway) use repression against their citizens. Kerkvliet's point, of course, is that we are best off adopting an empirical approach and considering carefully observable patterns of dissent, repression and, yes, "toleration." Indeed, developments in Vietnam since 2010 defy simple characterization. On the one hand, a number of regime dissidents have been sentenced to very lengthy prison terms, such as Trần Huỳnh Duy Thức (16 years) or Cù Huy Hà Vũ (seven years plus three of house arrest), while, on the other hand, scores more – including increasing numbers of young, internet-based activists – have been imprisoned or subject to regular harassment and abuse. During the first half of 2013, 46 pro-democracy activists and bloggers were arrested (Thayer 2013b).

But that is not the whole story. For Vietnam in a relatively short space of time has developed a more open political culture; one that has far-outpaced the evolution of the country's formal political institutions. No doubt, this has owed in large part to the development of a Vietnamese cyberspace. But it is more than that. Viewed sociologically, the developmental dynamics of Vietnam's incipient public political discourse can only be understood as the product of mutually constitutive interactions between the state and its social environment, an environment in which increasing numbers of Vietnamese, within and without the state apparatus, are taking an interest in politics and expressing their views. At the very least, Kerkvliet reminds us that, in any society, the state plays a vital role in structuring the space within which dissent occurs. This is not to assume the state is interested in promoting dissent by any means. Rather, it is to acknowledge that the state has significant agency in creating, and more or less effectively regulating, the social space in which dissent occurs. Undoubtedly, these issues are discussed at the very pinnacle of the CPV, in such agencies as the Party Committee on Education (Ban Tuyên Giáo). Today, in Vietnam, broadcasts of state-filtered news, whether through the precinct speaker system (loa phường) or 700 state-run newspapers, occurs within the social environment where Vietnamese are more able to access alternative views, albeit in a limited way.

Given the considerable interest in the politics of state repression in Vietnam, there has been strikingly little analysis of the apparatus of repression itself. Carlyle Thayer's contribution to this volume cuts through such claims with a crisp analysis of the quartet of Vietnamese agencies responsible for repressive functions. These include the Ministry of Public Security, the People's Armed Security Force, the General Directorate II (military intelligence), and the Ministry of Culture and Information. If Kerkvliet's chapter forces us to consider degrees of toleration in Vietnam's polity, Thayer's reminds us that Vietnam's repressive apparatuses are indeed extensive and constitute a major dimension of state governance. In his analysis, Thayer is struck by the extensiveness of repressive agencies, given the relatively "small number" of dissidents and activists. Thayer's suggestion that different factions within the Vietnamese state use repression to undermine each other is fascinating in its own right, particularly in the context of elite divisions. One wonders then, what will become of Vietnam's repressive agencies and their competitive behavior should the number of dissidents and activists in Vietnam grow, which appears to be occurring today.

How can we make sense of repressive aspects of Vietnamese authoritarianism in theoretical and comparative terms? There is a large literature on repressive institutions in China. One question to be explored is whether repressive agencies are any less decentralized than other parts of the state. There are interesting empirical questions to be asked about the extensiveness of repressive institutions. Thayer's widely cited analysis that one in six working-age Vietnamese is linked to the security apparatus – either as police or part of the sprawling military or as neighborhood security functionaries – is striking. Regular citizens across Vietnam are indeed widely carrying out public security functions (such as neighborhood defense brigades). Yet there has to date been no careful research on their activities (for a study of China, see Perry 2007). One might also juxtapose the Vietnamese experience with recent research by Lee and Zhang (2013), which has shed light on the manner in which the Chinese state employs non-security personnel, including networks of elderly persons, to bring pressure to bear on nonconformists.

Finally, we come to one of the most intriguing questions concerning politics in contemporary Vietnam: whether and to what extent the country is experiencing the rise of forms of autonomous forms of associational life; what some people refer to as "civil society." The relaxation of totalitarian controls that has unfolded in recent decades has permitted Vietnamese greater degrees of personal freedom, particularly in the areas of consumption and leisure activities. As Wells-Dang amply demonstrates, however, there are multiple forms of associational life springing up in Vietnam including many quasi-autonomous and practically autonomous social organizations that look, feel, and behave like civil society organizations in democratic polities. More important for our purposes, we have begun to observe the vigorous development of secondary associations of a distinctly political character, ranging from networks of independent journalists and bloggers to the "No-U Football Club (NUFC)," which brings together young persons opposed to China's legally baseless claims in the western Pacific.

The flowering of political associations in Vietnam occurs on thin ice. A clear example of these tensions was evident on Sunday, May 5, 2013, when a group of rights activists publicly called for human rights "picnics" at public parks in Hanoi, Nha Trang, and Ho Chi Minh City. Those participating were greeted by scores of police, who deployed multiple means to disperse the meetings. Several persons who were detained were subject to physical abuse and injury. In August 2013, young bloggers in Hanoi were the subject of a systematic campaign of threats, illegal detentions, and physical beatings. It seems that at the moment various activities represent what Bayat Asef has called "social 'non-movements'" (Bayat 2009).[2] Be that as it may, social "non-movements" whether in Vietnam or elsewhere can be socially significant and worthy of study. So too can further analysis of political discourse, including discussions of whether and under what conditions it is accompanied by political action.

Looking forward

How, then, should we characterize politics in contemporary Vietnam? This volume of chapters has not pretended to provide a comprehensive accounting of the state of politics in contemporary Vietnam. Nonetheless, the chapters in this volume permit degrees of confidence with respect to specific trends. Now into its eighth decade of existence, the CPV remains the leading force in Vietnam's politics, and is today faced with a qualitatively new set of challenges. While Vietnam's market economy has continued to grow, the Party has struggled to sustain economic growth and social order owing mostly to divisions and interests within the Party that dilute the force and coherence of its rule. The country's economic development remains geographically uneven, making the country's leadership and large swaths of the country's population dependent on a relatively small number of growth engines. Vietnam's formal representative institutions, though continuing to operate within the narrow confines of a single-party polity, maintain a unique position in Vietnam's polity. Within the past decade, the NA has gained stature as a forum for publicly addressing (if not always resolving) the stresses and strains of Vietnamese politics.

Perhaps the most salient development in Vietnam's politics has been in the realm of associational life. Dissent may be observed in any polity. Yet dissent within authoritarian contexts occurs within a hostile context. There seems little doubt that Vietnam in recent years has seen major changes in its political culture. While Vietnam has yet to develop any significant social movements, the country now exhibits (thanks mainly to increasing access to internet technologies) a vibrant political cyberspace in which dissenting views are presented and disseminated in an open manner. Nor are these discussions limited to cyberspace. On the other hand, the chapters in this volume demonstrate that open dissent in Vietnam carries many risks. The state sometimes tolerates dissent and sometimes crushes it by brutal means. While "civil society" remains a conceptually fraught term, empirical analysis suggests an increasing quasi-autonomous and practically autonomous associations now play a vital role in the social life of Vietnam and are transforming the character of the country's politics.

These and attendant changes introduce challenges to the study of politics in Vietnam. In contrast to the past, the study of politics in contemporary Vietnam is occurring in an age of big data, microblogs, and a 24-hour news cycle. To what extent does this enhance or hinder our ability to understand and explain political processes? The vastly increased flow of information in Vietnam gives one the sense that the velocity of politics has increased; but how can we know that we are indeed observing significant changes in the rules and compliance procedures governing power and authority relations in Vietnam? Is it the case that our understandings of politics in Vietnam are becoming more nuanced, or is it merely the case that we are experiencing changes in the manner in which we encounter politics in Vietnam? For scholars of politics in Vietnam, these are indeed interesting times.

As this book went to press, Vietnam's National Assembly had passed a revised constitution, with over 98 per cent approval, generating decidedly different reactions from across the political spectrum. Hailed by its champions, the constitutional vote was greeted with disdain by critics, including thousands of petitioners who had called for fundamental reforms. Just weeks later, Vietnamese observed International Human Rights Day with a series of events, including the inauguration of the Vietnam Bloggers Network. While in his 2014 New Year's Address, Vietnamese Prime Minister Nguyen Tan Dung raised eyebrows with a speech festooned with talk of the democracy and institutional reforms. These three examples, which transpired just within weeks of each other, remind us of how in the analysis of contemporary Vietnam's politics we confront questions both old and new. In this volume as in the past we have observed debates about the status of the CPV, featuring some accounts that emphasize decay and some that emphasize resilience and strength. As with the analysis of China, analysts of Vietnam often want to have it both ways. Indeed, they can. On the one hand, the CPV exhibits considerable fractiousness and incoherence and displays a leadership crisis at its peak. On the other hand, the Party and its constituent agencies remain a deeply institutionalized and dominant force in all spheres of social life, backed by a repressive apparatus that is formidable to say the least. Be that as it may, the events of the recent past suggest degrees of indeterminacy that are in my own view truly novel. Perhaps the greatest weakness of scholarship on authoritarian politics owes to the tendency for people within such regimes to conceal their preferences. For the present author, it is newly conceivable that very significant changes in Vietnam's political institutions could occur within five years' time.

Overall, this volume has depicted a country whose political institutions are evolving at a more rapid clip than in the past. The country's politics feels and is indeed less scripted than at any time in the postwar period. Vietnam's politics are fluid in a way that was hard to imagine just a few years ago. And they are more interesting than in the past, in part because the political scene is more open and uncertain than in the past. Certainly, many important themes have not been discussed in this volume. These include, but are not limited to, the rise of political activism, the shifting character of Vietnam's political links to the world system, the politics of class, gender, and ethnicity, and the politics of welfare, inequality, and citizenship. Be that as it may, the chapters in this volume have addressed key dimensions of politics in Vietnam at a momentous period in the country's political development. We hope and trust this volume contributes positively to existing understandings of contemporary Vietnamese politics and to situating Vietnam within the broader theoretical literature on comparative politics in Asia.

Notes

1. This sentiment was expressed at the conference to which these essays were initially submitted (Authoritarianism in East Asia, June 29–July 1, City University of Hong Kong).
2. I wish to thank Joerg Wischermann for calling this work to my attention.

References

Abuza, Zachary. *Renovating Politics in Contemporary Vietnam*. Boulder, CO: Lynne Rienner Publishers, 2001.

Alagappa, Muthiah. (ed.) *Civil Society and Political Change in Asia: Expanding and Contracting Democratic Space*. Stanford, CA: Stanford University Press, 2004.

Alesina, Alberto and Spolaore, Enrico,. "On the Number and Size of Nations." *Quarterly Journal of Economics* 112, no. 4 (1997): 1025–56.

An Dien. "Reforms in the Offing as Party Boss Apologizes." *Thanh Nien News*, October 9, 2012, available at <http://www.thanhniennews.com/index/pages/20121019-reforms-in-the-offing-as-party-boss-apologizes.aspx> Accessed 10/2012.

Arzaghi, Mohammad and Henderson,Vernon. "Why Countries Are Fiscally Decentralizing." *Journal of Public Economics* 89 (2005): 1157–89.

Ban Cong tac Dai bieu. "Vai tro cua Hoi dong Nhan dan trong phat trien kinh te-xa hoi o dia Phuong." [Role of People's Councils in Local Socio-Economic Development]. Hanoi: Chinh tri Quoc gia, 2009.

Bạch Ngọc Dương. "Những suy nghĩ về dân chủ đích thực cho Việt Nam." [Thoughts About Real Democracy for Viet Nam], October 20, 2007, available at Thông Luận Online <http://www.thongluan.org/vn/modules.php?name=News&file=article&sid=2196> Accessed October 26, 2007.

Baogang He and Thørgersen, Steig,. "Giving the People a Voice? Experiments with Consultative Authoritarian Institutions in China." *Journal of Contemporary China* 19 (September 2010): 675–92.

Bauxite Việt Nam. "Dự thảo Hiến Pháp 2013." [2013 Draft Constitution], alternate draft 2013, available at <http://boxitvn.blogspot.com> Accessed January 19, 2013.

Bayat, Asef. *Life as Politics: How Ordinary People Change the Middle East*. Stanford, CA: Stanford University Press, 2009.

BBC. "Ông Kiệt: Nên đối thoại sòng phẳng." [Kiệt: Need Honest Dialogue], May 7, 2007, available at <http://www.bbc.co.uk/vietnamese/vietnam/story/2007/05/070504_vo_van_kiet_part_two.shtml> Accessed May 15, 2007.

BBC Vietnamese. "An ninh VN phản đối Bộ Ngoại Giao Mỹ." [Vietnamese Security Object to US State Department], June 22, 2009, available at BBC Vietnamese website<http://www.bbc.co.uk/vietnamese/vietnam/2009/06/090620_us_tcan.shtml> Accessed June 22, 2009.

———. "Bà Trần Khải Thanh Thủy được thả." [Trần Khải Thanh Thủy Released], January 31, 2008, available at BBC Vietnamese website <http://www.bbc.co.uk/vietnamese/vietnam/story/2008/01/080131_trankhaithanhthuyrelease.shtml> Accessed February 11, 2008.

Beresford, Melanie. "Doi Moi in Review: The Challenges of Building Market Socialism in Vietnam." *Journal of Contemporary Asia* 38, no. 2 (2008): 221–43.

"Bóc trần dã tâm của bọn khủng bố." [Terrorists' Evil Intentions Exposed], April 21, 2009, available at CAND online < http://www.cand.com.vn/vi-VN/binhluan/2008/9/112115.cand> (accessed May 3, 2010).

Boix, Carles and Svolik, Milan. "The Foundations of Limited Authoritarian Government: Institutions, Commitment, and Power-Sharing in Dictatorships." *The Journal of Politics* 75, no. 2 (2013): 300–16.

Borton, Lady. *To Be Sure: Work Practices in Vietnam.* unpublished paper, 2001.

Bouquet, Mathieu. "Vietnamese Party-State and Religious Pluralism since 1986: Building the Fatherland?" *Sojourn* 25, no. 1 (April 2010): 90–108.

Brachet-Márquez, Viviane. "Domination, Contention, and the Negotiation of Inequality: A Theoretical Proposal." *Current Perspectives in Social Theory* 27 (2010): 123–61.

Brummitt, Chris. "Critics Pile on Government in Rare Debate." *Associated Press* (March 1, 2013b).

_____. "Vietnam Journalist Critical of Party Boss Fired." *Associated Press* (February 27, 2013a).

_____. "Vietnam Struggles to Crack Down on Activist Blogs." *Associated Press* (October 1, 2012).

Brzezinski, Zbigniew. *The Grand Failure: The Birth and Death of Communism in the Twentieth Century.* New York: Scribner, 1989.

Buchanan, James and Tullock, Gordon. *The Calculus of Consent.* Ann Arbor, MI: University of Michigan Press, 1962.

Bui, Thiem. "Liberal Constitutionalism and the Socialist State in an Era of Globalisation: An Inquiry into Vietnam's Constitutional Discourse and Power Structures." *Global Studies Journal* 5, no. 2 (2013): 43–52.

Bui Tin. *Following Ho Chi Minh*, translated by Judy Stowe and Đỗ Văn. Honolulu: University of Hawaii Press, 1995.

Bunce, Valerie. *Subversive Institutions: The Design and the Destruction of Socialism and the State.* Cambridge, UK: Cambridge University Press, 1999.

Case, William. "Low-Quality Democracy and Varied Authoritarianism: Elites and Regimes in Southeast Asia Today." *The Pacific Review* 22, no. 3 (2009): 255–69.

Chân Tín, Nguyễn Hữu Giải, Nguyễn Văn Lý, and Phan Văn Lợi. "Lời Kêu Gọi bầu cử Quốc Hội Đa Đảng." [Calling for Multiparty Elections for National Assembly], *Tự Do Ngôn Luận*, April 15, 2006: 3–4.

Cheng Li. *China's Leaders: The New Generation.* London: Rowman and Littlefield, 2001.

Chen Jian. "China and the First Indo-china War, 1950–1954." *China Quarterly* 133 (March 1993): 85–110.

Chinanet. "Vietnam Targets Bigger Realized FDI Capital in 2008." May 2, 2008 <http://news.xinhuanet.com/english/2008–05/02/content_8091903.htm>

CIVICUS. *State of Civil Society 2013: Creating an Enabling Environment.* World Alliance for Civic Participation, Johannesburg, 2013.

Clark, Helen. "Vietnam Party Congress: Where to Go from Here?" *Global Post* (January 20, 2011), available at <http://www.globalpost.com/dispatch/vietnam/110119/vietnams-communist-party-economy> Accessed 10/2012.

_____. "Can Vietnam Greens Block a Bauxite Mining Project?" *Time* (January 18, 2011).

Clarke, Simon and Pringle, Tim. "Can Party-Led Trade Unions Represent Their Members?" *Postcommunist Economies* 21, no. 1 (2009): 85–101

CODE. *Khai thác Bauxit và Phát triển bền vững Tây Nguyên [Bauxite Extraction and Sustainable Development in the Central Highlands].* Hanoi: Nhà xuất bản Tri thức, 2010.

Committee to Protect Vietnamese Workers. "Jailed Advocates' Families Ask Overseas Unions, Organizations to Help." October 26, 2010, available at <http://protectvietworkers.wordpress.com/2010/11/01/plea-for-help-letters-from-the-families-of-the-jailed/> Accessed May 25, 2011.

"Công An CS Hà Nội tiếp tục đàn áp dã man, khốc liệt gia đình nữ nhà báo tranh đấu Dương Thị Xuân." [Security Police Continue Ruthless Repression against Family of Dương Thị Xuân, an Activist Journalist], January 15, 2009, from Đối Thoại website <http://www.doi-thoai.com/baimoi0109_196.html> Accessed January 16, 2009.

Công An tinh Thừa Thiên Huế [Security Police, Thừa Thiên Huế Province]. "Bản Kết Luận Điều Tra – Vụ án: Nguyễn Văn Lý và đồng bọn – Tuyên truyền chống Nhà nước." [Investigation Report re. Nguyễn Văn Lý and Accomplices – Propaganda Against the State], March 13, 2007, available at Thông Luận Online <http://www.thongluan.org/vn/modules.php?name = Content&pa=showpage&pid=610> Accessed March 23, 2007.

"Constitution of the Socialist Republic of Vietnam." (1992), amended December 25, 2001.

"Country at the Crossroads Report: Vietnam." Washington DC: Freedom House, 2012, available at <http://www.freedomhouse.org/report/countries-crossroads/2012/vietnam> Accessed 10/2012.

"Cựu trung tá Trần Anh Kim, nhà tranh đấu và bất đồng chính kiến, bị công an bắt giữ 3 giờ đồng tại Hà Nội." [Hà Nội Security Police Detain for Three Hours Former Lieutenant Colonel Trần Anh Kim, Dissident and Fighter], April 30, 2006, available at Mạng Ý Kiến <http://www.ykien.net/> Accessed July 19, 2006.

Đài Việt Nam California Radio. "Phỏng Vấn Hoàng Minh Chính." [Hoàng Minh Chính interview], *Người Dân*, no. 71 (July 1996): 12–15, 34–5.

Dalpino, Catharin and Steinberg, David. *Georgetown Southeast Asia Survey 2004–2005*. Washington, DC: Georgetown University Press, 2005.

Dalton, Russell J. and Ong, Nhu-Ngoc. "Civil Society and Social Capital in Vietnam." In *Modernization and Social Change in Vietnam*, edited by Gerd Mutz and Rainer Klump, 30–48. Munich: Munich Institute for Social Science, 2004.

Dân Luận. "Nhà dân chủ Nguyễn Ngọc Quang khối 8406 được trả tự do." [Democracy Advocate of Bloc 8406, Nguyễn Ngọc Quang, Freed], September 5, 2009, available at Dân Luận <http://danluan.org/taxonomy/term/1755> Accessed January 15, 2010.

Dang Cong San Viet Nam [The Vietnamese Communist Party]. *Van Kien Dang Toan Tap* [The Complete Collection of Party Documents], v. 21, 491 and v. 37, 705.

Đảng Dân Chủ Nhân Dân [People's Democracy Party]. "Tuyên Ngôn." [Declaration], January 1, 2005, *Điện Thư*, no. 48 (July 2005): 1–7.

Đảng Thăng Tiến Việt Nam [Vietnam Progressive Party]. "Cương lĩnh tạm thời." [Provisional Policy Outline], September 8, 2006, available at *Tự Do Ngôn Luận* website <http://www. tdngonluan.com/tailieu/tl_dangthangtienvietnam_sept8.htm> Accessed September 29, 2006.

Đặng Văn Việt. "Kính gửi: Đại Hội X và Ban Chấp Hành Trung ương khóa IX." [Letter to the 10th Congress of Vietnam's Communist Party], February 12, 2006: 15, *Điện Thư*, no. 55 (February 2006b): 13–22.

_____. "Kính gửi Ủy ban Thường vụ Quốc hội…" [Letter to National Assembly's Standing Committee and Other Officials], September 10, 2006, *Tổ Quốc*, October 1 (2006a): 4–6.

Đặng Phong. "Stages on the Road to Renovation of the Vietnamese Economy: An Historical Perspective." In *Reaching for the Dream: Challenges of Sustainable Development in Vietnam*, edited by Melanie Beresford and Tran Ngoc Angie, 19–50. Copenhagen: Nordic Institute of Asian Studies (NIAS) Press, 2004.

Đặng Phong and Melanie Beresford. *Authority Relations and Economic Decision-Making in Vietnam: An Historical Perspective* (Vol. 38). Copenhagen: NIAS Press, 1998.

Dat Viet. "Siet chat cac du an san golf." June 2, 2008.

Department of Local Government, Ministry of Home Affairs. "Situation of Pilot for Non-Establishment of People's Councils at District and Ward Level." Ha Noi, ND.

Diamond, Larry. "Thinking about Hybrid Regimes." *Journal of Democracy* 13, no. 2 (2002): 21–35.

Điện Thư. "Tin Ghi Nhận" [News item], no. 39 (February 2005): 1.

Điện Thư. "Tin Ghi Nhận" [News item], no. 34 (December 2004): 1.

Đỗ Bá Tân. Letter from Đỗ Bá Tân, husband of Trần Khải Thanh Thủy, to Hà Nội city officials, October 15, 2009, available at Việt Tân website <http://www.viettan.org/spip.php?article9173>, via vnnews-l <vnnews-l@anu.edu.au> Accessed November 13, 2009.

Đỗ Mậu. "Tâm thư gửi đại hội." [Letter to Party Congress], *Điện Thư*, no. 57 (April 2006): 20–23.

Đỗ Nam Hải. "Phát biểu trong hội ngộ các thành viên của Phong trào yểm trợ Khối 8406." [Speech to Participants in the Block 8406 Movement], August 2008, available at Đối Thoại [Dialogue] website <http://www.doi-thoai.com/baimoi0308_288.html> Accessed April 4, 2008.

——. "Về việc 'Chấm dứt hợp đồng lao động' của tôi" [My 'work contract stoppage'], *Điện Thư*, no. 43 (April 2005): 4.

_____. [Writing under Pseudonym Phương Nam], "Việt Nam Tôi." [My Vietnam], *Điện Thư*, no. 28 (October 2004c): 15–47.

_____. "Thư ngỏ." [Open Letter to National Authorities et al.], December 10, 2004, *Điện Thư*, no. 34 (December 2004b): 1–4.

_____. "Little Saigon Radio Phỏng vấn Phương Nam." [Little Saigon Radio Interviews Phương Nam], December 14, 2004, *Điện Thư*, no. 35 (December 2004a): 1–4.

Drafting Committee for Revision of the 1992 Constitution. "Công văn về tiếp tục triển khai Nghị quyết của Quốc hội lấy ý kiến nhân dân về Dự thảo sửa đổi Hiến pháp." [Dispatch on Continuing to Implement the National Assembly's Decision to Consult the People on the Draft Revised Constitution], no. 250/UBDTSĐHP, March 6, 2013.

Duong Van Cu. "'Xã hội dân sự' – một thủ đoạn của diễn biến hòa bình." [Civil Society: A Trick of Peaceful Evolution], *Nhân Dân* [The People], August 31, 2012.

DVR Radio. "Phỏng vấn Vũ Hoàng Hải, thành viên Khối 8406 vừa đến Mỹ." [Interview with Vũ Hoàng Hải, Bloc 8406 member who recently arrived in the US], Westminister, California, February 17, 2010, available at Người Việt Online <http://www.nguoi-viet.com/absolutenm/ anmviewer.asp?a=108478&print=yes> Accessed March 3, 2010.

Edin, Maria. "State Capacity and Local Agent Control in China: CCP Cadre Management from a Township Perspective." *The China Quarterly* 106, no. 1 (March 2003): 35–52.

Ekiert, Grzegorz. *The State Against Society: Political Crises and their Aftermath in East Central Europe.* Princeton, N.J.: Princeton University Press, 1996.

Enikolopov, Ruben and Zhuravskaya, Ekaterina. "Federalism and Political Centralization." In *Political Institutions and Development: Failed Expectations and Renewed Hopes,* edited by Natalia Dinello and Vladimir Popov, 101–39. Cheltenham, UK: Edward Elgar, 2007.

FAO (Food and Agriculture Organization of the United Nations), available at <www.faostat.fao.org> Accessed February 12, 2011.

Fforde, Adam. "Vietnam's Informal Farmers' Groups: Narratives and Policy Implications." *Südostasien Aktuell* 1 (2008): 3–36.

Fforde, Adam and Paine, Suzanne. *The Limits of National Liberation.* London: Croom Helm, 1987.

Forum. *Journal of Vietnamese Studies* 5, no. 3 (Fall 2010): 192–243.

Freedom House. *Freedom in the World – Vietnam (2010),* available at <http://freedom-house.org/template.cfm?page+363&year=2010> Accessed May 29, 2011.

Fritzen, Scott. "Probing System Limits: Decentralization and Local Political Accountability in Vietnam." *Asia-Pacific Journal of Public Administration* 28, no. 1 (2006): 1–24.

Gainsborough, Martin. *Vietnam: Rethinking the State.* London: Zed Books, 2010.

_____."From Patronage to Outcomes: Vietnam's Communist Party Congresses Reconsidered." *Journal of Vietnamese Studies* 2, no. 1 (Winter 2007): 3–26.

_____. "Party Control: Electoral Campaigning in Vietnam in the Run-Up to the May 2002 National Assembly Elections." *Pacific Affairs* 78, no. 1 (2005): 57–75.

_____. "Ho Chi Minh City's Post-1975 Political Elite: Continuity and Change in Background and Belief." In *Beyond Ha Noi: Local Government in Vietnam,* edited by Benedict Tria Kerkvliet and David Marr, 259–84. Singapore: Institute of Southeast Asian Studies, 2004.

_____. "Key Issues in the Political Economy of Post Doi Moi Vietnam." In *Rethinking Vietnam,* edited by Duncan McCargo, 40–52. Oxford: RoutledgeCurzon, 2004.

Gainsborough, Martin, Dang Huong Giang, and Tran Thanh Phuong. "Promoting Efficient Interaction between the National Assembly and Civil Society in Vietnam." Report produced for the European Union. Hanoi: Konrad Adenauer Stiftung, 2011.

Gandhi, Jennifer. *Political Institutions under Dictatorship.* New York: Cambridge University Press, 2009.

Gandhi, Jennifer and Lust-Okar, Ellen. "Elections under Authoritarianism." *Annual Review of Political Science* 12 (2009): 403–22.

Gandhi, Jennifer and Przeworski, Adam. *Holding Onto Power by Any Means? The Origins of Competitive Elections.* Ms. Emory University (2009).

_____. "Authoritarian Institutions and the Survival of Autocrats." *Comparative Political Studies* 40, no. 11 (2007): 1279–301.

Garrett, Geoffrey and Rodden, Jonathan. "Globalization and Fiscal Decentralization." In *Governance in a Global Economy: Political Authority in Transition,* edited by Miles Kahler and David Lake, 87–109. Princeton, NJ: Princeton University Press, 2003.

Geddes, Barbara. "Why Parties and Elections in Authoritarian Regimes?" Paper presented at the annual meeting of the American Political Science Association, Washington, D.C., 2005.

Gehlbach, Scott and Keefer, Philip. "Private Investment and the Institutionalization of Collective Action in Autocracies: Ruling Parties and Legislatures." Working Paper, Department of Political Science, University of Wisconsin, Madison, 2010.

GiaoDuc Vietnam. "The National Assembly Does Not Need to Resolve the Situation of Deputy Hoang Huu Phuoc." February 21, 2013, available at <http://giaoduc.net.vn/Xa-hoi/Co-quan-Quoc-hoi-khong-can-phai-vao-cuoc-xu-ly-vu-DB-Hoang-Huu-Phuoc/278264.gd> Accessed 10/2012.

Gillespie, John. "The Juridification of Cause Advocacy in Socialist Asia: Vietnam as a Case Study." Conference paper (2012).

_____. "Understanding Legality in Vietnam." In *Vietnam's New Order. International Perspectives on the State and Reform in Vietnam.* New York: Palgrave Macmillan, 2007: 137–61.

Goodwin, Jeff. *No Other Way Out: States and Revolutionary Movements, 1945–1991.* Cambridge, UK: Cambridge University Press, 2001.

Goscha, Christopher. "Courting Diplomatic Disaster? The Difficult Integration of Vietnam into the Internationalist Communist Movement (1945–1950)." *Journal of Vietnamese Studies* 1, no. 1–2 (2006): 59–103.

Government of Vietnam. "Master Programme on Public Administration Reform for the Period 2001–2010." [Attachment to the Prime Minister's Approval Decision] NP.

Grossheim, Martin. "Revisionism in the Democratic Republic of Vietnam: New Evidence from the East German Archives." *Cold War History* 5, no. 4 (November 2005): 451–77.

GSO (General Statistics Office). "Number of Administrative Units as of 31 December 2008." available at <http://www.gso.gov.vn/default_en.aspx?tabid=466&idmid=3&ItemID=6138> Accessed January 28, 2010.

GSO and UNFPA (United Nations Population Fund). *The 2004 Vietnam Migration Survey: The Quality of Life of Migrants in Vietnam.* Ha Noi: Statistical Publishing House, 2006.

Hà Nội (2010). "Những trăn trở ẩn chứa sau hình ảnh nhà dân chủ." [Behind the Scenes Restlessness among Pro-Democracy People], available at VietLand: Voice of Freedom and Democracy for Vietnam <http://www.vietland.net/main/showthread.php?t=9808> Accessed January 7, 2010.

Hà Sĩ Phu. "Trả lời phỏng vấn của báo *Người Việt*." [Interview with *Người Việt* report], July 9, 2009b, available at Talawas blog <http://www.talawas.org/?p=7450> Accessed July 12, 2009.

_____. "Mất dân tộc còn tệ hơn mất nước." [Losing a Nation Is Worse Than Losing a Country], October 7, 2009a, available Tự Do Ngôn Luận website <http://www.tdngonluan.com/diendan/dd_matdantoc.htm> Accessed October 23, 2009.

_____. "Một mẩu đời thường." [A Bit of Everyday Life], September 9, 2008, available at Talawas <http://www.talawas.org/talaDB/showFile.php?res=14174&rb=0401> Accessed October 29, 2008. /D\Ha Si Phu\Mot Mau Doi Thuong 9 Sept 2008, p. 2/

_____. Transcript of interview by Đoàn Giao Thủy in Đà Lạt. June 2007b, available at Diễn Đàn <http://www.diendan.org/viet-nam/gap-ha-si-phu-o-111a-lat> Accessed July 11, 2007.

_____. "Cuộc giằng co về dân chữ còn kéo dài." [The Wrangle for Democracy Remains Protracted], August 23, 2007a, available at BBC website <http://www.bbc.co.uk/vietnamese/vietnam/story/2007/08/070822_hasiphu_interview.shtml> Accessed August 24, 2007.

Hai Cù Lần [probably a fictitious name]. "Luận bàn." [Discussion], *Điện Thư*, no. 39 (February 2005): 5–15.

Hannah, Joseph J. *Approaching Civil Society in Vietnam*. PhD diss., Department of Geography, Univ. of Washington, 2007.

Hansen, Peter. "Bac Di Cu: Catholic Refugees from the North of Vietnam and Their Role in the Southern Republic, 1954–1959." *Journal of Vietnamese Studies* 4, no. 3 (Fall 2009): 173–211.

Hardy, Andrew David. *Red Hills: Migration and the State in the Highlands of Vietnam* (Vol. 93). Copenhagen: NIAS Press, 2005.

Hayton, Bill. *Vietnam: Rising Dragon*. New Haven, CT: Yale University Press, 2010.

Heng, Russell. "Civil Society Effectiveness and the Vietnamese State – Despite or Because of the Lack of Autonomy." In Lee H.G. (ed.), *Civil Society in Southeast Asia*, 144–66. Singapore: Institute of Southeast Asia Studies, 2004.

Hicks, Natalie. "Facilitators of Rural Transformation and Development: The Role of Agricultural Extension Officers in Two Districts of Long an Province." In *Beyond Hanoi: Local Government in Vietnam*, edited by Benedict Kerkvliet and David Marr, 229. Copenhagen: NIAS Press, 2004.

"High Cost of Lifelong Commitment to Human Rights.", August 18, 2004, available at Amnesty International website <http://news.amnesty.org/index/ENGASA418182004> Accessed January 14, 2005.

Hiscox, Michael. "Political Integration and Disintegration in the Global Economy." In *Globalizing Authority*, edited by Miles Kahler and David Lake. Princeton, NJ: Princeton University Press, 2003.

Ho, Peter. "Introduction: Embedded Activism and Political Change in a Semi-Authoritarian Context." In Ho, P. and Edmonds, R.L. (eds), *China's Embedded Activism: opportunities and constraints of a social movement*, 1–19. London: Routledge, 2008.

Hoàng Bách Việt. "Những Chiến Sỹ Dân Chủ Chuyên Nghiệp." [Professional Fighters for Democracy], *Điện Thư*, no. 51 (October 2005): 1–6.

Hoang, Duy, Cuong Nguyen, and Angelina Huynh. 2009. *Viet Nam's Blogger Movement: A Virtual Civil Society in the Midst of Government Repression*. Washington, D.C.: Viet Tan Party, April 1, 2009, available at <www.Viet Nam.org/en> Accessed March 30, 2009.

Hoàng Hải. "Bạch Ngọc Dương lộ rõ chân tướng." [Bạch Ngọc Dương Showed His True Face], May 8, 2007, available at Đất Việt website <http://wwww.datviet.com/blogs/ forums/ba-nh-lua-n-tin-ta-c/141556-va-via-c-ba-ch-nga-c-dae-ae-ng-sang-campuchia.html> Accessed December 27, 2009.

Hoang Lan. "Bô xít Lâm Đồng sẽ xuất xưởng chậm hơn dự kiến." [Lam Dong Bauxite Will Be Extracted Slower than Planned], April 15, 2011, available at <http://bauxitevietnam.info/tin-tuc/bo-xit-lam-dong-se-xuat-xuong-cham-hon-du-kien.html> Accessed July 15, 2011.

Hoàng Minh Chính. "Tố cáo khẩn cấp việc bị cáo nhà báo Vũ Bình bị ngược tại nhà giam Hoả Lò Mới." [Denounce the Mistreatment of Defendent Vũ Bình in the Hoả Lò Mới Prison], April 22, 2004, *Điện Thư*, no. 19 (April 2004): 2–7.
_____. "Thư Ngỏ." [Open Letter], August 27, 1993, *Đối Thoại*, no. 3 (July–August 1994): 11–23.

Hoang Nghia. "Role of Civil Society Organizations in the Protection and Monitoring of Environmental." (sic). Paper prepared for the Vietnam Institute of Human Rights and IUCN Pilot Training Project on a Human Rights-Based Approach to Environmental Protection, 2011.

Hoàng Tiến. "Kẻ sĩ phải nói những điều ích nước lợi dân." [Scholars Should Say Things Useful for a Country to Benefit its People], *Thông Luận* (March 2005): 8–9.

Hội Nhân Dân Việt Nam Ủng hộ Đảng và Nhà Nước Chống Tham Nhũng. Open letter, dated September 2, 2001, available at Mạng Ý Kiến website <http://www.ykien.net/vdhchongtn.html> Accessed December 17, 2003.

Hongbin Li and Li-An Zhou. "Political Turnover and Economic Performance: The Incentive Role of Personnel Control in China." *Journal of Public Economics* 89 (2005): 1743–62.

Hongyi Lai. "Uneven Opening of China's Society, Economy, and Politics: Pro–growth Authoritarian Governance and Protests in China," *Journal of Contemporary China* 19 (November 2010): 819–35.

Hookway, James. "Vietnamese Premier Faces Fallout on Vinashin." *The Wall Street Journal*, November 2, 2010, available at <http://online.wsj.com/article/SB10001424052748703778304575589980974179868.html> Accessed 10/2012.

Huang Jing. *Factionalism in Chinese Communist Politics*. Cambridge, UK: Cambridge University Press, 2006.

Human Rights Watch. *World Report 2013*. New York: Human Rights Watch, 2013.
_____. *Montagnard Christians in Vietnam: A Case Study in Religious Repression*. New York: Human Rights Watch, 2011.

Huntington, Samuel P. *Political Order in Changing Societies*. New Haven, CT: Yale University Press, 1968: 146.

Huntington, Samuel P. and Clement Henry Moore. *Authoritarian Politics in Modern Society; The Dynamics of Established One-Party Systems*. New York: Basic Books, 1970.

Huy Duc. *Ben Thang Cuoc* [The Winning Side] (Vol. 1). Boston, MA: OsinBook, 2012.

Huynh Thanh Lap. "Hoat dong giam sat cua HDND TP Ho Chi Minh ve dau tu xay dung co ban." [Supervision Activities of Ho Chi Minh City's People's Council on Capital Construction]. N.D.

Huỳnh Việt Lang. "Dân chủ va văn hóa tổ chức." [Democracy and the Culture of Organization], *Điện Thư*, no. 58 (May 2006): 34–43.

"Internet Writer Bui Kim Thanh Released." August 13, 2008, available at International Pen website <http://www.internationalpen.org.uk/go/news/vietnam-internet-writer-bui-kim-th-nh-f-released> Accessed May 3, 2010.

iSEE. "Góp ý với dự thảo sửa đổi Hiến pháp 1992 của 7 nhóm xã hội, nhóm yếu thế và dễ bị tổn thương." [Suggestions on the Draft Revisions to the 1992 Constitution from Seven Weak and Vulnerable Social Groups], Hanoi, March, 2013b.

_____. "Kiến nghị của các tổ chức xã hội dân sự Việt Nam về dự thảo sửa đổi Hiến pháp 1992." [Recommendations of Vietnamese Civil Society Organizations on the Draft Revisions to the 1992 Constitution], Hanoi, March, 2013a.

_____. "Phản hồi bài báo 'xã hội dân sự' – một thủ đoạn của diễn biến hòa bình.", letter to the editor of *Nhân Dân* newspaper, September 12, 2012.

Ives, Mike. "In Surprise Move, Vietnam Asks Citizens for Public Comment on Their Constitution." *Christian Science Monitor*, March 26, 2013.

Jandl, Thomas. *Race to the Top: Global Integration and Contested Politics in Vietnam's Economic Success Story.* Lanham, MD: Lexington Books, 2013 (forthcoming).

_____. "Rent Seeking and Interest Group Contestation: A Harmony-of-Interest Approach to Vietnam's Economic Reforms." Dissertation, American University, 2011.

Kalyvas, Stathis. "The Decay and Breakdown of Communist One-Party Systems." *Annual Review of Political Science* 2 (1999): 336–40.

Kerkvliet, Benedict J. Tria. "Governance, Development, and the Responsive-Repressive State in Vietnam." *Forum for Development Studies* 37 (March 2010b): 33–59.

_____. "Workers' Protests in Contemporary Vietnam (with some Comparisons to those in the Pre-1975 South)." *Journal of Vietnamese Studies* 5 (Winter 2010a): 162–204.

_____. *The Power of Everyday Politics: How Vietnamese Peasants Transformed National Policy.* Ithaca, NY: Cornell University Press, 2005.

_____. "Introduction: Grappling with Organizations and the State in Contemporary Vietnam." In Kerkvliet, B., Heng, R., and Koh, D. (eds), *Getting Organized in Vietnam: Moving in and Around the Socialist State*, 1–24. Singapore: Institute of Southeast Asian Studies, 2003.

Kerkvliet, Benedict J. Tria and David Marr. (eds) *Beyond Hanoi: Local Government in Vietnam.* Copenhagen: NIAS Press, 2004.

Kerkvliet, Benedict J. Tria, Nguyễn Quang A., and Bạch Tân Sinh. *Forms of Engagement Between State Agencies and Civil Society Organizations in Vietnam.* Hanoi: NGO Resource Centre, 2008.

Khánh, Huỳnh Kim. *Vietnamese Communism, 1925–1945.* Ithaca, NY: Cornell University Press, 1986.

"Khi nhà nước đè bẹp công lý." [When the State Crushes Justice], March 25, 2009, available at Tiếng Nói Tự do Dân chủ website <http://tiengnoitudodanchu.org/modules.php?name=News&file=article&sid=7261> Accessed March 27, 2009.

Khối 8406, "Quyết định bổ nhiệm Đại diện Khối 8406 tại Hải ngoại." [Resolution Appointing a Foreign Representative for Bloc 8406], October 18, 2007, available at *Tự Do Ngôn Luận* website <http://www.tdngonluan.com/tailieu/tl_khoi8406_quyetdinhbonhiem daidienhaingoai.htm> Accessed February 22, 2008.

Koh, David. "Leadership Changes at the 10th Congress of the Vietnamese Communist Party." *Asian Survey* 48, no. 4 (2008): 650–72.

_____. "Political Reforms and Democratization in Vietnam." In *East Asian Democracy and Political Change in China*, edited by Zhengxu Wang and Colin Duerkop, 75–96, especially 79–82. Singapore: Konrad Stiftung, 2008b.

_____. "Urban Government: Ward-Level Administration in Hanoi." In *Beyond Hanoi: Local Government in Vietnam*, edited by Benedict Kerkvliet and David Marr, 197–228. Copenhagen: NIAS Press, 2004.

Lai, Bui Duc. "Dang lanh dao trong che do dan chu nhan dan." September 22, 2010, available at <http://vietnamnet.vn/chinhtri/201009/dang-lanh-dao-trong-che-do-dan-chu-nhan-dan-936926/> Accessed 10/2012.

Lai, Tuong. "Hanh trinh tu 'chuyen chinh vo san' den 'lam chu tap the' va 'Nha nuoc phap quyen Viet nam." *Nguoi Dai Bieu Nhan Dan*, September 12, 2006.

Landry, Pierre. *Decentralized Authoritarianism in China*. New York: Cambridge University Press, 2008.

Lee, Ching Kwan and Zhang, Yonghong. "The Power of Instability: Unraveling the Microfoundations of Bargained Authoritarianism in China." *American Journal of Sociology* 118, no. 3 (2013): 1475–508.

Lê Hồng Hà. "Đấu tranh vì phát triển và dân chủ hóa đất nước." [Struggle for National Development and Democratization], March 10, 2007b, available at Diễn Đàn <http://www.diendan.org/viet-nam/le-hong-ha-111au-tranh-vi-phat-trien-va-dan-chu-hoa-111at-nuoc/> Accessed July 11, 2007.

_____. "Ông Lê Hồng Hà." [Lê Hồng Hà], March 22, 2007a, available at RFA website <http://www.rfa.org/vietnamese/in_depth/2007/03/22/LeHongHaOverviews VCPArrangedParlamentVoting_VHung/> Accessed March 23, 2007

_____. Transcript of interview by Việt Tide, February 1, 2006, available at Đàn Chim Việt <http://www.danchimviet.com/php/modules.php?name=News&fil e=article&sid=1144> Accessed February 2, 2007.

_____. "Tiền đồ phát triển của đất nước và trách nhiệm của giới trí thức." [National Development Prospects and Intellectuals' Responsibilities], 2004, available at Mạng Ý Kiến <http://www.ykien.net/bnlhhtrithuc.html> Accessed March 3, 2004.

Lê Chí Quang. "Muốn chống tham nhũng, phải chống cái cơ chế ra tham nhũng." [To Fight Corruption One Needs to Fight the Structure That Produces it], August 19, 2001, in *Điện Thư*, no. 22 (June 2004): 1–6.

Lê Minh. "Bài viết về Lê Trí Tuệ." [About Lê Trí Tuệ], May 4, 2009, available at VietLand: Voice of Freedom and Democracy for Vietnam <http://www.vietland. net/main/show thread.php?t=9808> Accessed January 7, 2010.

Le Phuoc Tho. "Most so nhiem vu doi moi va chinh don Dang." *Tap chi Xay Dung Dang*, Special Issue (1982).

Lê Quang Liêm. "Làm thế nào Tiến đến Dân chủ hóa Việt Nam?" [How to Progress to Democratization in Vietnam], *Tự Do Ngôn Luận*, May 15 (2006): 17–18.

"Lê Trần Luật bị xóa tên trong danh sách Luật Sư Đoàn." [Lê Trần Luật's Name Erased from Bar Association List], November 1, 2009, available at Radio Free Asia website <http://www.rfa.org/vietnamese/in_depth/The-bar-association-of-ninh-thuan-province-deleted-the-name-of-lawyer-le-tran-luat-from-its-list-mlam-11012009120520.html> Accessed November 4, 2009.

"Lê Trí Tuệ đã lừa đào người lao động như thế nào?" [How Did Lê Trí Tuệ Swindle Workers?], *An Ninh Thế Giới*, May 16, 2007, available at CAND online <http://ca.cand.com.vn/VI-VN/anninhtrattu/tinANTT\2007\5\104774. cand?SearchTerm=Lê Trí Tuệ đã lừa> Accessed January 4, 2010.

Library of Congress. 1987. *Viet Nam*. Country Studies Series. Washington, D.C.: Federal Research Division. <http://lcweb2.log.gov/frd/cs> Accessed July 24, 2007.

Lien-Hang Nguyen. *Hanoi's War: An International History of the War for Peace in Vietnam*. Chapel Hill: University of North Carolina Press, 2012.

Linz, Juan J. "Further Reflections on Totalitarian and Authoritarian Regimes." In *Totalitarian and Authoritarian Regimes*, edited by Juan J. Linz, 1–48. Boulder, CO: Lynne Rienner, 2000.

Linz, Juan J. "An Authoritarian Regime: Spain." In *Cleavages, Ideologies and Party Systems. Contributions to Comparative Political Sociology*, edited by Erik Allardt and Yrjö Littunen, 291–341. Helsinki: Westermarck Society, 1964.

London, Jonathan D. "Market-Leninism." Working Paper, Southeast Asia Research Centre, City University of Hong Kong, Hong Kong, February 6, 2012.

_____. (ed.) *Education in Vietnam*. Institute of South East Asian Studies, 2011.

_____. "Viet Nam and the Making of Market-Leninism." *The Pacific Review* 22, no. 3 (2009): 375–99.

_____. 2004. "Vietnam's Mass Education and Health Systems: A Regimes Perspective." *American Asian Review* 21, no. 2 (2003): 125–70.

Lũ Phương. Transcript of interview by Đoàn Giao Thủy, July 2007, available at Diễn Đàn website <http://www.diendan.org/viet-nam/trao-111oi-voi-ban-111-oc-dien-111an/> Accessed August 31, 2007.

MacKinnon, Rebecca. "China's 'Networked Authoritarianism." *Journal of Democracy* 22 (April 2011): 32–46.

Magaloni, Beatriz. *Voting for Autocracy: Hegemonic Party Survival and its Demise in Mexico*. New York: Cambridge University Press, 2006.

Magaloni, Beatriz and Ruth Kricheli. "Political Order and One-Party Rule." *Annual Review of Political Science* 13 (2010): 123–43.

Mai, Pham Hoang. *FDI and Development in Vietnam*. Singapore: Institute of Southeast Asian Studies, 2004.

Malesky, Edmund J. "Paint-by-Numbers Democracy: The Stakes, Structure, Results, and Implications of the 2007 Vietnamese National Assembly Elections." *Journal of Vietnamese Studies* 4, no. 1 (2008): 1–48.

_____. "Straight Ahead on Red: How Foreign Direct Investment Empowers Subnational Leaders." *Journal of Politics* 70, no. 1 (January 2008): 97–119.

_____. "Push, Pull, and Reinforcing: The Channels of FDI Influence on Provincial Governance in Vietnam." In *Beyond Hanoi: Local Government in Vietnam*, edited by Benedict Kerkvliet and David Marr, 285–326. Copenhagen: ISEAS Press, 2004.

_____. "At Provincial Gates: The Impact of Locally Concentrated Foreign Direct Investment on Provincial Autonomy and Local Reform." Dissertation, Duke University, 2004b.

Malesky, Edmund, Anh Tran, and Paul Schuler. "Vietnam 2010: Familiar Patterns and New Developments Ahead of the 11th Vietnam Communist Party Congress." *Southeast Asian Affairs* (2011): 339–63.

Malesky, Edmund and Paul Schuler. "Star Search: Do Elections Help Non-Democratic Regimes Identify New Leaders?" *Journal of East Asian Studies* (December 2013).

_____. "Star Search: Do Elections Help Non-Democratic Regimes Identify New Leaders?" *Journal of East Asian Studies* 13, no. 1 (2012): 35–68.

_____. "The Single-Party Dictator's Dilemma: Information in Elections without Opposition." *Legislative Studies Quarterly* 36, no. 4 (2011): 491–530.

_____. "Nodding or Needling: Analyzing Delegate Responsiveness in an Authoritarian Parliament." *American Political Science Review* 104, no. 3 (August 2010): 1–21.

_____. "Paint-by-Numbers Democracy: The Stakes, Structure, Results, and Implications of the 2007 Vietnamese National Assembly Elections." *Journal of Vietnamese Studies* 4, no. 1 (2008): 1–48.

Marr, David. *Vietnam 1945: The Quest for Power*. Berkeley, CA: University of California Press, 1995.

Maskin, Eric, Yingyi Qian and Chenggang Xu. "Incentives, Information and Organizational Form." *Review of Economic Studies* 67, no. 2 (2000): 359–78.

McGee, Rosemary and John Gaventa. "Review of Impact and Effectiveness of Transparency and Accountability Initiatives: A Review of the Evidence to Date." Brighton, UK: Institute of Development Studies, 2010.

McGuire, Martin and Mancur Olson. "The Economics or Autocracy and Majority Rule: The Invisible Hand and the Use of Force." *Journal of Economic Literature* 34, no. 1 (1996): 72–96.

McKinley, Catherine. "Can a State-Owned Media Effectively Monitor Corruption? A Study of Vietnam's Printed Press." *Asian Journal of Public Affairs* 2, no. 1 (2008): 12–38.

Minh Chính. "Thư Gửi Ông Nguyễn Minh Triết." [Open letter to Nguyễn Minh Triết], April 26, 2006, Điện Thư, no. 58 (May 2006): 51–52.

Mitchell, Timothy. "Society, Economy and the State Effect." In Sharma, A. and Gupta, A. (eds), *The Anthropology of the State: A Reader*, 169–86. Malden, MA and Oxford: Blackwell Publishing, 2006.

Montinola, Gabriella, Yingyi Qian, and Barry Weingast. "Federalism, Chinese Style: The Political Basis for Economic Success." *World Politics* 48, no. 1 (1996): 50–81.

Morris-Jung, Jason. *Prospects and Challenges for Environmental Politics: The Vietnamese Bauxite Controversy*, paper presented at the Vietnam Update Conference, Australian National University, Canberra, November 17, 2011.

Munro, Robin. *China's Psychiatric Inquisition: Dissent, Psychiatry and the Law in Post-1949 China*. London: Wildy, Simmonds & Hill, 2006.

Nam Pham. "Ủy ban dự thảo sửa đổi Hiến pháp tiếp nhận bàn kiến nghị từ 7 nhóm Xã hội và các tổ chức Xã hội Dân sự." [Constitutional Drafting Committee Receives Recommendations from 7 Social Groups and Civil Society Organizations], blog article posted at <isee.org.vn>, March 29, 2013.

Nathan, Andrew. "Authoritarian Resilience." *Journal of Democracy* 14, no. 1 (2003): 6–17

Nguyễn Chính Kết. "Nguy cơ mất nước đã đến rất gần." [Threat of National Destruction is Near], April 5, 2009, available at Đối Thoại website <http://www.doi-thoai.com/baimoi0409_126. html> Accessed April 17, 2009.

_____. "Cuộc tranh đấu không cân sức giữa các nhà dân chủ trong nước và nhà cầm quyền cộng sản Việt Nam." [Vietnam's Uneven Struggle between Prodemocracy People and Communist Authorities], *Tự Do Ngôn Luận*, June 1, 2006b: 23–25.

_____. "Tình hình chính trị Việt Nam." [Vietnam's Political Situation], *Tự Do Ngôn Luận*, May 1 (2006a): 24–25.

Nguyen Dac Kien. "Vài lời với TBT ĐCSVN Nguyễn Phú Trọng." [A Few Words with General Secretary Nguyen Phu Trong], blog posting, February 28 <http://ttxva.org/tbt-dcs-vn-nguyen-phu-trong/> Accessed May 1, 2013.

Nguyen Hai Long. "Giam sat cua Hoi dong nhan dan o noi thuc hien thi diem khong to chuc Hoi dong nhan dan.", 2011, available at <http://www.nclp.org.

vn/y-kien-tu-co-so/giam-sat-cua-hoi-111ong-nhan-dan-o-noi-thuc-hien-thi-111iem-khong-to-chuc-hoi-111ong-nhan-dan>

Nguyễn Hải Sơn. "Dấu hỏi chấm than (...? !)." [Question and Exclamation Marks], *Diện Thư*, no. 32 (December 2004): 19–23.

"Nguyễn Khắc Toàn, kẻ vụ lợi bằng việc làm phán dân hại nước." [Nguyễn Khắc Toàn, a Mercenary Who Betrays the People and Damages the Country], June 8, 2009, available at Công An Nhân Dân Online <http://www.cand.com.vn/vi-VN/binhluan/2009/6/114397.cand> Accessed July 2, 2009.

Nguyễn Khắc Toàn. "Công An CSVN đàn áp đối lập trong ngày điều trân nhân quyền ở LHQ." [Security Police Repress Opposition While Testifying to the United Nations about Human Rights], May 11, 2009, available at Người Việt Online <http://www.nguoi-viet.com/absolutenm/anmviewer.asp?a=94755&z=157> Accessed May 14, 2009.

_____. "Trao đổi trong buổi làm việc với các sĩ quan an ninh của sở công an Hà Nội tại quán trà ngay sau Tết Nguyên Đán Mâu-Tý năm." [Exchanges with Local Security Police Officials at a Tea Shop Immediately after the New Year], March 5–6, 2008, available at Đối Thoại Online <http://www.doi-thoai.com/baimoi0308_174.html> Accessed March 19, 2008; <http://www.doi-thoai.com/baimoi0308_208.html> Accessed March 19, 2008; <http://www.doi-thoai.com/baimoi0308_323.html> Accessed April 4, 2008.

_____. "Phát biểu tại Hội thảo Bàn tròn." [Presentation to Roundtable Discussion], July 1, 2007, available at Đối Thoại Online <http://www.doi-thoai.com/baimoi0707_006.html> Accessed July 6, 2007.

_____. "Khác vọng tự do." [Craving Freedom], April 25, 2006, available at Mạng Ý Kiến <http://www.ykien.net/> Accessed June 20, 2006.

Nguyen Manh Tuong. *Ke bi mat phep thong cong, Hanoi 1954–1991: Ban an cho mot tri thuc*, translated from French by Nguyen Quoc Vy, available at <http://viet-studies.info/NMTuong/NMTuong_HoiKy.htm> Accessed 10/2012.

Nguyen Nam Khanh. "Thu cua Thuong tuong Nguyen Nam Khanh gui Lanh dao Dang ve su long quyen cua Tong cuc 2." [Letter from Major General Nguyen Nam Khanh to the Party Leadership Concerning the Abuse of Power by General Department II], June 17, 2004.

Nguyen Phu Trong. *Phát biểu của Tổng Bí thu bế mạc Hội nghị TU 6* [General Secretary's Closing Speech to the 6th Party Plenum], October 15, 2012.

Nguyễn Phương Anh. "Người Tù 4436Z." [Prisoner 4436Z], October 7, 2008, available at Mạng Ý Kiến <http://www.thongluan.org/vn/modules.php?name=News&file=article&sid=3162> Accessed October 13, 2008.

Nguyen Quang A. "Xã hội dân sự đâu có đáng sợ." [Civil Society Is Nothing to Be Afraid Of], *Lao Động Cuối tuần* [Labor Newspaper Weekend Edition], April 12, 2009, available at <http://www.chungta.com/Desktop.aspx/ChungTa-SuyNgam/Van-Hoa/Xa_hoi_dan_su_dau_dang_so/> Accessed August 16, 2010.

Nguyen Quang Dong. "NGO ở Việt Nam – anh là ai?" [NGOs in Viet Nam: Who Are You?], Paper circulated on the People's Participation Working Group email list, September 7, 2012.

Nguyễn Thanh Giang. "Bàn về Dân Chủ." [About Democracy], *Diện Thư*, no. 56 (March 2006): 8–51.

Nguyễn Thanh Giang. "Bộ Quốc Phòng rời bỏ nhiệm vụ chính của mình." [Ministry of Defence Has Abandoned Its Primary Responsibility], *Diện Thư*, no. 33 (December 2004): 1–10

Nguyen Thanh Tuan. "Xã hội dân sự: từ kinh điển Mác – Lê-nin đến thực tiễn Việt nam hiện nay." [Civil Society: From Classical Marxism-Leninism to Viet Nam's Present Conditions], *Tạp chí Công sản* [Journal of Communism] 132, no. 12 (2007), available at <http://www.tapchicongsan.org.vn/details. asp?Object=4&news_ID=6776787> Accessed August 27, 2008.

Nguyen Thi Huong (2012) "Pursuing Constitutional Dialogue within Socialist Vietnam: The 2010 Debate." *Australian Journal of Asian Law* 13(1): 1–18.

Nguyễn Thiện Tâm. "Thư gửi toàn dân Việt Nam." [Letter to all Vietnamese People], *Diện Thư*, no. 46 (June 2005): 14–34.

Nguyễn Văn Huy. "Hai vụ án thô bạo đáng lưu ý." [Two Bruttish Trials Worth Paying Attention To], *Thông Luận* (February 2009): 13–14.

Nguyễn Văn Lý. "Vì sao Tẩy Chay Quốc hội Độc Đảng 2007 Đủ sức Giải thể Chế độ CSVN hiện nay?" [Why Can Boycotting the 2007 Election for the Single Party National Assembly Bring Down the Communist Party Regime?] January 21, 2007, available at *Tự Do Ngôn Luận* website <http://www.tdngonluan.com/ tailieu/tl_visaotaychay.htm> Accessed January 31, 2007.

Nguyễn Văn May and Lê Thị Thúy Minh. Complaint letter from Nguyễn Văn May and Lê Thị Thúy Minh, parents of Nguyễn Phương Anh, to the Deputy Minister, Ministry of Security, December 22, 2007, available at Việt Báo online <http:// www.vietbao.com/?ppid=45&pid=45&nid=120781> Accessed March 15, 2010.

Nguyễn Vũ Bình. "Tương lai nào cho phong trào dân chủ Việt Nam?" [What's the Future for Vietnam's Democracy Movement?], February 28, 2008, available at Mạng Ý Kiến <http://ykien0711.blogvis.com/2008/02/29/t%c6%b0%c6%a1ng-lai-nao-cho-phong-trao-dan-ch%e1%bb%a7-vi%e1%bb%87t-nam/> Accessed March 6, 2008.

NH. "Những trăn trở ẩn chứa sau hình ảnh nhà dân chủ." [Behind the Scenes Restlessness Among Pro-Democracy People], April 3, 2008, available at VietLand: Voice of Freedom and Democracy for Vietnam <http://www.vietland.net/main/ showthread.php?t=9808> Accessed January 7, 2010.

Nhóm phóng viên Phong trào tranh đấu vì Dân chủ, Hà Nội." [Democracy Movement Journalists in Hà Nội], "Hà Nội: công an tiếp tục sách nhiễu các nhà dân chủ." [Security Police Continue to Harass Democracy Activists], June 4, 2008, available at Y Kien Blog <http://ykienblog.wordpress.com/2008/06/05/ ha-noi-cong-an-ti%e1%ba%bfp-t%e1%bb%a5c-sach-nhi%e1%bb%85u-cac-nha-dan-ch%e1%bb%a7/> Accessed June 18, 2008.

Ninh Kieu. "Bar to Be Raised on FDI." *Vietnam Investment Review*, January 28, 2008.

Ninh, Kim N. *A World Transformed: The Politics of Culture in Revolutionary Vietnam, 1945–1965.* Ann Arbor, MI: University of Michigan Press, 2002.

Nørlund, Irene. (ed.) *The Emerging Civil Society: An Initial Assessment of Civil Society in Vietnam.* Hanoi: CIVICUS, 2006.

Oates, Wallace. *Fiscal Federalism.* New York: Harcourt Brace Jovanovich, 1972.

O'Donnell, Guillermo. *Modernization and Bureaucratic-Authoritarianism: Studies in South American Politics* (Vol. 9). Berkeley, CA: Institute of International Studies, University of California, 1973.

Ogden, Suzanne. *Inklings of Democracy in China.* Cambridge, MA: Harvard University Asia Center, 2002: 3–7, 177–81, 345–52.

Olson, Mancur. "Dictatorship, Democracy and Development." *American Political Science Review* 87 (1993): 567–76.

O'Rourke, Dara. "Community-Driven Regulation: Toward an Improved Model of Environmental Regulation in Vietnam." In *Livable Cities? Urban Strategies for Livelihood and Sustainability*, edited by Peter Evans, 55–131. Berkeley, CA: University of California Press, 2002.

Oxfam and Oxford Policy Management. *Vietnam: Country Political Economy Analysis*. September 2012.

Parente, Stephen and Edward Prescott. *Barriers to Riches*. Cambridge, MA: MIT Press, 2000.

Pei, Minxin. *China's Trapped Transition: The Limits of Developmental Autocracy*. Cambridge, MA: Harvard University Press, 2006.

People's Participation Working Group. "Tổng hợp kết quả họp PPWG mở rộng." [Summary of Results of the Expanded PPWG Meeting], minutes circulated on the PPWG email list, September 6, 2012.

Perry, Elizabeth J. *Patrolling the Revolution: Worker Militias, Citizenship, and the Modern Chinese State*. Rowman & Littlefield, 2007.

Pham Bich San. "Kinh te va nhung gi ngoai kinh te sau 5 nam Viet nam gia nhap WTO." April 14, 2013, available at <http://songmoi.vn/kinh-te-tai-chinh/kinh-te-va-nhung-gi-ngoai-kinh-te-sau-5-nam-viet-nam-gia-nhap-wto> Accessed 10/2012.

Phạm Đình Trọng. "Thông báo về việc từ bỏ đảng tịch đảng viện đảng Cộng sản." [Announcement of a Communist Party Member Leaving the Party], November 20, 2009, *Tổ Quốc*, December 15 (2009): 2–8.

Pham Duy Nghia. "Luat phap truoc suc ep." *Thoi Bao Kinh Te Sai Gon*, February 12, 2007.

Phạm Hồng Sơn. "Đấu tranh bất bạo động: tại sao không?" [Non-violent Struggle: Why Not?], *Thông Luận* (July and August 2009b): 5.

———. "Ngày Độc Lập, Nghĩ về Độc lập Tư duy." [Independence Day Reflections about Independence], *Thông Luận* (September 2009a): 8–10.

Phạm Hồng Sơn and Thu Lệ. "Vài dòng Tâm sự." [A Few Intimate Lines], a preface to *Thế Nào là Dân Chủ* [What Is Democracy; A Translation], January 2002, available at Mạng Ý Kiến <http://www.ykien.net/bnphsthenaodc.html> Accessed October 10, 2003.

Phạm Quế Dương. "Một bài viết có tầm chiến lược cho phong trào dân chủ." [An Article of Strategic Relevance to a Democracy Movement], *Thông Luận* 9 (2007): 15.

———. "Về Bản Cáo Trạng Lê Chí Quang." [Regarding Charges against Lê Chí Quang], October 20, 2002, available at Mạng Ý Kiến <http://www.ykien.net/tl_lcq15> Accessed October 23, 2003.

Phạm Quế Đương and Trần Khuê. "Hội Nhân Dân Việt Nam Chống Tham Nhũng." [Vietnamese Association against Corruption], *Điện Thư*, no. 18 (March 2004): 1–3.

Phạm Văn Hải. "Ai chống đối nhà nước CHXHCN?" [Who's Opposing the Socialist Republic?] May 2, 2009, available at Thông Luận Online <http://www.thongluan.org/vn/modules.php?name=News&file=article&sid=3734> Accessed June 2, 2009.

Phan, Diep and Ian Coxhead. "Inter-Provincial Migration and Inequality during Vietnam's Transition." Staff Paper #507. Madison, WI: Department of Agricultural and Applied Economics, University of Wisconsin. Draft, July 12, 2007.

Phan Đình Diệu. "Một số suy nghĩ về con đường tiếp tục đổi mới của đất nước ta." [Thoughts About Our Country's Continuing Renovation], *Điện Thư*, no.33 (December 2004): 18–22.

"Phát biểu của tướng Trần Độ." [Speech by General Trần Độ], *Tivi Tuần San* (Melbourne), January 13 (1999): 16, 44.

Porter, Gareth. *Vietnam: The Politics of Bureaucratic Socialism*. Ithaca, NY: Cornell University Press, 1993.

Puddington, Arch. "The Erosion Accelerates." *Journal of Democracy* 21, no. 2 (2010): 136–50.

Phuc Son. "Kho khan va giai phap trong viec nang cao chat luong to chuc co so Dang va Dang vien." *Tap chi Xay Dung Dang*, 11 (2007), available at <http://www.xaydungdang.org.vn/details.asp?Object=4&news_ID=51178442> Accessed 10/2012.

Pike, Douglas. *History of Vietnamese Communism, 1925–1976*. Stanford: Hoover Institution Press, 1978.

Quinn-Judge, Sophie. "Rethinking the History of the Vietnamese Communist Party." In *Rethinking Vietnam*, edited by Duncan McCargo, 27–39. New York: RoutledgeCurzon, 2005.

Radio Free Asia. "Ông Trần Anh Kim bị tuyện án 5 năm rưởi tù giam." [Trần Anh Kim Sentenced to Five and a Half Years Imprisonment], December 29, 2009, available at Tiếng Nói Tự do Dân Chủ website <http://tiengnoitudodanchu.org/modules.p hp?name=News&file=article&sid=8516> Accessed December 28, 2009.

———. "Lê Hồng Hà: cuộc phỏng vấn." [Interview with Lê Hồng Hà], February 1, 2007b, available at Thông Luận Online <http://www.thongluan.org/vn/ modules.php?name=Content&pa= showpage&pid=493> Accessed February 2, 2007.

———. "Kỹ sư Bạch Ngọc Dương thuật lại chuyện bị công an hành hung." [Engineer Bạch Ngọc Dương Relates Instances of Beatings by Security Police], February 9, 2007a, available at RFA website <http://www.rfa.org/vietnamese/in_ depth/2007/02/09/BachNgocDuongDeportedToHaiPhong_VHung/> Accessed February 15, 2007.

———. "Anh Nguyễn Ngọc Quang thuật lại các buổi lời thầm vấn công an." [Nguyễn Ngọc Quang Relates Security Police Interrogation Sessions], August 9, 2006b, available at <http://www.rfa.org/vietnamese/in_depth/2006/08/09/ Interview_NNQ_member_of_democracy_group_TMi/> Accessed August 11, 2006.

———. "Anh Vũ Hoàng Hải." [Mr Vũ Hoàng Hải], August 4 and 9, 2006a, available at RFA website <http://www.rfa.org/vietnamese/in_depth/2006/08/04/ InterviewPhamBaHaiQuestionedByPolice_TMi/> and <http://www.rfa.org/ vietnamese/in_depth/Interview_member_of_Democracy_group_Beaten_by_ Police_VHung-20060809.html> Accessed August 11, 2006.

———. "Nguyễn Xuân Nghĩa." September 27, 2005, available at Mạng Ý Kiến, <http://www.ykien.net/tl_viettrung91.html#dhX050928a> Accessed October 30, 2005.

———. "Nạn Tham nhũng tại Việt Nam theo Quan điểm của Đại tá Phạm Quế Dương." [Vietnam's Corruption Catastrophe According to General Phạm Quế Dương], November 25, 2004, available at Le Phai website <http://www.lephai. com/dt20041203d.html> Accessed January 7, 2005 or <http://www.ykien.net/ tl_viettrung91.html#dhX050928a> Accessed October 30, 2005.

Read, Benjamin and Robert Pekkanen. (eds) *Local Organizations and Urban Governance in East and Southeast Asia: Straddling State and Society*. London: Routledge Studies on Civil Society in Asia, 2009.

Reuter News. "Vietnam priest given a year of medical parole.", March 16, 2010, available at <http://in.reuters.com/article/worldNews/idINIndia-46947 120100316> Accessed March 16, 2010.

Riker, William. *Federalism: Origins, Operation, Significance*. Boston: Little, Brown & Co, 1964.

Salemink, Oscar. "Translating, Interpreting and Practicing Civil Society in Vietnam: A Tale of Calculated Misunderstandings." In *Development Brokers and Translators*, edited by David Lewis and David Mosse, 101–26. Bloomfield, CT: Kumarian Press, 2006.

Schedler, Andreas, Larry Diamond, and Marc Plattner. (eds) *The Self-Restraining State: Power and Accountability in New Democracies*. Boulder and London: Lynne Rienners Publishers, 1999.

Schmitter, Philippe C. "Civil Society: East and West." In *Consolidating the Third Wave Democracies: Themes and Perspectives*, edited by Larry Diamond et al., 239–62. Baltimore, MD: Johns Hopkins University Press, 1997.

Schmitter, Philippe C. and Terry Lynn Karl. "What democracy is...and is not." *Journal of Democracy* 2, no. 3 (1991): 75–88.

Schuler, Paul. "Deliberative Autocracy: Managing the Risks and Reaping the Rewards of Partial Liberalization in Vietnam." Dissertation, University of California, 2013.

Shambaugh, David. *China's Communist Party: Atrophy and Adaptation*. Washington, DC: Woodrow Wilson Center Press, 2008.

Shanks, Edwin, Cecilia Luttrell, Tim Conway, Manh Loi Vu, and Judith Ladinsky. *Understanding Pro-Poor Political Change: The Policy Process – Vietnam*. London, Overseas Development Institute, 2004.

Shih, Victor, Christopher Adolph, and Mingxing Liu. "Getting Ahead in the Communist Party: Explaining Advancement of Central Committee Members in China." *American Political Science Review* 106, no. 1 (2012): 166–87.

Shirk, Susan L. *The Political Logic of Economic Reform in China* (Vol. 24). Berkeley, CA: University of California Press, 1993.

Sidel Mark. "Maintaining Firm Control: Recent Developments in Nonprofit Law and Regulation in Vietnam." *International Journal of Not-for-Profit Law* 12, no. 3 (May 2010): 52–67.

_____. *The Constitution of Vietnam: A Contextual Analysis*. Oxford: Hart Publishing, 2009.

_____. *Law and Society in Vietnam: The Transition from Socialism in Comparative Perspective*. Cambridge, UK: Cambridge University Press, 2008.

_____. "New Directions in the Study of Vietnamese Law." *17 Michigan Journal of International Law 705* (1996) (Review of Carl Thayer and David Marr. (eds) *Vietnam and the Rule of Law*. Canberra: Australian National University, 1993).

Sikor, Thomas. "Local Government in the Exercise of State Power: The Politics of Land Allocation in Black Thai Villages." In *Beyond Hanoi: Local Government in Vietnam*, edited by Benedict Kerkvliet and David Marr, 167–96. Copenhagen: NIAS Press, 2004.

Slater, Dan. "Can Leviathan Be Democratic? Competitive Elections, Robust Mass Politics, and State Infrastructural Power." *Studies in Comparative International Development* 43, no. 3–4 (2008): 252–72.

Smith, Benjamin. "Life of the Party: The Origins of Regime Breakdown and Persistence under Single-Party Rule." *World Politics* 57 (April 2005): 450.

Snyder, Richard. "Beyond Electoral Authoritarianism: The Spectrum of Nondemocratic Regimes." In *Electoral Authoritarianism: The Dynamics of Unfree Competition*, edited by Andreas Schedler. Boulder, CO and London: Lynne Rienner Publishers, 2006.

Socialist Republic of Vietnam. 1999. Penal Code, No. 15/1999/QH10, *Official Gazette*, no. 8 (February 29, 2000): 3–96.

Socialist Republic of Vietnam. *Viet Nam's National Defense in the Early Years of the 21st Century*. Hanoi: Ministry of [National] Defense, 2004.

Solnick, Steven. *Stealing the State: Control and Collapse in Soviet Institutions*. Cambridge, MA: Harvard University Press, 1998.

"So phan cua nong nghiep co phai la dang chet?" [Does the Agricultural Sector Deserve to Die?], September 17, 2009, available at <http://www.tuanvietnam.net/news/InTin.aspx?alias=thongtindachieu&msgid=5841> Accessed 10/2012.

Stern, Lewis M. *Renovating the Vietnamese Communist Party: Nguyen Van Linh and the Programme for Organizational Reform, 1987–91*. Institute of Southeast Asian Studies, 1993.

"Sự thật về 'tờ báo lậu' Tổ Quốc." [The Truth About the Underground Newspaper *Tổ Quốc*], December 7, 2008, available at Công An Nhân Dân Online <http://www.congan.com.vn/phong_su_dieu_tra/2008/12/20081205.55165.ca> Accessed December 15, 2008.

Svolik, Milan W. "Authoritarian Reversals and Democratic Consolidation." *American Political Science Review* 102, no. 2 (2008): 153–68.

Svolik, Milan W. *The Politics of Authoritarian Rule*. Cambridge, UK: Cambridge University Press, 2012.

Tập San Tự Do Dân Chủ. "Kỹ Su Đỗ Nam Hải tại Sài Gòn." [Engineer Đỗ Nam Hải in Sài Gòn], April 7 (2010): 29–34.

Tap chi Xay Dung Dang. "Nang cao chat luong doi ngu can bo trong cac doanh nghiep tu nhan o thanh pho Ho chi Minh." 4 (2008), available at <http://www.xaydungdang.org.vn/details.asp?Object=4&news_ID=7461228> Accessed 10/2012.

Taylor, William, Nguyen Thu Hang, Pham Quang Tu, and Huynh Thi Ngoc Tuyet. *Civil Society in Vietnam: A Comparative Study of Civil Society Organizations in Hanoi and Ho Chi Minh City*. Hanoi: The Asia Foundation, 2012.

Teerawichitchainan, Bussarawan. "Trends in Military Service in Northern Vietnam, 1950–1995: A Sociodemographic Approach." *Journal of Vietnamese Studies* 4, no. 3 (Fall 2009).

Thayer, Carlyle A. "Vietnam: National Assembly's First Confidence Vote (3)." *Thayer Consultancy Background Brief* June 12, 2013a.

_____. "Vietnam's Conflicted Human Rights Policy." *Asian Currents* [Asian Studies Association of Australia], August (2013b): 9–12.

_____. "Military Politics in Contemporary Vietnam: Political Engagement, Corporate Interests and Professionalism." *The Political Resurgence of the Military in Southeast Asia: Conflict and Leadership*, edited by Marcus Mietzner, 63–84. London: Routledge, 2011.

_____. "The Trial of Le Cong Dinh: New Challenges to the Legitimacy of Vietnam's Party-State." *Journal of Vietnamese Studies* 5, 3 (2010b): 196–207.

_____. "Political Legitimacy in Viet Nam: Challenge and Response." *Politics and Policy* 38, no. 3 (2010a): 423–44.

_____. "Vietnam and the Challenge of Political Civil Society." *Contemporary Southeast Asia* 31, no. 1 (2009b): 1–27.

_____. "Political Legitimacy of Viet Nam's One Party-State: Challenges and Responses." *Journal of Current Southeast Asian Affairs* 28, no. 4 (2009a): 47–70.

_____. "Viet Nam." In *PSI Handbook of Global Security and Intelligence: National Approaches (Vol. 1), The Americas and Asia*, edited by Stuart Farson, Peter Gill, Mark Phythian, and Shlomo Shapiro, 300–317. Westport: Praeger Security International, 2008.

_____. "Vietnam: The Tenth Party Congress and After." *Southeast Asian Affairs* (2007): 381–97.

_____. "Political Dissent and Political Reform in Viet Nam, 1997–2002." In *The Power of Ideas: Intellectual Input and Political Change in East and Southeast Asia*, edited by Claudia Derichs and Thomas Heberer, 115–132. Copenhagen S: Nordic Institute of Asian Studies Press, 2006.

_____. "Political Developments in Viet Nam: The Rise and Demise of Le Kha Phieu, 1997–2001." In *Consuming Urban Culture in Contemporary Viet Nam*, edited by Lisa B.W. Drummond and Mandy Thomas, 21–34. London: RoutledgeCurzon, 2003.

_____. "Mono-Organizational Socialism and the State." In *Vietnam's Rural Transformation*, edited by B. Kerkvliet and D.J. Porter, 39–64. Boulder, CO: Westview Press, 1995.

_____. *Vietnam and the Rule of Law*. Canberra: Australian National University, 1993: 189.

_____. "Renovation and Vietnamese Society: The Changing Roles of Government and Administration." In *Doi Moi: Vietnam's Renovation Policy and Performance*, edited by Dean Forbes. Canberra: Department of Political and Social Change, Australian National University, 1991.

_____. "The Regularization of Politics: Continuity and Change in the Party's Central Committee, 1951–1986." In *Postwar Viet Nam: Dilemmas in Socialist Development*, edited by David Marr and Christine White, 77–89. Ithaca, NY: Cornell Southeast Asia Program, 1988.

_____. "Vietnam's Sixth Party Congress: An Overview." *Contemporary Southeast Asia* 9, no. 1 (1987): 12–22.

_____. "Development in Vietnam: The Fourth National Congress of the Vietnam Communist Party." *Asian Profile* (June 1979): 275–82.

Thayer, Carlyle A. and David Marr. (eds) *Vietnam and the Rule of Law*. Canberra: Australian National University, 1993: 189.

Thân Văn Trường. "Anh Đoàn Huy Chương bị Công an Bắt [Security Police Arrest Đoàn Huy Chương], February 13, 2010, available at Vietnam Exodus <http://www.vietnamexodus.info/vne0508/modules.php?name=News&file=article&sid=4323> Accessed May 25, 2011.

The Nation (Thailand), January 13, 2011, available at <vnnews-l@anu.edu.au> Accessed January 12, 2011./in chronological folder Socialism, ldrship, Communist Party, Jan 2011/

Thông Luận [Thorough Discussion], 7–8 (2004): 2.

"Tiến sĩ Phan Đình Diệu." [Dr. Phan Đình Diệu], available at Việt Tân website <http://www.viettan.org/article.php3.html> Accessed March 31, 2005.

Tiebout, Charles. "A Pure Theory of Local Expenditures." *Journal of Political Economy* 64 (1956): 416–24.

Tien Phong. "Day manh phat trien Dang trong khoi kinh te tu nhan." January 11, 2007.

_____. "Len chuc ong ngoai van lam bi thu Doan xa." July 3, 2006.

Tilly, Charles. *Contention and Democracy in Europe, 1650–2000.* Cambridge, UK: Cambridge University Press, 2004.

Tong, James. "Anatomy of Regime Repression in China: Timing, Enforcement Institutions, and Target Selection in Banning the Falungong, July 1999." *Asian Survey* 42 (November–December 2002): 795–820.

Tống Văn Công. "Đổi mới đảng, tránh nguy cơ sụp đổ." [Renovate the Party, Avoid Danger of Being Overthrown], September 23, 2009, available at Diễn Đàn <http://www.diendan.org/viet-nam/111oi-moi-111ang-tranh-nguy-co-sup-111o> Accessed October 2, 2009.

Tonnesson, Stein. *The Vietnamese Revolution of 1945.* London: SAGE Publications, 1991.

Tran, Angie Ngọc. "Contesting 'Flexibility': Networks of Place, Gender, and Class in Vietnamese Workers' Resistance." In *Taking Southeast Asia to Market,* edited by Joseph Nevins and Nancy Lee Peluso, 56–72. Ithaca, NY: Cornell University Press, 2008.

_____. "The Third Sleeve: Emerging Labor Newspapers and the Responses of Labor Unions and the State to Workers' Resistance." *Labor Studies Journal* 32 (September 2007): 257–79.

Trần Anh Kim. "Lời Cảnh Báo." [Warning], available at Mạng Ý Kiến website <http://www.ykien.net> Accessed April 7, 2006.

Trần Bảo Lộc. "Góp ý với tác giả Nguyễn Gia Kiểng." [Sharing Opinions with Nguyễn Gia Kiểng], July 14, 2007, available at Đối Thoại [Dialogue] website <http://www.doi-thoai.com/baimoi0707_332.html> Accessed August 2, 2007.

Trần Đại Sơn. "Cần phải cân nhắc thiệt hơn." [Need a More Honest Assessment of Pros and Cons], *Điện Thư,* no. 8 (October 2003): 8–9.

Trần Độ. "Nhật ký Rồng Rắn." [Diary of a Dragon-Snake], Part 1, *Điện Thư,* no. 29 (11/2004): 2–16.

_____. "Nhật ký Rồng Rắn." [Diary of a Dragon-Snake], Part 3, *Điện Thư,* no. 31 (November 2004): 1–12.

Trần Dũng Tiến. "Góp ý với dự thảo sửa đổi Hiến Pháp." [Suggestions for Revising the Constitution], August 25, 2001, available at Mạng Ý Kiến <http://www.ykien.net/bntdthienphap.html> Accessed February 4, 2004.

Trần Khải Thanh Thủy. "Thừa giấy làm chi chẳng vẽ voi." [When Paper Is Aplenty Why Not Draw an Elephant], December 11, 2006, available at Đàn Chim Việt Online <http://www.danchimviet.com/php/modules.php?name=News&file=print&sid=2695> Accessed January 15, 2007.

Trần Khuê. "Đinh Quang Anh Thái phỏng vấn ông Trần Khuê." 2001, available at Mạng Ý Kiến <http://www.ykien.net/dtanhthai.html> Accessed December 4, 2003.

Trần Lâm. "Sự Thay đổi đã Đến gần." [Change is Near], November 30, 2009b, available at Thông Luận Online <http://www.thongluan.org/vn/modules.php?name=News&file=article&sid=4377> Accessed January 29, 2010.

_____. "Phải chăng đã đến hồi bĩ cực?" [Could Misfortune Be Ending?], *Tổ Quốc,* May 1, 2009a: 5–7.

_____. "Những đòi hỏi cấp thiết: phải mở rộng tự do dân chủ." [Urgent Demands: Expand Freedom and Democracy],October 4, 2006, available at Thông Luận <http://www.thongluan.org/ vn/modules.php?name=News&file=article&sid=1 166> Accessed December 1, 2006.

_____. "Phong trào dân chủ Việt Nam." [Vietnam's Democracy Movement], December 2005b, available at Mạng Ý Kiến <http://www.ykien.net/> Accessed May 19, 2006.

_____. "Tủi hổ quá Việt Nam ơi!" [Vietnam, How Shameful!], June 16, 2005a, from Mạng Ý Kiến <http://www.ykien.net/> accessed May 19, 2006.

Trung Hiếu. "Thấy gì qua Bài viết...của Nhà văn Hoàng Tiến?" [What Do We Find in Writer Hoàng Tiến's Essay?], November 24, 2006, available at *Thông Luận* Online <http://www.thongluan.org/vn/modules.php?name=News&file= article&sid=1282> Accessed January 5, 2007.

Truong Huyen Chi. "Winter Crop and Spring Festival: The Contestations of Local Government in a Red River Delta Commune." In *Beyond Hanoi: Local Government in Vietnam*, edited by Benedict Kerkvliet and David Marr, 110. Copenhagen: NIAS Press, 2004.

Truong Son. "Deputy Writes Blog Attacking Duong Trung Quoc." *VNExpress*, February 19, 2013, available at <http://vnexpress.net/tin-tuc/xa-hoi/dai-bieu-quoc-hoi-viet-blog-cong-kich-ong-duong-trung-quoc-2426576.html> Accessed 10/2012.

Tsai, Lily L. *Accountability without Democracy*. Cambridge, UK: Cambridge University Press, 2007.

Tsang, Steve. "Consultative Leninism: China's New Political Framework." *Journal of Contemporary China* 18 (November 2009): 865–80.

"Tước giấy phép hoạt động văn phòng luật sư pháp quyền." [Law Office Stripped of License], March 26, 2009, available at Công An Nhân Dân Online <http://www.cand.com.vn/vi-VN/thoisu/2009/3/110862.cand> Accessed April 22, 2009.

Tuoi Tre. "Mot nong dan Dong Nai kien Vedan.", July 13, 2010.

_____. "Tam su cua Bi thu Doan xa tuoi 44.", September 11, 2006c.

_____. "Can bo dia phuong ban dat cong bua bai nhu ban mo rau, con ca.", July 8, 2006b.

_____. "Sai pham dat dai chu yeu lien quan den can bo.", June 20, 2006a.

Turner, Robert F. *Vietnamese Communism: Its Origins and Development* (Vol. 143). Stanford University, CT: Hoover Institution Press, 1975.

Turley, William. "The Military Construction of Socialism: Postwar Roles of the People's Army of Vietnam." In *Postwar Vietnam: Dilemmas in Socialist Development*, edited by David Marr and Christine White, 195–212. Ithaca, NY: Southeast Asia Program, Cornell University, 1988.

"Tuyên Ngôn Tự do Dân chủ cho Việt Nam" April 8, 2006, available at Mạng Ý Kiến [Opinion Net], http://www.ykien.net/ Accessed May 12, 2006.

UNDP. "Deepening Democracy and Increasing Popular Participation in Viet Nam." *UNDP Viet Nam*, June 30, 2006, available at <http://www.undp.org.vn/ digitalAssets/4/4856_Grassroot_democracy.pdf> Accessed September 30, 2013.

United States Department of State. *Country Reports on Human Rights Practices for 2011: Vietnam* (Washington, D.C., 2012).

_____. *2010 Country Reports on Human Rights Practices: Vietnam* (Washington, D.C., 2011).

"Ủy ban Nhân Quyền Việt Nam." [Vietnam Human Rights Committee]. "Cực lực phản đối việc nhà cầm quyền Việt Nam hành hung gây thương tích trầm trọng đối với ông Nguyễn Phương Anh." [Strenuously Oppose Vietnam Authorities' Violent Acts That Gravely Injured Nguyễn Phương Anh], 1 November 2007, *Thông Luận*, 11/2007: 25–26.

Vasavakul, Thaveeporn. "Report on the Analysis of Vietnam's Current Legal Framework for People's Councils: A Perspective from Ninh Thuan." A study prepared for Oxfam-Great Britain, Hanoi, 2009.

_____. "From Fence-Breaking to Networking: Interests, Popular Organisations, and Policy Influences in Post-Socialist Vietnam." In *Getting Organized in Vietnam: Moving in and Around the Socialist State*, edited by Benedict Kerkvliet, Russell Heng, and David Koh, 25–61. Singapore: Institute of Southeast Asian Studies, 2003.

_____. "Vietnam: Sectors, Classes, and the Transformation of a Leninist State." *Morley, J., Ed* (1999): 59–82.

_____. "Sectoral Politics and Strategies for State and Party Building from the VII to the VIII Congresses of the Vietnamese Communist Party (1991–1996)." In *Doi Moi: Ten Years after the 1986 Party Congress*, edited by Adam Fforde, 81–135. Canberra: Department of Political and Social Change, Australian National University, 1997.

_____. "Politics of Administrative Reform in Post-Socialist Viet Nam." In Suiwah Leung (ed.), *Vietnam Assessment: Creating a Sound Investment Climate*, 42–68. Singapore: Institute of Southeast Asian Studies, 1996.

_____. "Vietnam: The Third Wave of State Building." *Southeast Asian Affairs* (1997): 337–63.

Vi Đức Hồi. "Đối mặt." [Opposite Side], November 25, 2008, available at Thông Luận Online <http://www.thongluan.org/vn/modules.php?name=News&file=article&sid=3301> Accessed November 26, 2008.

VietCatholicNews. "Dissident writer tried for hooliganism." *VietCatholicNews*, February 5, 2010, available at vnnews-1 <http://mailman.anu.edu.au/mailman/listinfo/vnnews-l> Accessed February 6, 2010.

VietnamNet. "PM Acknowledges Personal Responsibility for Vinashin case.", November 24, 2010, available at <http://www.lookatvietnam.com/2010/11/pm-acknowledges-personal-responsibility-for-vinashin-case.html> Accessed 10/2012.

_____. "Bắt giam Lê Công Định là công việc nội bộ của VN." [Lê Công Định's Imprisonment Is an Internal Matter for Viet Nam], June 23, 2009a, available at VietnamNet <http://www.vietnamnet.vn/chinhtri/2009/06/854535/> Accessed May 19, 2010.

_____. "Nhieu bi thu, pho bi thu tinh bi xem xet ky luat.", November 3, 2009.

Vietnam Sydney Radio. "Công an Hà Nội đàn áp gia đình chị Dương Thị Xuân." [Security police abuse family of Dương Thị Xuân], January 14–15, 2009, available at Tiếng Nói Tự Do Dân Chủ website <http://tiengnoitudodanchu.org/modules.php?name=News&file=article&sid=6923> Accessed January 29, 2009.

Võ Đồng Đội. "Giới Thiệu Bộ Chính Trị, Ban Chấp hành Trung ương ĐCSVN về tên lưu manh Nguyễn Chí Vịnh." [Introducing the Communist Party's Political Bureau to Hooligan Nguyễn Chí Vịnh], *Diện Thu*, no. 41 (March 2005): 22–26.

Vo Nguyen Giap. "Kinh qui: Ban Chap hanh Trung uong, Dong chi Tong Bi thu, cac dong chi trong Bo Chinh tri, Ban Bi thu va Uy Ban Kiem tra Trung uong." [Letter to Central Committee, Comrade Secretary General, Comrades on the Politburo, the Secretariat and Central Control Committee], January 3, 2004, available at <http://www.fifthcolumnmag.com/1204/domino.htm> Accessed April 13, 2005.

Vo Nhan Tri. *Vietnam's Economic Policy since 1975*. Singapore: Institute of Southeast Asian Studies, 1990.

Vo X. Han. "Vietnam in 2007: A Profile in Economic and Socio-Political Dynamism." *Asian Survey* 48, no. 1 (2008): 29–37.

Voice of America Online. "Luật sư Công Nhân." [Attorney Công Nhân], March 12, 2010b, available at Dân Luận < http://danluan.org/node/4397#comment-10309> Accessed April 13, 2010.

_____. "Gia đình Nguyễn Tiến Trung lên tiếng." [Nguyễn Tiến Trung's Family Speak Out], January 22, 2010a, available at VOA online <http://www.voanews.com/vietnamese/2010–01–20-voa42.cfm> Accessed January 22, 2010.

Voice of America. Nguyễn Dân Quế Interview, February 4, 2006, available at VOANews http://ww.voanews.com/uspolicy/Ontheline/2006–02–03-voa3.cfm?renderforprint=1 Accessed February 7, 2006.

Vogel, Ezra. *Deng Xiaoping and the Transformation of China*. Cambridge, MA: The Balknap Press, 2011.

"Vụ án Nguyễn Đan Quế." [Nguyễn Đan Quế's Case], July 29, 2004, available at Mạng Ý Kiến <http://www.ykien.net/tl_ndq.html> Accessed September 24, 2004.

Vũ Hoàng Hải. "Bản Tường Trình về việc bị công an hành hung." [Report about Being Beaten by Security Police], August 9, 2006, available at Mạng Ý Kiến <http://www.ykien.net/> Accessed August 11, 2006.

Vũ Hùng. "Thư Tố Cáo." [Accusation], May 8, 2008, available at Thông Luận Online, <http://www.thongluan.org/vn/modules.php?name =Content&pa=showpage &pid=1038> Accessed August 21, 2008.

Vu, Tuong. "The New Nationalism in Southeast Asia: Causes, Missions, and Significance." *TRaNS: Trans-Regional and National Studies of Southeast Asia* 1, no. 2 (forthcoming).

_____. *Paths to Development in Asia: South Korea, Vietnam, China, and Indonesia*. New York: Cambridge University Press, 2010.

_____. "To Be Patriotic Is to Build Socialism: Communist Ideology in Vietnam's Civil War." In *Dynamics of the Cold War in Asia: Ideology, Identity, and Culture*, edited by Vu Tuong and Wasana Wongsurawat. New York: Palgrave-Macmillan, 2009b.

_____. "It's Time for the Indochinese Revolution to Show Its True Colours: The Radical Turn of Vietnamese Politics in 1948." *Journal of Southeast Asian Studies* 40, no. 3 (2009a).

_____. "Dreams of Paradise: The Making of a Soviet Outpost in Vietnam." *Ab Imperio* 2/2008 (August 2008): 255–85.

_____. "Workers and the Socialist State: North Vietnam's State-Labor Relations, 1945–1970." *Communist and Post-Communist Studies* 38 (September 2005): 329–56.

Vuving, Alexander. "Vietnam: A Tale of Four Players." *Southeast Asian Affairs* (2010): 367–91.

Weingast, Barry. "The Economic Role of Political Institutions: Market-Preserving Federalism and Economic Development." *The Journal of Law, Economics and Organization* 11, no. 1 (1995): 1–30.

Wells-Dang, Andrew. *Civil Society and Climate Change in Vietnam: Actors, Roles and Possibilities*. Hanoi: Pact Vietnam, April 2012b.

_____. *Civil Society Networks in China and Vietnam: Informal Pathbreakers in Health and the Environment*. Basingstoke: Palgrave Macmillan, 2012a.

_____. "Environmental Networks in Vietnam: A New Form of Civil Society?" Policy report, IUCN, September 2011.

_____. "Political Space in Vietnam: A View From the 'Rice-Roots'." *Pacific Review* 23, no. 1 (2010): 93–112.

Wischermann, Jörg. "Governance and Civil Society Action in Vietnam: Changing the Rules From Within – Potentials and Limits." *Asian Politics and Policy* 3, no. 3 (2011): 383–411.

_____. "Civil Society Action and Governance in Vietnam: Selected Findings from an Empirical Survey." *Journal of Current Southeast Asian Affairs* 2 (2010): 3–40.

_____. *Vietnam Development Report*. Hanoi, 2008b.

_____. *Taking Stock: An Update on Vietnam's Recent Economic Development*. Hanoi, 2008a.

_____. *Private Capital Flows to Developing Countries*. Washington, 1997.

Wright, Joseph. "Do Authoritarian Institutions Constrain? How Legislatures Affect Economic Growth and Investment." *American Journal of Political Science* 52, no. 2 (2008): 322–43.

Wright, Teresa. "The China Democracy Party and the Politics of Protest in the 1980s–1990s." *China Quarterly*, no. 172 (December 2002): 906–26.

Xi Chen. "The Power of 'Troublemaking': Protest Tactics and their Efficacy in China." *Comparative Politics* 41 (July 2009): 451–71.

Xuan Dien. "Kiến nghị về bảo vệ và phát triển đất nước trong tình hình hiện nay." [Recommendations on Protecting and Developing the Country in the Present Circumstances], 10 July, 2011, petition posted on <http://xuandien-hannom.blogspot.com/2011/07/toan-van-kien-nghi-khan-cap-ve-bao-ve.html> Accessed January 31, 2012.

Xu huong lao dong va xa hoi Vietnam 2009/2010. Hanoi: Bo Lao Dong Thuong Binh Xa Hoi, 2010.

Yongshun Cai. "Power Structure and Regime Resilience: Contentious Politics in China." *British Journal of Political Science* 38 (2008): 411–32.

Yumin Sheng. "Authoritarian Co-optation, the Territorial Dimension: Provincial Political Representation in Post-Mao China." *Studies in Comparative International Development* 44, no. 1 (2009): 71–93.

Yu Zheng. "Incentives and Commitment: The Political Economy of Special Zones in China." Paper presented at the 50th Annual Convention of the International Studies Association, New York, February 15–18, 2009.

Zinoman, Peter. "Nhân Văn-Giai Phẩm and Vietnamese 'Reform Communism' in the 1950s." *Journal of Cold War Studies* 13 (Winter 2011): 60–100.

_____. "Nguyễn Huy Thiệp's 'Vàng Lửa' and the Nature of Intellectual Dissent in Contemporary Vietnam." *Vietnam Forum*, no. 14 (1994): 36–44.

Legal Documents

Decree 86/2006/ND-CP. "On the Performance of Rights and Duties of the State Owner Over State Companies." Vietnamese Government, Hanoi: August 21, 2006.

Government of Vietnam. *Nghị định ban hành Quy chế quản lý và sử dụng viện trợ phiChính phủ nước ngoài* [Decree on Issuance of Regulations on Management and Use of Foreign Nongovernmental Organization Aid], no. 93/2009/NĐ-CP, October 22, 2009.

_____. *Nghị định về tổ chức và hoạt động của tổ hợp tác* [Decree on Organization and Operation of Collaborative Groups], no. 151/2007/NĐ-CP, October 10, 2007.

Law 05/2003/QH11. "On Oversight of the National Assembly." National Assembly, June 17, 2003.

National Assembly of The Socialist Republic of Vietnam. *Resolution 561/2013/ UBTVQH13.* "Guidelines for the implementation of certain articles in Resolution 35/2012/QH13 on confidence preferential ranking and confidence voting of persons elected and/or approved by the National Assembly and/or People's Councils." Standing Committee of the National Assembly. Hanoi, January 16, 2013.

_____.*Constitution of the Socialist Republic of Vietnam (Amended in 2013)*, draft version. English translation, January, 2013.

_____. *Law on the Viet Nam Fatherland Front*, English translation, June 23, 1999, no. 14/1999/QH10.

Van Phong Quoc Hoi. *Giu moi lien he cua dai bieu dan cu voi cu tri o Viet Nam: thuc trang va kien nghi.* Hanoi, June 2008.

Index

print media, 163
prison conditions, 127
prison terms, 124–7
private investment, 74
pro-democracy activists, 141–2, 154
professionalism, 86–7, 88
professional organizations, 166–7
protests, 102
provinces
  autonomy for, 71
  autonomy of, 77–9
  competition among, 66–7, 70, 76–7
  contributions to central budget by,
    70–1, 72, 80
  economic reforms and, 75–7
  FDI in, 69–70, 71, 75, 78
  inter-provincial migration flows, 76
  poverty in, 75
provincial leaders, 8, 32, 188
provincial PCOs, 49–62
Provincial People's Councils (PPCOs),
    45
  accountability functions of, 51–9
  budgetary funding approval by,
    53–4
  decision-making authority of, 52–3
  legal appraisal by, 54
  public consultation and, 56–9
  supervision by, 54–6
public accountability, 44–9
public administration reform, 8–9
Public Administration Reform (PAR)
    Index, 46
public consultation, 56–9
public denunciation, 149–51
public officials
  career paths of, 77–9
  corruption and, 104–6
  rent seeking by, 80–1

Radio Free Asia, 146
rations, 69
reforms
  agricultural, 69–70
  in China, 82
  constitutional, 176–9
  economic, 69–75, 187–8
  education, 107
  institutional, 42, 194

market, 64, 72–5, 187–8
  NA, 88
refugees, 110
regime dissidents, *see* dissidents
regional differences, 66–7, 70
religion, 36
rents, 6, 22, 31, 33, 35, 37
rent seeking, 80–1
representative institutions, 9–11
repression, 2, 11–13, 135–61
  apparatus of, 135–61, 191
  in China, 191
  of civil society, 181
  components of, 145–56
  of dissidents, 100–34, 189–90
  groups targeted for, 141–5
  monitoring and surveillance as,
    145–8
Resolution Four, 186
revenue collection, 50–1, 70–1, 72, 80
revolutionary violence, 33–4, 36,
    38n3, 111, 186
Riker, William, 83
rule of law, 44

Schedler, Andreas, 43
Schuler, Paul, 10–11
secondary associations, 11–13
secrecy, 18
sectoral leaders, 32
security forces, 11, 18, 38, 115, 116,
    135, 137, 145–8, 153, 191
Sheng, Yumin, 67–8, 79–80
Shih, Victor, 17, 67, 68, 80–1
Shirk, Susan, 73
Sidel, Mark, 7
Singapore, 19, 107
single-party dictatorships, *see*
    one-party regimes
Smith, Benjamin, 33, 38n2
social autonomy, 162
social conditions, 3
social inequalities, 1
socialism, 23, 109
social media, 140, 163
social mobility, 35
social organizations, 162–5, 170–1
social research, 3
social services, 9

CPSIA information can be obtained
at www.ICGtesting.com
Printed in the USA
BVOW06*1359301117

501626BV00012B/451/P